Influencer Marketing

FOR

DUMMIES®

A Wiley Brand

Influencer Marketing

FOR DUMMIES®
A Wiley Brand

by Kristy Sammis, Cat Lincoln, and
Stefania Pomponi with Jenny Ng,
Edita Gassmann Rodriguez, and Judy Zhou

Influencer Marketing For Dummies®

Published by: **John Wiley & Sons, Inc.,** 111 River Street, Hoboken, NJ 07030-5774, www.wiley.com

Copyright © 2016 by John Wiley & Sons, Inc., Hoboken, New Jersey

Published simultaneously in Canada

For general information on our other products and services, please contact our Customer Care Department within the U.S. at 877-762-2974, outside the U.S. at 317-572-3993, or fax 317-572-4002. For technical support, please visit www.wiley.com/techsupport.

Wiley publishes in a variety of print and electronic formats and by print-on-demand. Some material included with standard print versions of this book may not be included in e-books or in print-on-demand. If this book refers to media such as a CD or DVD that is not included in the version you purchased, you may download this material at http://booksupport.wiley.com. For more information about Wiley products, visit www.wiley.com.

Library of Congress Control Number: 2015955445

ISBN 978-1-119-11409-3 (pbk); ISBN 978-1-119-11392-8 (ebk); ISBN 978-1-119-11405-5 (ebk)

Manufactured in the United States of America

10 9 8 7 6 5 4 3 2 1

Contents at a Glance

Table of Contents

Introduction

*I*f you work in marketing, or have a product or service to sell, you've probably realized by now that you need to establish an online presence in some shape or form. You also need to keep your online audience engaged in order to establish brand awareness and grow your business.

But the world of social media is vast, and there are so many platforms to choose from when it comes to publicizing your brand. New tools pop up everyday, and the social media landscape can easily become overwhelming! You've probably heard about the benefits of word-of-mouth marketing and perhaps even heard the term *influencer marketing* bandied about as a strategy to consider. Maybe you're just curious to learn more about word-of-mouth marketing, what makes someone "influential" online, and whether working with influencers can help your business grow. If so, you're in the right place!

We wrote this book with the goal of demystifying influencer marketing and all the various components that make it successful.

About This Book

This book is a reference. That means you don't need to read it in order from front to back. Instead, feel free to skip to the sections that are most relevant to your brand and interesting to you. For information on a specific topic, check the table of contents or refer to the index.

Within this book, you may note that some web addresses break across two lines of text. If you're reading this book in print and want to visit one of these web pages, simply key in the web address exactly as it's noted in the text, pretending as though the line break doesn't exist. If you're reading this as an e-book, you've got it easy — just click the web address to be taken directly to the web page.

Foolish Assumptions

As we wrote this book, we made certain assumptions about you:

- ✔ You already have an established web presence (a website and/or brand-owned social channels).

- ✔ You're interested in learning more about how to work with online influencers and identifying who they are.

- ✔ You have established clear business and marketing/PR goals, which may or may not yet include social media activations.

- ✔ You're trying to decide whether using influencer marketing will help you meet your business goals.

- ✔ You have a passion for social media, or you're at least open to learning more about how it can elevate your brand marketing campaigns.

Icons Used in This Book

To make your reading experience easier, we use various icons in the margins to identify special categories of information:

Anything marked with the Tip icon may help streamline your marketing efforts. We've learned through trial and error so you don't have to!

Material marked with the Remember icon serves as a quick reminder of information, including best practices that we've shared elsewhere in the book. Review it to refresh your memory on content that's already been covered previously.

When we throw up a Warning icon, it's our way of steering you away from tactics that may derail your influencer marketing plans. We urge you to consider these bits of information carefully to avoid being blindsided by poor outcomes.

Beyond the Book

In addition to the content contained within this book, we have curated additional companion digital content that's available to you online. These include the following:

✔ **Cheat Sheet** (`www.dummies.com/cheatsheet/influencermarketing`): Here you can find information like how much influencers make, what influencer marketing can't do, influencer marketing tactics that'll get you in trouble, and more.

✔ **Web Extras** (`www.dummies.com/extras/influencermarketing`): Each parts page contains a link to Dummies.com and articles that extend the content covered in the book. Here, we offer free articles on everything from tips on sending products to influencers, a year's worth of themes for engaging social content, how to get influencers to advocate for your brand, and more.

Where to Go from Here

We hope that this book proves to be an invaluable tool as you start or continue your influencer marketing journey. The road can be long at times, but you'll start to get the hang of it soon. Start small, conquering one social platform at a time while building up your key influencer relationships. To be sure, there are always new platforms sprouting up, so your skillset will continue to evolve.

If you're brand new to the concept of influencer marketing, we highly recommend starting with Chapters 1 and 2 to get the lay of the land. If you're already somewhat familiar with influencer marketing tactics, you might want to jump to Chapter 4 or review the different social platforms methodically (Part III).

No matter where you start, we wish you much success in your influencer marketing endeavors! If you have comments and feedback to share, please feel free to email us at `info@clevergirlscollective.com`.

Part I
Getting Started with Influencer Marketing

In this part . . .

- Learn the origins of influencer marketing and how it evolved.
- Get acquainted with the six primary influencer platforms.
- Discover how to make influencer marketing work for you and your brand.

Chapter 1

Influencer Marketing 101

. . . .

In This Chapter

▶ Getting the lay of the land

▶ Approaching social media platforms like a pro

▶ Redefining "influence"

▶ Knowing what your business needs to launch successful programs

. . . .

Congratulations! You've arrived at the era of influencer marketing: an exciting, interesting, fresh, ever-changing, and *seriously fun* time to be a marketer! You're gonna love it here.

What makes influencer marketing so compelling? For one thing, it simply couldn't have existed before now. Influencer marketing brings together age-old concepts but gives them a modern, social media twist, and then distributes them across platforms that change almost daily. And the results are stunning.

We believe that influencer marketing is unprecedented and truly differentiates itself from the old marketing practices. In fact, it challenges most of them. This new medium pushes traditional boundaries — and that's a good thing! Consumers (the folks we're marketing to) are savvier than ever. It's our job to keep up.

In this chapter, we give you an overview of what influencer marketing is and why it matters to you — whether you know it or not!

Defining Influencer Marketing

So, what is influencer marketing exactly, and why are we so darn excited about it? *Influencer marketing* is the art and science of engaging people who are influential online to share brand messaging with their audiences in the form of sponsored content.

Advertisers have always used celebrity endorsements as a way to increase awareness and improve perception of a brand, because people tend to trust celebrities they admire, and sometimes aspire to be like them. Influencer marketing is similar in concept, but it has ushered in a new way to define *celebrity*. In addition to TV and movie stars, pro athletes, and musicians, celebrities of the social media world exist now, too. People can build big, engaged audiences on social media, such as blogs or Instagram. And those *social media influencers* wield influence over their audiences, akin to celebrity influence. Brands then work with these social media influencers to create a new kind of celebrity endorsement.

For example, maybe a new energy drink has just come out, and they want to market themselves as a "perfect boost for busy women." They decide that — in addition to email blasts, online display ads, and in-person events — they're going to reach out to influential female bloggers who write about their busy lives (and include information about the new energy drink). To engage these influencers, the energy drink's marketing team will

- ✔ Find bloggers who meet their target demographic.
- ✔ Reach out to the bloggers in an effective and professional way so that both parties are happy with and clear about their upcoming partnership.
- ✔ Send the bloggers samples of the drink.
- ✔ Enjoy the results of a fantastic social media campaign! The bloggers' readers are thrilled to have learned about their favorite online friend's good experiences with this energy drink, and they comment that they're going to try it themselves.

Of course, influencer marketing is not quite that simple, and these are actually quite time-consuming and involved (which is why we've written a whole book about them!), but the idea is sound.

So why a whole book about influencer marketing? What makes it so impossible to have done before and so hot right now?

- ✔ Social media today gives access to anyone to become an influencer; anyone who builds an audience can influence that audience. This means there's a huge pool of influencers available for brands to work with.
- ✔ There are more tools than ever before to help brands find and engage with influencers. There are resources for turnkey influencer programs now that simply didn't exist a year ago.
- ✔ Influencers exist on any channel or platform; they aren't limited to one format or another.

- ✔ Consumers have little trust in advertising. No one clicks banner ads anymore! But consumers *do* trust their friends and family when it comes to product recommendations and purchasing decisions — and consumers consider social media acquaintances to be friends.

- ✔ When executed well, influencer marketing programs have proven to be one of the most cost-effective and powerful tools in a marketer's arsenal.

Identifying the Primary Influencer Platforms

There are a slew of social media platforms out there, but in this book, we focus on the six big ones. The ones we've selected are

- ✔ **The most established:** Programs on these platforms are replicable and scalable based on years of data and case studies.

- ✔ **The most marketing-friendly:** Marketers know they can expect good results from programs on these platforms. The Snapchats of the world are fun, but they haven't yet proven to yield demonstrable results for most businesses.

Regardless of how many new tools emerge, when you've mastered the basics of these six platforms, you can manage influencers *anywhere*.

Blogs

Blogs were arguably the first form of user-generated content that attracted advertisers. When the web evolved from *top-down editorial content* (content that was published on websites, much like magazines and newspapers were published, without any way for audiences to interact or respond to that content), bloggers were the first people to attract true, measurable, engaged audiences. Blogs allowed for commenters, which meant bloggers (publishers) were interacting with their audiences. This two-way communication was revolutionary, and entire communities formed around blogs. Advertisers followed.

Over the last 15 years, blogs have evolved from being primarily text-heavy outlets for sharing opinion and personal stories, to a dizzying world of highly visual, readily shared content.

Blogs are still a mainstay of influencer programs. Here's why:

- ✔ There are popular blogs for every topic under the sun.
- ✔ Traffic and activity from blogs (page views, visits, time on site, and so on) are easy to measure.
- ✔ Influential bloggers can create gorgeous content and tell beautiful, true stories in a way that brands simply can't.
- ✔ The "evergreen" nature of blog content means sponsored posts will be discovered long after programs have been completed.

Instagram

No other social media tool has enjoyed Instagram's meteoric rise to prominence. People of all ages (especially under the age of 34) love perusing and sharing snapshots of people's lives, whether they know them IRL (in real life) or not. Instagram is fun and easy to use, and though marketers were once hesitant to believe that fleeting photos on Instagram could do much for brands, nearly 95 percent of retailers are now on Instagram!

Working with influencers on Instagram is fabulous because

- ✔ Users want visual content that's easy to digest, which is why Instagram is so popular. Engaging Instagram influencers to ensure that brand content is prominent on Instagram is a no-brainer!
- ✔ Simple photos are a great way to bring your product to life, for others to see it in action. A picture really is worth a thousand words.
- ✔ Many tools are available to track Instagram programs simply by using a unique hashtag, so measuring program success is easy (and some of these tools are even free!).
- ✔ Instagram's audience is broad, and often different from the audiences who are reading story-based blogs. Instagram offers a fantastic additional channel to get sponsored content in front of as many people as possible.

Twitter *more active*

Twitter has changed the news cycle, and the way social media-savvy users consume news. Any event will be discussed and shared as it unfolds in real-time on Twitter. Twitter is the platform for the world's social commentary, whether it's serving as a political megaphone for citizens reporting live from the trenches, or a humorous collection of ongoing reactions to this season's *Bachelor* finale.

Facebook is where social media users check in and check up on family and friends (mostly people they know in real life). Twitter is where users go to find out — or share — what's happening in the world at large with thousands of users they (mostly) don't know. Therefore, Twitter is great for

- ✔ Hosting chats or "parties" with a wide cross-section of people who have a common interest.

- ✔ Disseminating information about a new product launch or anything newsworthy.

- ✔ Brands that are interested in actively engaging with users. Facebook is more passive — comments may go unanswered for long periods of time, for example. Twitter users expect responses quickly. As a brand, if you can't engage in near real-time conversations with followers, working with influencers who can do it on your behalf is a fantastic option.

Facebook

Although Facebook isn't quite as popular as it once was among the under-25 crowd, millions of Americans check Facebook daily. Marketers have to be there! But being there can be tricky. Facebook changes its algorithms, policies, and ad serving regularly — what worked today may not work tomorrow. It's tough — but critical — to keep up.

For that reason, when it comes to Facebook, working with influencers is fantastic. Here's why:

- ✔ People who are popular on Facebook know how to navigate the tool to ensure that their posts are seen as widely as possible. Working with influencers means working with experts.

- ✔ If you've already created branded content and you just want to disseminate it, engaging Facebook influencers is your perfect solution. Facebook is incredibly powerful for sharing brief, to-the-point messages, such as coupons, in-store sale info, or branded images or videos.

Running a company Facebook page is completely different from engaging influencers to post sponsored content to Facebook.

Pinterest

After soaring onto the scene a few years ago, fueled by users who couldn't get enough of the beautiful, educational, and aspirational tool, Pinterest has established itself as an absolute must for any product-based brand. Pinterest drives more traffic to online retailers than any other site.

Here's why Pinterest is great for influencer marketing:

- Influencers love to create beautiful content and post it to Pinterest. The more beautiful the content, the more extensive the pin's reach will be.

- Working Pinterest into an influencer marketing program means thinking about the brand in a visual way, which ultimately makes the program more successful. For example, how do you make a child's plastic bucket visually beautiful and pinworthy? By adjusting the program content to work for Pinterest — for example, images of sand castles that influencers made with the plastic bucket or by posting a list of 13 outdoor activities for kids under 5 (and all you need is a bucket!).

- Unlike other platforms, pins tend to live on and on and on, because they're are pinned and repinned in perpetuity.

Video

Video influencers are, in some ways, the holy grail of social media influencers. In some cases, their videos reach millions of adoring viewers who can't wait for the next installment — and to be told what products to try. A popular beauty expert who makes a video about the perfect bronzer will directly affect sales of that bronzer.

In the influencer marketing world, video is its own special entity. The most popular video influencers are often quickly scooped up by agents or agencies, which makes it difficult for brands to work directly with them. Popular video influencers can also command much higher compensation than other types of influencers, especially if they have six- and seven-figure followings.

The good news is, as video production tools continue to become more ubiquitous, more affordable, and easier to use, there are more up-and-coming video influencers than ever before. Now that you can film nearly theater-quality movies with your camera, more and more people are entering the video influencer world and amassing thousands of viewers who aren't necessarily reading blogs, checking Pinterest, or using Twitter or Facebook. And when done well, a sponsored video can be as beautiful as a TV ad, while being more authentic and compelling to viewers.

To make the most of video influencer programs,

- **Don't focus too narrowly on YouTube stars.** There is video talent everywhere! For example, there are thousands of Vine users, who have tremendous followings even though their videos are only seconds long.

- **Keep your eyes open for new talent.** When a video talent is discovered by the masses, she's less likely to work one-on-one with brands or marketers.

✔ **Allow influencers great creative freedom.** Building up a video audience isn't easy to do, and the influencer knows her audience best. If you want her to incorporate brand product or messaging into her work, you have to be willing to allow her the flexibility to do it her way.

If you're working with highly inexperienced and less popular video influencers, be willing to offer help — from editing resources to script ideas — and expect more back-and-forth communication throughout the process.

Engaging Stellar Influencers

You may have the most creative, most stupendous ideas for an influencer program. Hooray! But your fabulous ideas won't make a lick of difference if you don't know which influencers to engage or how to engage them. In this section, we give you the seven keys to engaging stellar influencers.

∗ Start with women

Women influence up to 90 percent of purchasing decisions in U.S. households. So, it almost doesn't matter what you're selling — appealing to women simply makes sense.

This doesn't mean you should ignore male influencers in favor of working with female ones. It just means that it makes sense to start by identifying female influencers. The good news here is that women use every social media platform as much as (if not more than) men, share more product information online than men, and make a greater number of purchases as a direct result of social sharing than men do. (See Chapter 3 for details.)

Find people who create great content

Search for influencers who create great content that is (at least somewhat) related to your brand and who demonstrate engagement with their audiences — as evidenced by comments; followers on Facebook, Instagram, or Twitter; and social shares per post.

Beyond engagement, relevancy is critical. It seems perfectly reasonable and logical for a marketer to want to go after the "biggest" influencers they can find, but big doesn't mean relevant. For instance, say we have a client who is launching a new gluten-free protein bar, ideal for people who are fit and athletically inclined. At the outset, it might seem like a great idea to try to work with a prominent gluten-free food blogger on this program. But what if that blogger never writes about fitness and never recommends packaged products? She may have 300,000 monthly blog visitors, but it's not likely that any of them care about prepackaged fitness foods, even if they're gluten-free.

Compare that to a blogger who may only have 25,000 monthly visitors, but whose stories are focusing on her new gluten-free lifestyle as she trains for a marathon. In this case, you'd be better off working with the smaller blog. Even if the numbers won't look as great in some reports, we know the program will gain more traction with the smaller blog's audience.

If you're tempted to find the biggest influencers, keep this in mind:

- ✔ Relevancy of a blog or influencer content is more important than size.
- ✔ Prominent influencers often command much higher compensation.
- ✔ Popular influencers are routinely inundated with brand offers. Your offer needs to be compelling. Even then, you must be willing to be treated as though you're doing the influencer a favor. (This isn't always true, but we want you to know it happens often!)
- ✔ The audience of prominent influencers who do a lot of sponsored work get fatigued by sponsored messages and start tuning them out.

If you're a marketer and you need to show impressive numbers in your program report, keep in mind that there's a lot of ways to make a dollar. If your program goal is to meet a million social impressions, you can get there with one prominent influencer whose blog garners a million monthly visitors. But you could also get there with four bloggers, each of whom gets 250,000 visitors a month — or, better yet, with 100 bloggers, each of whom has 25,000 visitors per month. At the end of the program, the 1 million number would look the same, but you'd have 100 different pieces of content from 100 different perspectives and 100 different audiences.

Perfect your pickup

Influencers are human beings. You want to approach working with influencers professionally, but not so professionally that you come across as a robot (or worse, a spambot).

As we explain in Chapter 4, reaching out to influencers to ask them to work for you is not as simple as sending a mass PR mailing. Outreach should be personal, thoughtful, and tell the influencer what's in it for them. Putting in the time to craft customized outreach is time-consuming, but it will always yield better results than a spray-and-pray approach.

Sign a contract

This may sound like a small, tactical concern, but it's not. Bringing a contract into your influencer relationship makes sense for myriad reasons:

- ✔ **You're emphasizing that this is a professional relationship between the influencer and your brand.**

- ✔ **You want the influencer to create authentic content that will resonate with her audience, but you don't have to lose complete control of the entire creative process.** Use a contract to provide some rules of the road for the influencer about what she can and can't say, do, or post with respect to your brand.

- ✔ **You're not leaving deliverables up to chance.** The "old" influencer model — where, say, a company would send product to influencers with no note at all, in the hopes that the influencer would write, well, *anything* about the product — is dead. As a brand you have every right to spell out exactly what coverage you expect (a blog post, a Facebook post, three Instagram images, and so on) and by a set deadline.

- ✔ **A contract ensures there is no ambiguity about compensation.** Include what the compensation is, how it will be delivered, and by what date.

Pay influencers for their time and effort

When influencer marketing was still a new phenomenon in the social media sphere, brands that compensated influencers for their work were considered shady. By the old public relations standards, that's not how things were supposed to work. As we explain in Chapter 2, brands would simply send publications information or products in the hopes that the publications would feature them. PR folks applied the same approach with bloggers.

The industry has moved past this. Influencers expect to receive compensation in return for their work. Plus, compensation should reflect that the influencers are doing work on behalf of brands regardless of how the content "performs." If an influencer goes to the store, buys a new salad dressing, creates a beautiful dinner featuring that salad and salad dressing, blogs her salad recipe, and features gorgeous photos of the salad, all her work deserves compensation regardless of how many comments her blog post receives.

When it comes to compensation, cash is almost always preferred by influencers. It may be acceptable for a brand to offer products or services instead of cash, as long as those products or services have a monetary value equal to or greater than the cash equivalent; even then, some influencers may take offense at being offered "payment" that won't actually pay the bills. "Paying" influencers in "blog traffic" by featuring them on a brand site is not acceptable.

Outsource your influencer marketing to a marketing firm

Much like social media marketing in general, influencer marketing takes time, resources, and strategy. If your brand hands off influencer marketing to the intern, chances are, your programs won't gain much traction. You may also run the risk of a PR crisis or backlash if an inexperienced person is running the show and doesn't truly understand protocol.

Influencer marketing isn't something you can automate, either. Although there are many tools on the market now to help brands manage their influencer marketing programs, any successful program still requires a lot of planning, and — when it comes down to it — a lot of hand-holding of the influencers. Influencers are people; the more personal your interaction with them, the more personal the content they're creating for you will be, and the more it will resonate with their readers.

If your brand doesn't have the resources needed to truly manage influencer marketing, we recommend you outsource to an agency that specializes in it until you do. As we outline in Chapter 5, there are many ways to partner with influencer agencies to ensure your efforts are successful and cost-effective.

Measure the right stuff

Measuring the right stuff doesn't just help your influencer marketing programs; it helps you recruit the right kind of influencers.

Never, ever begin an influencer program before you can answer the question, "What will success look like?" If you don't know how you'll measure success, how will you know if you got there? And if you don't know what your goals are, how will you know what to measure?

We devote Part IV of this book to dealing with metrics and return on investment (ROI) of influencer programs, but here are some guidelines to consider:

✔ You can only truly measure ROI if you take the cost of your entire marketing program and its effect on sales into consideration. What percentage of budget that was allocated for influencer marketing? How does that budget compare to sales results?

✔ "Success" can be measured in sales results, but linking purchases back to a series of blog posts is incredibly difficult. How can you track someone who saw a tweet about a new mascara, went to the blog post about it, took down the name of the mascara in her phone, and then purchased it the next time she was in her corner drugstore weeks later? Our ability to use technology to track these purchase paths is improving, but we're not there yet. (This is why we have to estimate ROI as a percentage of sales compared to percentage of budget.)

✔ "Success" can be measured in ways other than sales results, including the amount of content created, increases in a brand's social followings (Facebook, Instagram, and so on), site traffic, coupon downloads, engagement (comments, shares, and so on), overall share of voice before and after a program, overall social mentions, and brand sentiment.

An effective approach to measuring a program's efficacy matters to influencers because it guides what they need to do. If you're clear on what you're trying to achieve, you can be clear about which influencers you need, and what you'll ask them to produce. (Trust us, influencers don't want to create useless content any more than you want it created!)

Being upfront with influencers about what you're trying to achieve makes your offer more compelling, and helps the influencers feel that they're in a true partnership with you.

Making Influencer Marketing Work for You

No matter what size business you have or what kind of marketing or PR background you come from, you can make influencer marketing work for your business — as long as you keep in mind what influencer marketing can and cannot do! The various approaches outlined in this section can serve as the foundation for the influencer programs you'll build.

If you're an established consumer brand

If you represent a large, established brand and you're looking to launch or enhance your influencer marketing programs, you likely have the experience, resources, and budget to regularly run large-scale programs.

Leveraging your advantages

If you're an established brand, you've obviously been successful with your marketing and PR programs. Way to go! You have systems and processes in place for your marketing efforts, you know what works, and you have a budget in place for ensuring your campaigns are successful. You should be able to implement all our tips and tricks in your influencer marketing efforts. Use your scale and experience to your advantage!

You probably already have access to more data and metrics for influencer marketing than you realize. Many social media metrics tools — the ones you're already using to monitor your social media programs — have add-ons for measuring influencer activity. Research what your current tools can already do to help save budget while ensuring you're measuring your programs' successes.

Speaking of measuring success, according to a 2015 study performed by influencer marketing agency Tomason, businesses are, on average, making $6.50 for each $1 spent on influencer marketing. That's quite a statistic! Data like these support influencer marketing ROI figures and should make an easy case for diverting more marketing budget to influencer marketing.

Given the demonstrable ROI, hiring a dedicated person to oversee influencer marketing makes sense. Just as businesses were once reluctant to hire full-time social media resources and now have entire social media teams *and* agencies, influencer marketing is deserving of full-time strategizing and implementation.

Think of influencer marketing as an addition to your current programs, not a standalone effort. Start with your overall marketing plan: What are your goals? Your key messages? Your key milestones? Your social media efforts will be coordinated with your more traditional tactics (digital, print, TV, radio, and so on). There's no reason for influencer marketing to be any different. Influencers should amplify your efforts, not compete with them!

As an established brand, the best reason to use influencer marketing is to help give your brand a fresh perspective. Allowing influencers to tell your story lets other consumers see your brand through their eyes. Handing over the "storytelling keys" to influencers breathes new life and personality into brands that may otherwise feel too staid to consumers.

Avoiding common mistakes

Larger brands with bigger budgets and teams can run into trouble with influencer marketing by taking too much of a "hands-off" approach. There are, of course, ways to scale influencer marketing programs, but avoid rushing to automation! Don't fall into one of these traps:

✔ **Even if you build your own internal pool of influencers, or outsource your programs to an influencer agency, don't underestimate the amount of work that goes into making influencer campaigns successful.** The very reason influencer marketing works is because influencers are real, live human beings — not display ads. There are ways to scale your programs, but influencer marketing is not programmatic. Don't approach it as though it were.

✔ **Don't under-budget!** You're working with individuals (not machines or ad exchanges). No matter how sophisticated your process or tools may be, every influencer campaign will be different, and each will require a larger investment of time and resources than a campaign that only involves "flipping a switch."

✔ **Don't try to control everything.** More established brands frequently have a more rigid way of doing things, and are often used to owning — and controlling — their own media. Yes, an influencer campaign would be more automated and controlled if a company simply provided the influencers the exact copy they were supposed to publish — except that's not influencer marketing. Don't try to control the messages in the name of efficiency or fear of losing control. Otherwise, you're just forcing a different kind of display advertising into a medium where it will fall flat. (Bloggers' audiences don't want to read a prewritten press release!)

✔ **Treat your influencers like individuals.** The more impersonally you treat your influencers (something that's easy to do when you're a large organization), the less personal and less effective their work will be.

Finding an approach that works for you

As a large and (we're going to assume) sophisticated company, you have greater flexibility to really leverage influencer marketing and make it work for you. Here's how:

✔ **Your overall marketing initiatives can lay the foundation for hugely successful influencer marketing campaigns.** You can use influencer marketing to supplement, enhance, and amplify your existing efforts. For example, say you've created a two-minute ad spot but only 30 seconds of it will air on TV. Use influencers to showcase the full video across social channels, while everyone uses the same hashtag.

✔ **Don't limit your perception of influencer marketing to "something someone else creates over there."** Use and repurpose the amazing content you worked so hard with your influencers to create! Spend the time, energy, and budget to create large, high-quality influencer programs. We're talking about the kind of programs where the writing and photos and captions and posts are striking, where influencers clearly can and do produce outstanding content for you. And then repurpose that content all day long! Use it in display ads, via social media channels, on your website, even on TV. Be sure to build content usage terms into your influencer contracts.

Influencer marketing works in two directions: We mostly focus on how influencers do a great job of introducing *their* readers to a new brand or product — to grow brand awareness, purchase intent, and (ultimately) purchase. But influencer marketing also works well for consumers who are already in the purchasing intent phase. For instance, a guy who's looking to buy a new vacuum cleaner is going to start by searching online for something like "best family vacuum cleaners." Imagine how compelling it would be for him to stumble upon a series of blog posts written about a specific vacuum cleaner, especially if those posts were balanced and visually attractive. He's never heard of these bloggers before, but this demonstrates the long-term impact of influencer marketing programs.

What's more, this man may then further investigate the vacuum he's read about by going to an online retailer and looking up the model to read reviews. It's extra powerful to have influencers write reviews directly on retail sites (with full disclosures that they're being paid for their reviews) to help move the customer from intent to purchase.

If you're a small to midsize consumer brand

You don't have all the experience and budget of the major brands, but that doesn't mean you can't rock influencer marketing! In some ways, you're actually more likely to be able to enjoy success with this new marketing medium *because* you're more nimble and better able to try new things. You can absolutely use your size and lesser-known brand name to your advantage!

Leveraging your advantages

What you may lack in resources (budget and human capital) will impact the size and length of your influencer programs — you simply won't have the ability to run giant programs again and again.

Instead of breadth of programs, focus on depth of relationships. In other words, do more with less. Spend time upfront identifying influencers who really embody your brand, and develop true, one-on-one working relationships with them. If you can't pay them in cash, "pay" them with valuable products, insider information, and attention. Treat them as extensions of your workforce. Consider developing brand ambassador programs that span several months.

If you have a lesser-known brand, you have more creative freedom. The social media influencer sphere is attracted to innovation and self-expression. The less forced influencer marketing is (that is, the less a brand insists on stringent brand and editorial guidelines when working with influencers), the more likely the program will be to garner users' attention. Take chances and let your influencers get creative with their assignments!

As you're working to create more awareness of your brand, you're building out your social media presence. Influencer marketing is especially useful at helping companies build their social media followings on Twitter, Facebook, Pinterest, Instagram, and so on.

Focusing your influencer marketing goals on shorter-term wins, such as building up your social media following, means you'll be better able to track successes. "Brand awareness" is a good goal, but it's tricky to measure and expensive to achieve on a broad, national scale. Influencer marketing goals need to be realistic and achievable, especially if your resources are constrained.

Avoiding common mistakes

Some approaches to influencer marketing simply won't work, regardless of the size of the company trying to implement them. But we've found a disappointing pattern among small to midsize organizations trying to implement influencer marketing for the first time. Don't fall into these traps:

- ✔ **Don't underestimate the cost of running influencer marketing programs.** Too many companies turn to influencer marketing because they mistakenly think it's a cheap, easy alternative to other marketing tactics. It's not! Producing amazing and demonstrably valuable campaigns takes dedicated time and resources. That doesn't mean you can't get great bang for your buck (as we outline in this book), but don't approach influencer marketing as though it's a quick fix for marketing ails.

- ✔ **Ensure that influencer marketing is only a portion of your marketing budget.** We recommend no more than 20 percent of your total marketing budget for smaller organizations. *Remember:* Influencer marketing amplifies traditional marketing efforts, but it doesn't replace them.

- ✔ **Think about what your success metrics are going to be and how you'll get there.** Are you tracking sentiment, brand lift, coupon distribution, social media followers? With what tools and benchmarks? Whatever your goals, start with a small, in-house program with a handful of influencers and let them serve as your benchmark. Too many organizations throw together influencer programs with unrealistic expectations ("Our hashtag will go *viral!*") and no way to measure success.

Finding an approach that works for you

You want to get the most out of your investment, especially since your marketing dollars are likely to be spread thin. Keep these tips in mind as you approach influencer marketing:

- **Given your more limited resources, focus on influencer marketing programs that truly amplify your other marketing efforts rather than programs that operate completely independently from them.** If you have a product promo code or sale, use influencers to get that code spread far and wide. If you're launching a product in stores, coordinate your influencer efforts to launch at the same time. Do you have TV, YouTube, radio, or podcast content you're proud of? Work with influencers to share that content with their audience.

- **Use influencer marketing to increase awareness of and followers to your social media channels or to increase your email marketing list.** This is easier to do if your influencers have one simple, clear, and consistent message.

- **Keep your goals realistic, measurable, and short term.**

- **Nurture the relationships you develop with your influencers.** You want them to become vocal advocates for your brand — both online and off — even when they aren't being paid to do so.

- **Reuse the content that your influencers create!** Their content can populate your other social channels and resonate with your audience because the content came from users and not just the brand. This is especially true for Facebook, where you're constantly searching for new content that will engage your readers; posting images and blog links is fast and easy, and very relatable.

If you're a startup brand

Being a startup is tough in every way. You're struggling to build something great internally, while ensuring that potential customers know you exist. Often startups turn to influencer marketing because they think it's a fast, cheap (read: free) way to get a lot of traction with brand awareness. And although that's not exactly true, there are ways to make influencer marketing work for startups.

Leveraging your advantages

The very best advantage you have as a startup is that you're new and fresh. Maybe you want to be first to market with a cool new concept. Maybe you can do something no one has seen before!

Find influencers who care about being trendy and who want to know, see, or do things before their peers, and appeal to this desire — you've got something no one else has. If you can't pay them, offer them first looks, tours of your workspace, beta versions of products before they're on the market, or stock/equity in your company.

Be creative! As you're trying to get your brand name out there, you have tons of freedom to try new things. PR "stunts" are safer to try. Consider collaborating with potential influencers to do something radical!

You don't have to limit your influencer activity to writing reviews of your product. Consider reaching out to influencers and using them as beta testers. Bloggers can make amazing virtual focus groups. Sometimes, early feedback makes all the difference between a startup succeeding or failing. If you don't have the resources to pay an influencer to write a public-facing review, the influencer may still be willing to work with you to give you private feedback.

Avoiding common mistakes

Startups tend to make the following mistakes when it comes to influencer marketing. Avoid doing the following:

- **Assuming influencer marketing is quick or cheap:** Influencer marketing takes a lot of time and resources, two things most startups don't often have. Unless there is a clear strategic marketing goal that influencers can help you achieve (such as beta testing), don't waste your startup energy.

- **Trying influencer marketing if your product is an app:** If you're promoting an app, you may want to reconsider influencer marketing. Yes, it can be a fabulous tool for long-term boosts in searches — if you engage a handful of bloggers to include your app as part of a blog series on "perfect apps for kindergarteners," you can be sure that parents who search for "kindergarten apps" will discover those posts. But you won't see a surge of downloads directly from blog posts. Don't max out your marketing budget hiring 50 bloggers to write about your app thinking you'll see thousands and thousands of downloads as a result. Influencer marketing is not direct response — it will never convert at the rate a startup app needs.

Finding an approach that works for you

If you're limited in resources and budget, be very deliberate in how to leverage influencers and know exactly what you're going to get out of a program before you start one.

Chapter 2

Digging Deeper into Influencer Marketing

In This Chapter

▶ Seeing where marketing started

▶ Understanding how influencer marketing came about

▶ Looking at the future of influencer marketing

▶ Determining whether influencer marketing is paid, owned, or earned media

All successful marketing or advertising is reliant on influence. Brands want to *influence* consumers to become aware of, consider, and eventually purchase their products. Consumers are *influenced* by all manner of brand communications, whether from the brand directly through traditional advertising (TV ads, print ads, online display ads, radio spots, and so on) or from word-of-mouth endorsements from friends and family.

The entire marketing ecosystem is dependent on influence. But in our current advertising-everywhere climate, where consumers are constantly bombarded with brand noise and competing messaging, who gets heard? How do consumers decide who to listen to? Who actually wields the power to influence?

We answer all those questions in this chapter. But before we talk about influencer marketing, let's go back a bit and look at what let up to influencer marketing.

A Brief History of Marketing and Public Relations

Influencer marketing is a relatively new form of marketing, but it has its roots in the earliest days of public relations. In this section, we give you a quick tour of the history that led up to influencer marketing.

In the beginning was the word: The purpose of public relations

"Let's get people talking about us!" That's the goal of all public relations (PR). PR firms have existed since at least the year 1900, serving as something of the right hand to advertising's left. For decades, the distinction between the two was easy to understand: Advertising was something you paid for, and publicity was something you earned.

The job of a PR agent is to build awareness for her client by "earning" it, which means creating press or buzz that builds organically. For example, a PR agent representing a new line of organic makeup might pitch editors at beauty magazines. She sends the editors makeup samples along with information about the products in the hopes that the editors will love what they get. If the editors love the products, they might feature the makeup line in an unpaid, editorial section of the magazine — in other words, an article. Maybe the founders of the new makeup line will be featured in an article about industry innovators. Or maybe one of the products will make it onto an "Editor's Picks" list, featuring the best new products on the market.

Landing a feature in the Editor's Picks list is *earned* placement: The cosmetics company didn't pay for it — they earned the respect of the magazine editors based on the merits of their product. You can imagine how much this type of endorsement would mean for a brand! A glossy ad in a magazine might grab a reader's attention, but the reader might not believe the ad's claims. After all, the reader knows the ad was designed by advertising professionals, and she knows the cosmetics company paid for it. On the other hand, she loves the Editor's Picks list. She trusts that the editor spent time and effort considering which products to include on that list and recognizes the editor as an authority in the industry. She may even tear out the list and bring it with her the next time she goes shopping for makeup. She'll definitely try this product.

This is essentially how press mentions have worked for years. Magazine editors at all kinds of publications receive press releases and products every day from people who want their clients, companies, brands, products, or ideas noticed. They want to be written about favorably by authoritative figures who readers trust.

Word of mouth: The holy grail of marketing

If you see a flyer for a new café that just opened downtown claiming to serve "the best sandwiches ever," you may or may not believe the café's claim. Of course the café is going to say that, right?

But what if your best friend tells you he just ate "the best sandwich ever" at the new café downtown? Not only would you be more likely to believe his claim, but you might make a point to remember the café's name and consider it the next time you're eating lunch nearby.

That's word-of-mouth marketing at its most basic: People trust recommendations from friends and family. Friends and family influence our purchasing decisions. Word-of-mouth recommendations are incredibly effective.

Unfortunately, brands face two great challenges when trying to generate great word of mouth:

- ✔ **They can't guarantee that any given consumer will mention their product or brand, even if the consumer truly enjoys their products.** Data shows that people are far more likely to share bad brand experiences than good ones.

- ✔ **There is no way to force word-of-mouth marketing to happen on a grand scale.** Getting dozens, hundreds, or thousands of people to know about your company, let alone talk about it, is difficult.

As brands tried to solve for these challenges, they planted the seeds for today's influencer marketing.

Enter social media: Take it to the people!

Blogging was the foundation of social media, but it took several years and many failed attempts for PR professionals to truly understand how working with bloggers could revolutionize word-of-mouth marketing. At first, it was just kind of messy.

Blogging came to prominence in the United States at the turn of the 21st century. Political blogging gained traction and credibility during the tumultuous post-9/11 era, when bloggers began covering the news in ways traditional media outlets weren't (ironically, becoming newsworthy themselves in the process). In the first few years of the century, blogging ushered in a new era of Internet usage:

- ✔ **More and more people gained high-speed Internet access, including at the office, and the demand for fresh content surged.** Sites like Gawker (www.gawker.com), which launched in 2002, were instantly popular.

- ✔ **Modern web design made it easier than ever for people to create blogs and to comment on them.** WordPress (www.wordpress.com) and Blogger (www.blogger.com), two popular blog platforms still widely used today, were launched in 2003. They allowed people to publish blogs without needing to know how to build or design a web page.

- ✔ **Blog readers loved the ability to comment and enter into discussions with blog writers and other readers.** The concept of active online engagement took hold. Users were no longer passive; they were part of the conversation.

By 2005, *The New York Times* reported that more than 30 million Americans were reading blogs regularly. Advertisers and PR professionals took notice. A whole new world had opened up to these industries. Almost overnight, a new way of reaching consumers had come into existence. Instead of having to work with the editors in charge of print or online publications, PR agents could work directly with prominent bloggers directly.

So they tried.

On the surface, blogs didn't look much different from traditional media. Instead of magazine editors, there were bloggers. Instead of print circulation numbers, blogs had daily or monthly visitors. And just like traditional publications, blogs focused on specific, sometimes niche topics that made it easy to target the right client with the right publication.

Except it turned out that blogging is actually *vastly* different from traditional press, for many reasons — reasons that PR professionals learned the hard way. Because, despite the fact that blogging was a truly new online medium (with so many possibilities for changing traditional PR), most PR agencies managed bloggers and blogger outreach exactly the same way they'd been managing press outreach for decades. And it didn't work very well:

- ✔ **Bloggers aren't media outlets — they're human beings telling personal stories on personal websites.** Back when blogging was new, bloggers didn't understand why a PR rep would interrupt or "invade" their personal space with impersonal requests.

- ✔ **PR reps often got bloggers' names wrong, or wouldn't take time to learn about a blogger's niche.** This further alienated bloggers from wanting to work with PR companies.

- ✔ **Bloggers aren't journalists looking for the next big "scoop."** They don't need content suggestions from companies.

- ✔ **For the most part, if a blogger is going to voluntarily write about a product she loves, she'll do so without prompting.** If a brand reaches out to a blogger with the express intention of the blogger writing about them, the brand needs to approach the blogger as a professional, and enter into a professional relationship.

The rise of the "mommyblogger"

While blogging was still relatively new, different types of blogging niches formed along with their respective, devoted communities. The first blogs to gain widespread acknowledgement (and yes, notoriety) from mainstream press tended to be political blogs and tech blogs.

You might remember how bloggers were portrayed by the mainstream media in the early days. Bloggers were all supposedly nerdy boys living in their parents' basements, socially inept and unemployable. Bloggers were accused of being pajama-clad, entitled, self-aggrandized commentators with too many opinions and zero journalistic integrity.

In fact, despite the mainstream media's skewed portrayals, thousands of blogging communities were alive and thriving by 2005 — many of them with giant audiences and many of them women-focused. In response to a mainstream media article that rhetorically asked where all the women bloggers were, the BlogHer organization was formed. In the summer of 2005, 300 female bloggers gathered at the inaugural BlogHer Conference in San Jose, California, to meet each other and learn about the state of the female blogosphere.

What transpired was transformative: Women bloggers were everywhere male bloggers were, covering the same topics (politics, tech), as well as many others. Some women had amassed huge audiences, writing on all kinds of topics — from lifestyle and beauty, to health and fitness, to craft and do-it-yourself (DIY). And many women bloggers were writing about parenting.

The 2005 BlogHer Conference brought to light, in a nonvirtual way, three prominent, emerging trends that were happening in the online world:

✔ **Women had discovered blogging and were actively participating in the blogosphere in huge numbers.** Women represented at least half of the social media producers and consumers.

✔ **Some of the most popular blogs were written by moms, and blogs that focused on parenting were labeled "mom blogs."** Prominent mom bloggers (or "mommybloggers") were reaching millions of readers every month and wielding tremendous influence. All anyone had to do was visit one of these mom blogs to witness a vibrant, active community of commenters who clearly trusted and cared about what the bloggers had to say.

✔ **Brands, PR agencies, and advertisers realized that mom bloggers were attracting millions of readers and were incredibly influential.** Almost every brand of consumer product on the market wants to reach moms. The rise of mom blogging sparked widespread interest among brand advertisers and their PR agencies. For those of us who were in the blogging/marketing/PR industry at the time, it seemed that suddenly *everybody* was rushing to find a way to leverage the unprecedented influence of mom bloggers.

Today, *mommyblogger* is an outdated and limiting term. Just as it's inaccurate to portray social media experts as basement-dwelling nerds, it's inaccurate to define influential women by their parental status. Not all popular female bloggers are moms, and not all moms who blog focus on their children. Plus, the term *mommy* is a term of endearment; marketers who use it come across as inauthentic, condescending, or both.

Because of this, most of the first PR pitches to bloggers fell on deaf ears, went unanswered, or (worst of all!) were published on public blogs and circulated among bloggers as what *not* to do. When a well-respected tech blogger known for her childfree, vegan lifestyle was approached by a meat company touting child-friendly recipes, you can bet she posted that pitch on her blog!

Of course, PR reps and brands eventually learned how to win favor with bloggers. And those early mistakes paved the way for what would eventually become influencer marketing.

The Beginning of Influencer Marketing

Influencer marketing is the result of influencers and PR agencies refining how they work together to harness the power of social media. In this book, we show you how, when done correctly, influencer marketing is far more effective, controllable, measurable, and exciting than traditional approaches to word-of-mouth marketing.

Influencer marketing is the art and science of engaging people who are influential online to share brand messaging with their audiences in the form of sponsored content.

What influencer marketing is

Let's break down the definition of influencer marketing and dig a little deeper:

- ✔ **"The art and science of engaging people . . .":** What makes influencer marketing so special is that it's about engaging real people. The Internet in general, and social media platforms in particular, have made it easy for anyone to be an expert or build a community over which she has influence. Influence is no longer the sole territory of celebrities, newscasters, athletic stars, politicians, big brands, or publications.

    The challenge is that real people aren't necessarily marketers. They aren't companies. They aren't even press. Real people don't tend to have professional relationships with brands.

    So, brands and marketers can't reach out to real people to engage with them the way they would reach out to magazine editors. Instead, they have to approach real people in a human way.

- ✔ **". . . who are influential online . . .":** Just who, exactly, is influential online? Who is a "social media influencer"? The answer depends on why you're asking, who you're trying to influence, and what you want them to do. Sometimes, influence can be measured by statistics (like number of followers), but more often than not, true influence is measured in qualitative data as much as (if not more than) quantitative data. Numbers tell one story; specifically, that a person posts enough content of interest to attract a certain number of readers. But we don't always know where those numbers come from. Maybe an influencer posted one story that generated a lot of followers, but readers never came back? Or maybe a blogger attracts many monthly followers because of great search engine marketing, but readers aren't "sticky" (they don't stay on the site long or return to the site). Qualitative data, such as regular commenters who are deeply engaged with a blogger's content, tells a much fuller story than numbers alone.

✔ **". . . to share brand messaging with their audiences in the form of sponsored content":** The message brands want influencers to share may be very specific and boilerplate, or it may be very loose and fluid. For example, a brand may:

- *Offer a downloadable coupon and ask influencers to share that coupon with their audience.*

- *Create a video and ask influencers to share that video.* Or the brand may want influencers to watch the video, and then offer their opinions of the video while also sharing it with their readers.

- *Ask bloggers to sample and write a review of a product.* That review may have to include specific language about the product (provided by the brand). Or the brand may give the blogger complete flexibility in the language he uses. (This is still considered "brand messaging" because the blogger's message is about the brand's product.)

- *Ask social media influencers to photograph or write a story about a concept that reinforces a brand's message:* For instance, say a beverage brand is eager to be perceived as fun and stylish. Instead of seeking reviews, the brand may engage influencers to creatively showcase their relevance using a brand-approved hashtag.

The idea of influencer marketing is that, once an influencer shares something, her audience is inspired to take action. Action may take the form of something small, such as noting and remembering a brand name (which may lead to brand recognition, familiarity, and purchase at a future date). Action may be immediate, such as a blog reader commenting on a sponsored blog post or sharing an influencer's post on Facebook. In some cases, an audience member may be inspired to purchase a reviewed product then and there, and take action in the form of clicking a "Buy Now" link. Each of these actions may be a desired outcome of an influencer marketing program.

Influencer marketing leverages our ability to communicate with the world at once through any number of platforms. Specifically, influencer marketing solves almost all traditional PR problems, as well as the more modern PR and marketing challenges that emerged along with social media.

People trust word-of-mouth marketing more than any other kind of marketing, but it's challenging for PR professionals because it's hard to predict and impossible to guarantee. Online influencers changed all this. Sponsored blog posts, tweets, Facebook updates, and Instagram pictures are all forms of word-of-mouth marketing. It makes sense for brands to enter into relationships with influencers where both their participation and the results (how many people they'll reach on any given medium) are guaranteed. Press releases and traditional media outlets never gave this kind of guarantee.

Plus, influencer marketing is a boon to the influencers themselves. Unlike back in the early days of blogging, when a blogger's only hope for revenue came from banner ads over which she had no creative control, today anyone who has developed an online audience can expect to work with brands collaboratively, and to be paid accordingly for their work.

What influencer marketing is not

In some ways, influencer marketing seems like the next generation of celebrity endorsements — except instead of glossy ads, we're talking about endorsements that occur online and through social media. But the difference between the old and new world of endorsements isn't just a matter of technological advances: Audiences everywhere are far more media savvy today than they ever were, and the success of online influencers is dependent on their transparency and authenticity.

Celebrities aside, most people who've grown to be influential online have done so because they connect to their audiences in genuine ways. They tell honest stories, share real-life photos, and make videos that resonate with everyday people.

There are two primary misconceptions about what influencer marketing is or should be. We tell you what influencer marketing is *not* in the following sections.

Influencer marketing is not a commercial

An influencer marketing program will only be successful if the influencers are allowed to do what they do best: Connect with their audiences. The more authentic the brand allows an influencer to be, and the more freedom an influencer has to share brand message in her voice, the more the message will resonate with the influencer's fans. The more scripted or forced the message becomes, the less effective it will be.

When your friend is recommending the new café downtown, he uses his own language, his own unique way of communicating with you:

> "Dude, I just had the best sandwich *ever* at that new place on the corner of Main. I'm not sure what they put in it, but the melted cheese was the best I've ever had. You gotta go! Oh, they gave me a coupon, too! Want one?"

Now imagine if, instead, your friend spoke like this:

> "Did you know that Melt, the new café on Main Street, is open for business? Come on in and try one of their new lunch melts, available in four varieties! It's an excellent spot for lunch with the guys, or for a quick bite when you're on-the-go. Outdoor patio available! Here's a coupon, good through the end of next week!"

You'd be put off if your friend started speaking in what's obviously marketing-ese. It'd feel uncomfortable and weird — and you'd wonder what the heck had happened to your pal. The same goes for influencer marketing. People aren't engaging on social media to be sold something or to interact with scripts. People use social media to be social.

Brands that spend time and money trying to use the paid advertising/commercial model in the influencer marketing world risk inefficacy and unfavorable backlash. And social media influencers who allow themselves to be used in this way by brands risk losing the audiences they've built over months and years.

Influencer marketing is not pay-for-play

People who are new to online sponsorships and the world of influencer marketing are often skeptical. They think that brands that engage with influencers are paying influencers to post positive reviews or say things they don't mean. The good news is, that's not how it works.

First, brands that work with influencers *do* usually offer compensation, but not in exchange for positive reviews. Influencers are compensated for the work that they're being asked to do. Entering into an agreement with a brand, receiving a product, trying it out in real life, taking photos of it, and writing a blog post that is even-handed, true to the influencer's voice, and valuable to the brand takes time.

If brands are using influencers as part of their marketing strategy, those influencers are an extension of the brand's marketing team. They deserve to be compensated for their time, energy, and finished product. In this respect, influencers are more like freelance marketers than celebrity endorsers.

Diving In: The Present Landscape of Influencer Marketing

The entire world is connecting online through social media, so we're seeing a convergence of PR, marketing, advertising, and digital and social media. Influencer marketing is on the forefront of this convergence, because it straddles aspects of all these media formats. More excitingly, influencer marketing has a huge potential for growth!

We're currently experiencing all of the following:

- **Platform explosion:** Blogging has changed considerably since it rose to prominence in the early 2000s. Long-form storytelling isn't as popular as it used to be, but that doesn't mean blogs aren't still popular. In fact, some of the world's most popular websites started off as blogs, and still feature regularly updated stories, memes, and articles from their original authors (think The Huffington Post, ScaryMommy.com, or Mashable). Ree Drummond (a.k.a. The Pioneer Woman) began as a blogger, and she has now written several best-selling cookbooks, is a renowned photographer, and has her own series on The Food Network. She still maintains her "storytelling" content in addition to her lifestyle guides.

  But blogs aren't the only platform in town. Today we have established platforms like YouTube, Twitter, Facebook, Instagram, and Pinterest, and newer video-based formats like Vine, Snapchat, and Periscope. Social media may change more rapidly than media of the past (TV, radio, print), but there's good news here: Yes, it may be difficult to keep up with the changing landscape, but as long as there are social media platforms, there will be social media influencers!

- **Technology advances:** The tools available to engage in and monitor influencer marketing grow more sophisticated by the day. It's easier than ever for brands to use these tools to do the following:

  - Listen to social media as it pertains to their industries and companies

  - Identify target influencers and identify where they are

  - Engage with influencers quickly and easily

  - Monitor the work that the influencers do

  - Track how effective their influencers have been — following the path from an influencer's post to its amplification through his network through the ultimate conversion or sale

- **Budget growth:** Blogger relationships were once the sole province of PR, and the budgets allocated for influencer outreach were minimal to nonexistent. (After all, the thinking used to go, social media is free.

Why should anyone have to pay for social media programs?) Today social media marketing is part of everyone's plan. Social media marketing budgets may live with marketing, digital advertising, PR, or often all three departments or agencies. And influencer marketing, as a subset of social media marketing, does, too. A widely circulated study conducted by Tomoson, a company focused on providing influencer marketing software, nearly 60 percent of marketers plan to increase their spending on influencer marketing between 2015 and 2016.

✔ **Success:** Influencer marketing is powerful! Studies show time and time again that influencer marketing — when done right — moves the needle better than any other form of marketing. Want proof?

- According to a 2014 McKinsey Study, "marketing-inspired word-of-mouth" generates more than double the sales of paid advertising, and these customers have a 37 percent higher retention rate.

- According to the 2015 BRANDERATI study, offers shared by trusted advocates convert at four to ten times higher rate than offers sent by brands.

- According to the 2014 Burst Media Influencer Marketing Benchmarks Report, on average, marketers who implemented an influencer marketing program in 2014 received $6.85 in earned media value for every $1.00 of paid media.

Paid, Owned, Earned: A Messy Media Landscape

As influencer marketing is poised for explosive growth across channels, platforms, departments, agencies, and more, market forces will need to iron out one particular challenge: defining influencer marketing as paid, owned, or earned media.

✔ **Paid media:** Media you pay for. It covers anything considered "traditional advertising," like banner ads or TV commercials. Paid media uses a one-to-many model. A brand or agency has creative control over the entire ad unit and sends it out into the world to reach consumers on a mass scale. Consumers are ignoring these types of messages more than ever.

✔ **Owned media:** Media completely owned by a brand or advertiser. A company website, blog, or social media channel is completely owned and controlled by the company. Owned media works in tandem with paid media to build brand awareness, share brand messaging, entice new customers to explore and build trust in a brand, and interact with existing customers. And although owned media isn't "free" (because internal resources still must be spent in order to create and maintain these assets), it's not anywhere near as expensive as paid media. For the most part, there is little to no cost to distribute owned media (such as a brand's Facebook page).

✔ **Earned media:** Brand mentions created by consumers themselves, outside of the control of the brand. This includes independent blog posts, reviews, mentions on Twitter or Facebook, or even comments/responses to a brand's social media efforts. Earned media is a great test for how well a brand's paid and owned media are performing.

Brands and marketers disagree on whether influencer marketing is paid, owned, or earned. And that's because influencer marketing doesn't clearly fall into one category. Those who try too hard to narrowly define it will ultimately fail at influencer programs, either because of oversimplified assumptions or misaligned expectations. The biggest barriers to the growth of influencer marketing are those who misunderstand its unique nature.

In the following sections, we look at the three forms of media and how influencer marketing aligns with each.

Paid media

You could argue that if a brand is paying influencers to write about them following brand guidelines, then yes, it's paid media. What's the difference between paying a top-influencing Instagrammer to photograph a product and post it to her account, and paying an advertising agency to photograph a product and post it as an ad online?

On the other hand, influencers aren't advertising agencies. They're real people and the only way their posts will be considered effective is if they seem real to their audiences. A brand can't control the message the influencer creates — otherwise, the message misses the point. Plus, there's no easy way to scale influencer marketing at the same rate you can with an ad. Advertisers can use a marketplace and, for a fee, click a button to have a single ad served millions of times. It's much more time consuming to work with individual influencers to create content that's custom to them and their readers.

When brands assume that influencer marketing must be paid media,

✔ Brands want complete creative control of the content, as opposed to handing the reins to the influencers.

✔ Content becomes too ad-like and, therefore, less effective.

✔ Advertisers get frustrated over lack of scalability. Instead of working with one agency on one creative plan, you're working with as many influencers as you choose — sometimes hundreds — and they all have their own creative processes.

Owned media

Brands are engaging with influencers, asking them to behave as an extension of their own social media marketing efforts. Influencers may be asked to amplify a brand's social media posts or to comment on them. It's very easy to see how hiring social media influencers could fall under the umbrella of a brand's owned social media — especially if the content that influencers create is then repurposed or syndicated on the brand's own media channels.

On the other hand, even though brands are paying and instructing influencers to create media, brands still don't "own" the content the way they would if they were creating it themselves. For instance, if a food brand contracts a blogger to create a unique recipe and post it to her blog, is that content "owned" by the brand or the influencer? They may have a legal agreement stating that the brand may *use* her content, but the content has authentic value to consumers specifically because it was *not* created by the brand. Plus, if a brand is used to considering owned media more or less free (except for staffing/resource expenditures), it's nearly impossible to justify cash outlays for influencers.

When brands assume that influencer marketing must be owned media,

- ✔ There is little to no budget or resource allocation for managing the influencer program.
- ✔ Brands want to own the content the influencers create.

Earned media

Brands engage influencers so that their audiences will take action. One way brands measure success of influencer marketing programs is by how much engagement they receive. For example, consider the case of a food brand that contracts a blogger to create a unique recipe and post it to her blog. Say the blog post received 15 comments, was retweeted 257 times on Twitter, and pinned over 5,000 times on Pinterest. That's a tremendous amount of earned media!

Sometimes brands don't require that influencers do anything. Just as with the old public relations model, sometimes brands simply send bloggers a product. There is no guarantee the blogger will review that product or mention it on her social media channels. If she decides she wants to, that's entirely her choice — and *definitely* earned.

On the other hand, when the influencer has been contracted and compensated by a brand, the influencer's audience creates the "earned" media, not the influencer herself. Her content is paid, but when her readers share her content with *their* readers, those shares are earned. So if, for example, a blogger is paid to promote a new ice cream and shares a coupon with her readers, and then her readers share the coupon with their friends on Facebook, those Facebook shares may be considered earned.

When a brand sends a product or press release to an influencer with no contracted expectation of coverage, this approach tends to yield poor, inconsistent results. The very reason influencer marketing is gaining traction is because brands can move away from the earned approach and experience amazing results.

When brands assume that influencer marketing must be earned media,

✔ They approach influencers with a "spray and pray" mindset (throw tons of pitches out to influencers willy-nilly and hope that some of them take desired actions).

✔ The program results are mixed and inconsistent.

✔ Influencers don't take the opportunity seriously. It's easy to blow off or ignore.

The Exciting Future of Influencer Marketing

Influencer marketing is all about human interaction. A brand can work with influencers to build awareness for the brand, get people excited about their product, reach the brand's ideal customers where they want to be reached, and ultimately drive a brand's success.

Influencer marketing is possible because real people are able to interact with other real people in ways never imagined before. Influencer marketing is successful because real people trust other real people more than they trust brands.

Influencer marketing isn't really like any form of marketing that came before — and that's a good thing! When we stop trying to force influencer marketing to be something that was or something it's not, the possibilities are truly exciting!

Part II
Identifying Influencers

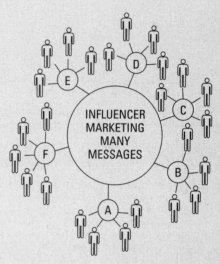

Find tips for sending products to influencers in a free article at www.dummies.com/extras/influencermarketing.

In this part . . .

- ✓ Learn why women are the most influential demographic for the majority of brands today.

- ✓ Determine when you should do it yourself or hire an agency to help with your influencer marketing campaign.

- ✓ Learn how to engage influencers in the right way to get the best results.

- ✓ Get the inside scoop on how to compensate influencers fairly.

Chapter 3

The Best Influencers: The Power of Women on Your Bottom Line

In This Chapter

▶ Seeing the influence women have on their households

▶ Recognizing the power of women in social media

▶ Appreciating how on-point women are when it comes to social trends

*I*f you've decided that influencer marketing is the right tool for you, the next step in carrying out your marketing strategy is to identify which influencers are right for your brand.

So, how exactly do you determine who the most successful influencers will be specific to your needs? Each situation and product will call for a unique set of influencers and campaign offerings, but it's almost always a safe bet to start with female influencers.

In this chapter, we explain the powerful role that women play in their households, in social media, and in social trends. When you fully appreciate the power of women, you'll be able to work with them to accomplish your marketing goals.

Women Rule the Household

Traditionally women have taken on the primary role within the household. Although gender roles are changing, women still rule the household when it comes to making purchasing decisions.

Young women are exceeding their male counterparts in education and earnings in many metropolitan areas in the United States. They're also holding a greater percentage of jobs as compared to a couple decades ago. All these factors in turn, lead to an overall increase in spending and purchasing power.

TIME reports that there has been an 8 percent increase in the number of women ages 25 to 29 holding a bachelor's degree or higher from 1999 to 2009. In addition, almost 50 percent of non-farm jobs in the United States today are held by women, and they own nearly one-third of companies. Furthermore, in 2008, 64 percent of mothers with kids under 6 years old worked outside the home, compared to 39 percent back in 1975.

Another significant statistic reported by *TIME:* In 47 out of the 50 largest U.S. metro areas, single childless women in their 20s make more money than their male peers. Women are outearning their male counterparts by 117 percent in New York City, 121 percent in Atlanta, 119 percent in Memphis, 115 percent in San Diego, and 116 percent in Sacramento. In 2008, 35 percent of wives outearned their husbands, compared to 25 percent in 1990.

Not only has female purchasing power changed over the decades, but female purchasing habits have changed as well. The Female Factor, a study by Women@NBCU, reports that over the past couple of decades, women have become more involved in family finances and decision making when it comes to big-ticket purchases. Women today are doing more financial planning, negotiating, purchasing stock to make a profit, and buying into traditionally male-dominated spending areas.

Susan Malfa, senior vice president of sales for Bravo, Oxygen, and Women@NBCU reports: "Women are not only buying in the typical categories like groceries, home, and family items, but are also shopping for traditionally male and big-ticket items such as financial products and flat-screen TVs."

As female purchasing habits have changed over time, the public has recently focused in on this opportunity to target specific female influencer groups as a marketable demographic who not only make their own household purchasing decisions, but also hold a tremendous amount of power in helping both men and other women make their purchasing decisions as well.

Women drive purchasing decisions

According to the *Harvard Business Review,* women are the ones making a majority of household purchasing decisions. They report that women are the decision makers for 94 percent of home furnishings purchases, 92 percent of vacation purchases, 91 percent of home purchases, 60 percent of car purchases, and 51 percent of consumer electronics purchases.

What is it about women that makes them the authorities when it comes to household consumer decisions? According to *Forbes,* it's actually because women are multiple markets rolled up into one. Although traditional gender roles are changing in today's American society, in the majority of societies, women still have very traditional roots of being the caretakers of families. They're the primary caretakers of children and the elderly in most societies around the world, giving them the jurisdiction to decide what to buy for kids, in-laws, parents, and grandparents.

Plus, women aren't just buying for themselves, their kids, and their parents. They're also influencing and buying for their significant others. Savvy male-dominated brand marketers are now building female bloggers and influencers into their marketing strategies. Categories that you think would normally target a male audience — such as male grooming — are now also turning to female influencers to drive sales because they recognize the power that women have on pushing their products.

Women running successful households with a lot of purchasing power often-times share the knowledge they've gained along the way. If you're thinking, "Can female bloggers really make my bottom line look fatter?," the simple answer is, "Yes!" And if you've never considered working with female bloggers, it's a group you should definitely consider as part of your next strategy.

So-called "mommy bloggers" (not a preferred term by moms who blog) were one of the first groups of blogger types that emerged when blogging started to become popular (see Chapter 2). And their popularity has not diminished. Brands still desperately try to reach female bloggers, researching mothers' spending habits and daily routines to find ways to get this demographic and niche community to promote their products.

In fact, President Obama met with a group of female bloggers in the spring of 2015 to talk about gender and finance issues. Political opinions aside, there is no denying that this once demeaning title of "mommy blogger" has given rise to a powerful, influential group of women who have a lot of sway in our economy.

Women trust other women

What specifically about moms is it that makes them such a profitable target? According to a 2011 Scarborough USA study, 14 percent of mothers blog, and that number may very well be higher now that blogging has blown up bigger than ever.

Why are female bloggers — particularly mothers — so successful? First, they're relatable. Motherhood is an instant bond shared by all moms, relevant across countries and societies. It's like an inner elite that you fall into and hold membership in for life. Women bond over the difficulties and the joys of motherhood, and they're always looking for ways to make their own lives, as mothers, better and easier. Who do they turn to as a resource? Other moms who are doing it successfully.

If you aren't a mother, or even a woman, and you're reading this thinking "How is motherhood relevant to me?," don't worry. At some point in your life, you've had contact with a mother — whether it was your own mom or a friend's mother, or a friend or colleague who is a mother. Maybe without your even realizing it, those mothers have had an impact on your purchasing decisions. Your mother may have taught you what laundry products to use when she sent you off to college. Your colleague who is a mother may have advised you on the best lunch places around the office. Most likely, you trusted their opinions. In fact, men value women's advice more than the advice of other men!

TalkTrack (www.kellerfay.com/solutions/talktrack), a large research project that monitors conversations about products and brands between consumers with a survey, reports that when men receive consumer advice from a woman, they deem that advice highly credible 58 percent of the time. In comparison, when men receive consumer advice from a man, only 50 percent of them consider that advice highly credible.

The U.S. Census reports that there are about 44.2 million mothers in the United States. If you think about how many people those mothers interact with on a daily basis (kids, spouses, parents, and so on), that gives them a *lot* of influence.

When it comes to mom bloggers, people look to them as a resource for giving advice on running a model household. These moms are the ones who are doing it right. A part of it may also be aspirational — if a mom sees one mom who has all the steps to running a successful household, career, and family, she wants to know her secrets! Just as we read magazines for tips and advice, when blogging started, women discovered and shared tricks of the trade through their own experiences and trial and error.

Women Rule Social Media

Women make up a greater percentage of social media users than men do, which is why it's a natural step to use a predominantly female influencer base to drive your marketing campaign.

Women are the top social media users for every social media channel except for LinkedIn. According to a report by Ruby Media Corporation and FinancesOnline, 76 percent of women use Facebook (compared with 66 percent of men), 54 percent of women use Tumblr (compared with 46 percent of men), 33 percent of women use Pinterest (compared with 8 percent of men), 20 percent of women use Instagram (compared with 15 percent of men), and 18 percent of women use Twitter (compared with 17 percent of men). For LinkedIn, 19 percent of women are on the platform (compared with 24 percent of men).

Not only are more women on some of the biggest social media channels (except for LinkedIn), but they're also more active on those channels. In a 2014 study sponsored by the American Marketing Association and the Word of Mouth Marketing Association, 70 percent of brand marketers said their company would increase spending on social media, more than any other marketing channel. So, it makes sense for brands to focus on women as a priority to drive more impressions and engagement for them.

In 2012, *The Next Web* reported the following stats about online marketing and social media usage as it pertains to women:

- ✔ As early as 2000, women were found to have surpassed men in Internet usage.
- ✔ Seventy-eight percent of women in the United States use the Internet for product information before making a purchase.
- ✔ Thirty-three percent of women research products and services online before buying offline.
- ✔ Women account for 58 percent of all total online spending.
- ✔ Twenty-two percent of women shop online at least once a day.
- ✔ Ninety-two percent of women pass along information about deals or finds to others.

A survey by Women's Marketing, Inc., and SheSpeaks also reported that 55 percent of women are more likely to purchase from brands they follow on social media.

What do all these stats translate to? That having a strong presence on social media works as a strategy for brands.

The power of oversharing

We live in a world where oversharing has become the norm. When you scroll through Twitter or Instagram, you probably know where your friends went for dinner, who they're working out with, when their kids celebrated another year of birth, and what art form their latte foam took that morning. But you know what? That's also how you discover what cool new restaurants just opened, what fashion trends are currently #onfleek, and how to make your own lip sync video with Dubsmash. And without this constant oversharing of information, people around the world wouldn't be able to keep up on the latest and greatest products and trends.

Do you remember that dress? The one that started social wars over whether it was actually white and gold or black and blue (www.buzzfeed.com/catesish/help-am-i-going-insane-its-definitely-blue)? If there were no social media, that dress would've forever stayed one friend group's color recognition dilemma. Instead, it gained organic coverage across all the major news outlets and received millions of views on Buzzfeed.

A user on Tumblr first uploaded the image of the dress, which got picked up by Buzzfeed. Buzzfeed then tweeted asking what color the dress was, and the rest is history.

Buzzfeed shared stats on how one original tweet about the dress got picked up and shared across all other social media channels. It gained 339,000 views on Facebook, 214,000 views on Twitter, 147,000 on *dark social* (content occurring outside of what's easily measured by web analytics), and 284,000 on the other social channels combined. This resulted in more than 975,000 views from one tweet. It was the power of oversharing that helped extend the reach of that one tweet, making it one of the most talked about social media events of 2015.

And that is the power of oversharing. Just imagine what a phenomenon like that dress could've done for a paid campaign.

Sharing on social media is basically word-of-mouth marketing. And each time something gets shared again, the effectiveness of word of mouth increases. Therefore, the more times a product or brand gets shared, the more impressions that product or brand receives. Marketers rely on this multiplier effect, combined with the effectiveness of word-of-mouth marketing, and turn to influencers as a strategy to get the word out about their brand or product.

Now, how does over sharing specifically relate to women? Well, women have been statistically proven to be better at sharing than men. The Pew Research Center reports that as of May 2013, 74 percent of women used social networking sites, as compared with 62 percent of men.

Furthermore, women are more active on social media on a daily basis than men. According to Ruby Media Corporation, 30 percent of women report that they use social media several times per day (compared to 26 percent of men who report the same habit).

Because we've already identified that women are dominating almost all the social channels, and we know that they're more active on social media, we can conclude that more women are sharing and receiving information via social media. For brands, this again points to the fact that female influencers will generally make a stronger impact when it comes to their bottom lines.

Women Rule Social Trends

Earlier in this chapter, we tell you how women rule social media because they dominate all the major social channels except one *and* are more active on those channels in general. In this section, we explain how they rule social trends as well.

First, we explain the difference between social media and social trends. *Social media* is the content that is being served up on various social channels. *Social trends* are how that content is being served up and how people are interacting with that content. So, when we refer to women ruling social trends, we're saying that women are dominating on three of the biggest trends in social: mobile, brand interaction, and visual media.

Mobile

Social media originated on desktop computers, but today much of social media content creation and sharing is done via mobile. In fact, some of the most popular social media platforms today — such as Instagram and Snapchat — were created specifically *for* mobile and the desktop counterparts of those platforms can't even serve the same functionality as their mobile apps. With the advancement of technology in portable devices, there has been a major shift in how we engage with social media and digital marketing, and that's how mobile became a social trend.

Ruby Media Corporation reports that in 2013, 46 percent of women (compared with 43 percent of men) used their smartphones for social media, and 32 percent of women (compared with 20 percent of men) used their tablets for social media.

More women than men use mobile devices for social media, but in addition to use, more women view their mobile devices as the most important devices in their lives. According to a study by Time, Inc., and Nuance Digital Marketing, 60 percent of women listed their mobile devices as their number-one device in terms of importance, while only 43 percent of men reported feeling the same way.

In addition to using mobile devices for social media, an increasing number of people are also using mobile devices to make online purchases. A report by *e-Marketer* shows the dollar increase in mobile sales over the past few years, along with projected growth through 2018. The dollar value of sales via mobile device is on a steady rise, with tablets leading the way as the main platform for sales.

According to *e-Marketer,* in 2012, $24.78 billion was spent via mobile commerce (excluding travel and event tickets). In 2013, this number jumped to $42.13 billion, followed by $57.79 billion in 2014. In 2015, it was projected to be at $76.41. By the year 2018, the total amount of Internet purchases made via mobile devices is projected to be at $132.69 billion, and growth does not appear to be slowing down.

As for mobile purchasing habits, women lead as well. According to *Adweek,* men use mobile devices to make purchases, but a higher percentage of women use mobile devices for all aspects of the buying process, including researching products, collecting coupons, making shopping lists, and even sharing pictures of their purchases. As a result, there are more opportunities for brands to reach more women along the purchasing process.

Brand interaction

According to Burst Media Online Insights, the main ways that people interact with brands via social media are

- ✔ Showing support
- ✔ Accessing offers or coupons
- ✔ Staying current
- ✔ Sharing information
- ✔ Learning about brand content
- ✔ Offering opinions or comments

Women dominate four of these categories. More women interact with brands to show support of the brand. A significantly higher number of women than men also interact with brands to access special brand offers or coupons. More women interact with brands just to stay current. And more women interact with brands to offer opinions or comments.

So, what drives brand interaction? *MediaPost* reports that based on a survey by Burst Media, among what they call the "social influencer segment" (participants ages 18 to 34 years old), online ads have greater effectiveness than TV ads at driving social engagement with brands (67.6 percent versus 60.6 percent, respectively). The difference is also most noticeably higher with women ages 18 to 34, of whom 73.9 percent say digital ads with social media calls to action are effective in motivating them to interact with brands.

Just because the brand interaction happens on social media doesn't mean that it has to be prompted by social media. Based on the Burst Media survey, digital ads were most highly reported as effective in driving social brand interaction, being reported from 61 percent of respondents. However, 58.7 percent also said TV ads are effective, followed by 52.4 percent for print ads, 41.5 percent for radio ads, and 39.4 percent for outdoor ads.

In total, 54.2 percent of women and 48.6 percent of men have engaged in a brand-related social sharing activity based on something seen on or in an ad, which is how women also rule brand interactions on social media. Brands over the years have also steadily increased their presence on social media. And, of course, one way of doing so is by using social influencer marketing.

Visual media

Although there are many types of channels for visuals on social media, Instagram, Pinterest, Tumblr, and Polyvore are some of the social media platforms that center on image-based content (and Snapchat may soon be added to the mix). A 2014 study by Ruby Media Corporation reports that over the course of a year, Instagram, Pinterest and Tumblr gained 10 million users, making the "visual web" the fastest growing social media type.

To further drive the point home, more women are dominating these visual channels than men, with more women on Tumblr, Pinterest, and Instagram (see "Women Rule Social Media," earlier in this chapter).

In order to be successful on these channels, content is generally beautiful and emphasizes aesthetics. Areas of interest that tend to do well include fashion, food, and scenery.

Because women are most active on these channels, it makes sense in most cases to use female influencers to reach this audience. These channels are also valued at billions of dollars, with Pinterest in the lead. As of 2013, Pinterest is valued at $7.7 billion, followed by Instagram at $5 billion and Tumblr at $1.1 billion.

Pinterest (now that it has a sponsored feature) is a marketer's dream when it comes to elevating visibility of household brands. Women are authorities and resources when it comes to the household. Because a big portion of Pinterest is dedicated to accessible recipes, crafts, and fashion turned into beautiful projects, the audience reach spans widely. And because pins are able to be directly linked out to another page, the content can easily translate to sales and brand engagement.

This is one of the main reasons Pinterest is valued higher than Instagram, even though Instagram is a more popular network across audiences. Women are, for the most part, dictating the future of these billion-dollar platforms because they're the main content creators, curators, and consumers.

Chapter 4

The New Rules of Engagement

The overwhelming majority of influencers, especially the ones brands should be targeting, are not celebrities. They don't have agents. They aren't corporate entities. They may not have any corporate (let alone marketing or advertising) experience to speak of. They're real, genuine people who have amassed an online following simply by being themselves.

Reaching out to influencers, getting them to respond, and ultimately getting them to do what you want is possible . . . but it's not as easy as automated transactions. You can't "order" engaging, personal, and authentic sponsored content the way you can buy ad space or hire a celebrity endorser who will ultimately read from a script. And you can't reach out to influencers as though they're press or as though they understand (or care about) your corporate-ese.

Mastering influencer outreach, relationship building, and program execution isn't hard as long as you keep the three C's in mind: communicating, contracting, and compensating. In this chapter, we've got you covered.

Communicating Like a Pro

When you've decided that you're ready to work with social media influencers, you may spend quite a bit of time finding the right influencers for you. Don't let it all fall apart by screwing up your communication. In this section, we tell you how to reach out to influencers in a way that will reflect well on your brand, whether the influencers decide to work with you or not.

Making your communication personal

The number-one mistake marketers make is sending the same generic email to every influencer. According to iBlog Magazine's 2015 Women's Blogging Industry and Business Report, bloggers said that more than 74 percent of the pitches they receive don't fit their blog's style, theme, tone, or business.

We can't stress strongly enough how personal social media is. People connect through dozens of different channels every day to stay in touch with friends, family, their communities, and the world. Social media outreach needs to be personal, too.

Each influencer is special in her own way. Each influencer has cultivated a unique audience and deserves to be recognized accordingly.

If you want a successful influencer outreach program, start by contacting individuals (not mass email lists). Find an influencer you believe will do good work for you and tell her why — read her blog, understand what she blogs about and who her audience is, and tell her why you think she'd be the ideal influencer for your company. Approach influencers as you would potential partners — not as potential hires who didn't even know you had a "help wanted" sign on your window! This means doing your research and putting in a lot of upfront work. But we promise it will be worth it!

To make your outreach personal, follow these tips:

- ✔ **Remember that most influencers take their work personally.** They consider their relationships with their readers personal as well. If you want to interrupt their regular flow of content to have them showcase your sponsored messaging, the very least you can do is recognize that's what you're asking of them.

- ✔ **Do not address your email to "blogger" or "writer of such-and-such blog."** Find the name of the person behind the account, or at least how he refers to himself.

- ✔ **Avoid marketing-speak.** You're reaching out to a person, not a corporation. Approach your target with respect and professionalism, but also as a human being.

- ✔ **Don't forget that you're asking them to do something for you, not the other way around.** Even if your product is the best, even if you're only contacting the very top of the top-tier influencers, even if you're planning to pay them well, never lose sight of the fact that you are the one asking for *their* help.

Making your offer compelling

You want to leverage each influencer's voice and brand and the influence she's established among her community to further your brand message. Why would an influencer want to do that for you? Unless you can answer that question, you're not likely to get very far, no matter how personal your message.

As influencer marketing expands as a viable marketing approach, influencers are in higher and higher demand. As a brand, your offer needs to be compelling. Simply having a great product may not be enough. Never approach an influencer if you haven't thought through a good response to the question, "What's in it for the influencer?"

In the following sections, we walk you through several key ingredients you may be able to offer to sweeten the deal: stuff, status, and creative freedom.

Offering free stuff

The simplest and most obvious offer brands make to influencers is a *quid pro quo:*

> We'll send you our product for free in exchange for your writing a review of the product on your blog.

Makes sense, right? In many cases, this approach works well. For example, many beauty bloggers, Instagrammers, and YouTubers receive makeup samples in exchange for including those samples in their makeup photos and tutorials.

If your product doesn't have much retail value, or you don't have enough product samples to send to every potential influencer, this approach isn't the right one for you.

Offering status

Offering "insider" information about your company and products is a great way to engage fans on social media. Liking a brand page on Facebook may give someone access to behind-the-scenes information, advance notice of cool announcements, and even special discounts or coupons.

A similar tactic can work well with influencers. If an influencer is someone who would likely use your product or like your company, you could offer her special "insider" status in return for writing about your brand. In fact, you could even offer her an ambassador role.

A *brand ambassador* is an influencer who partners with a brand and works almost as an extension of the company. Her role is to promote a brand online over an agreed-upon amount of time (although it's possible that she'll be so enamored of your company that she'll continue to promote it after her ambassadorship is over).

Many influencers enjoy being Brand Ambassadors as long as the brands follow through on their end of the bargain — that is, they ensure the role of brand ambassador is actually compelling. Here are some tips for how to make a brand ambassador or "insider" offer compelling:

✔ Offer your ambassadors sneak peeks at upcoming products or announcements as you would with employees.

✔ Engage in regular communication with your ambassadors to share behind-the-scenes information, such as photos of the company or product that isn't otherwise available to the public.

✔ Send your ambassadors product(s) to sample before the product is available in stores.

✔ Offer your ambassadors special coupons or discounts or (even better!) give your ambassadors codes that they can give away or pass on to their readers at their discretion.

✔ Cross-promote the content that your ambassadors create on your own social channels — you can repost her photos on Instagram, retweet her tweets, even feature her blog or images on your brand's Facebook page.

Offering creative freedom

You're selecting your influencers because you like the content they produce. Unfortunately, too many companies make the mistake of engaging with an influencer only to tell her exactly what she is supposed to do — from the photos she should post, to the language she should tweet, to the features and benefits she should highlight.

Not giving an influencer her space to create an authentic-sounding, crafted-by-her message dilutes the whole reason you want to use influencers in the first place. Brands that give the influencers gentle guidance but then let them "do their thing" are much happier with the results.

You're working with influencers so that they tell your brand's story in their own unique way. The more you try to control their message, the more like an ignorable "ad" the message becomes. You also risk damaging the influencer's reputation with her audience if you force her to use your marketing language while framing it as though it's her own.

In addition, consider brainstorming *with* the influencers about the kind of content they want to create! Don't be afraid to invite your influencers to your company's creative table and be part of the campaign planning from the beginning. After all, who knows what will resonate on your influencers' social media channels better than the social media influencers themselves?

Keeping it real: Do's and don'ts

When it comes to influencer outreach, put yourself in the mindset of the influencer. Social media is founded on authenticity, so as much as you're able to, leave your jargon and marketing hype out of the equation.

Online influencers are popular because their audience relates to them. They aren't corporate entities — if you want these influencers to respond to you, you need to speak to them like the people they are. This may seem obvious, but it's harder than it seems!

Here are the do's and don'ts of keeping it real in influencer outreach:

- ✔ **Don't make false claims about your brand or company.** For example, don't call a product "life-changing" if it isn't (and let's be honest, few products are).

- ✔ **Do explain why your company, brand, or product is worthy of being promoted.**

- ✔ **Don't make the message or request confusing.** The influencer shouldn't have to guess at what you're asking them to do! Don't send an email saying, "I thought you'd want to know about this product" with no call to action if what you really want them to do is write a blog post reviewing the product.

- ✔ **Do keep your message clear and simple.** Ask for what you'd like the influencer to do.

- ✔ **Don't expect your product, message, or social media campaign to go viral.** Yes, influencers have caused virality but there's no way to predict what, when, or how something — especially a sponsored piece — will hit it big.

- ✔ **Do be realistic in what results you can expect from your influencer.** We have an entire chapter devoted to metrics, because there are many different ways to set goals for influencer marketing programs. Unfortunately, "We want it to go viral" is not a realistic or useful one.

✴

✔ **Don't expect the influencer to create an ad.** Influencer-generated content is *not* a glossy print ad, it's not a press release, it's not a graphically designed display ad. You're asking the influencer to create a sponsored message in her own authentic way. If you want to control every aspect of what the influencer produces (her language, her post design, editing her photos), you're no longer engaging in influencer marketing, you're defaulting to a purely paid media model.

✔ **Do provide clear editorial guidelines and standards (things the influencers should or should not do) and let them tell your story their way.**

✔ **Don't ask your influencers to jump through hoops.** The harder you make the program, the more room there is for errors and incomplete assignments. For instance, don't require that your influencers download a coupon, print it out, take it to a specific store miles and miles away from them, purchase the item, bring it home, demo it, write an extensive review, take tons of photos, and post everything to their blogs, Twitter, Facebook, and Instagram with only a few days' notice.

✔ **Do be considerate of your influencers.** The easier your request, the better the odds that you'll have a successful program.

Upping Your Game: Creating an Influencer Contract

One of the most important things you can do to ensure a successful influencer marketing program is to establish a contract with your influencers. This should be a simple but legally binding contract between the hiring entity (that's you, or your marketing agency if you hired one) and each and every influencer that entity is engaging.

Use an online service such as EchoSign (www.echosign.adobe.com) to send and sign contracts electronically with no need to print, fax, or mail anything.

Setting up a simple contract can mean the difference between the "spray and pray" approach — where you reach out to dozens of influencers and hope they produce something of quality — and knowing exactly what results you can expect.

Nothing is preventing you from entering into a professional relationship with your influencers. You are, essentially, hiring them to function as an extension of your marketing team. You'd never hire someone (even a freelancer) without a written agreement, so contracting with influencers just makes good business sense.

Setting expectations

Don't leave your influencer marketing program to chance. When you've reached out to your influencers and established mutual interest, it's in all parties' best interests to write out exactly what is expected, when, and for how much.

Forget the idea of writing an influencer to say, "I thought you'd want to know about . . . " without actually asking them to do anything specific. Be as clear as possible, and don't be afraid to ask for what you want.

Controlling what you need to control

Many brands harbor some fear of bloggers and influencers in general. For as far as social media has come, some companies still hate the loss of control that comes with engaging with the masses on platforms they don't own and can't completely steer.

With one-way communication (where companies controlled everything about their brand image and messaging, before social media allowed consumers to "talk back"), companies didn't have to worry about anything being "off-brand."

When you hire influencers to produce sponsored content, you're walking a fine line. You want the message the influencers create to be on-point, but you can't have the message seem too corporate or it'll sound inauthentic (because it is!). But if you allow someone to produce brand content for you, you risk that influencer going "off-brand."

We have good news for the nervous. The entire point of influencer marketing is to let the influencers do what they do best: Craft your story in a way that's best for their readers. Fortunately, this doesn't mean giving the influencers carte blanche. With a contract, you can give your influencers express guidelines that should help them stay within the bounds you feel comfortable with.

- content guardrails
- authentic w/ readers

Protecting yourself and your brand

A contract doesn't just help the influencers understand what's expected of them, it helps protect you, your company, and your brand.

From a simple legal standpoint, if the influencer you contract with doesn't fulfill her end of the deal, you're under no obligation to compensate her. If the work she produces isn't up to your standards, or is in violation of the guidelines you provided, you have recourse to ask her to change her work and bring it up to snuff.

You may be wondering what happens if you hire a blogger and she hates your product. What if she writes terrible things about your company? Can you make her sign something that says she won't say anything bad? The short answer is "no," but the longer answer is "nor should you want to."

You *can* draft a contract that clearly states that the influencer may not post content that is false. However, it's unethical to require a positive review. What's more, if an influencer posts an unbalanced review of a product or company, it'll come across as inauthentic. Her readers will know she's not being genuine — *especially* because influencers are required to disclose that they've been sponsored to create brand content.

Avoiding problem influencers

Not only is it unethical to require positivity in a contract, it's largely unnecessary. Consider why an influencer may write something damaging to a brand so you can avoid putting yourself in harm's way:

- ✔ **The influencer genuinely doesn't like or understand the product.** Make sure you're targeting the right influencers and that they're a good match for your product before you enter into a contract, and you'll likely avoid this problem.

- ✔ **The influencer receives a shoddy product that doesn't work, doesn't meet claims, or doesn't live up to its hype.** If you don't make claims about a product that it can't live up to, you'll prevent this problem. And if the product just isn't very good (which sometimes happens), we recommend you use another form of marketing instead of asking for honest feedback from influencers.

- ✔ **The influencer feels frustrated, undervalued, or angry with how the program has been managed.** Make sure your expectations have been communicated clearly and are outlined in a contract which both parties have signed. The more respect and professionalism you show the influencers, the better the quality of the work they'll produce. Having a contract in place helps solidify your partnership and prevents influencers from retaliating — because they have nothing to retaliate against.

Knowing what to include in a contract

Have a lawyer create your contract with all the standard elements needed to ensure your contract is legally binding. That said, here are the nonstandard contract elements your influencer contract should include:

- ✔ **The influencer's legal name.**

- ✔ **The influencer's social media addresses where you expect her to post (for example, her blog URL, Instagram handle, Twitter handle, and so on).**

- ✔ **Specific deliverables with deadlines.** For example, "Write one blog post between July 6 and July 17, 2016, including what you enjoyed about the product, why other families might enjoy the product, three to five high-quality photos that complement your post, and top and bottom disclosures (provided separately) in compliance with FTC guidelines."

- ✔ **Language about who will own the sponsored content that the influencer creates for you.** We recommend that you allow the influencer to always own her content, but that she grants you and your brand rights to use or repurpose her content.

- ✔ **Professional standards.** Here's your opportunity to make sure the influencer doesn't post anything illegal, false, or defamatory; doesn't use profanities; doesn't plagiarize; provides error-free work; and attributes photos properly.

- ✔ **How you prefer to communicate and how you'll confirm that the influencers' work has been completed.**

- ✔ **What the influencer will be paid, dependent on what, by which means, and by when.**

Compensating Influencers Fairly

Paying influencers is something of a controversial topic, but there are no two ways about it: *You must compensate your influencers.*

Some PR and marketing professionals believe that the old, spray-and-pray method is the best way to approach influencers. They still believe that the best way to get "organic" (or "earned") media placements is to send product samples or press releases to as many influencers and possible and just *hope* to get something good in return.

But influencer marketing isn't only about *earned* media, it's about *earned, owned, and paid-for media.* There is no reason to limit how you approach influencers, and there should be no controversy about paying them. In this section, we walk you through how to pay your influencers fairly.

Understanding why you need to pay influencers

If you're still not convinced that you need to pay your influencers, here's why:

- ✔ **Not compensating your influencers sends a clear message: "We don't value your work."** You want influencers to produce good content in a timely manner that supports your brand goals. In other words, you're asking them to work for you . . . for free.

- ✔ **Some influencers may promote you out of the goodness of their hearts, but most will not.** Influencers who do agree to promote a brand "for free" do so with the expectation that they'll be compensated down the road.

- ✔ **Brands that don't compensate influencers fairly risk getting a bad rap among influencers.** One of the most prominent bloggers in the country, Jenny Lawson (a.k.a., The Bloggess), has an entire section of her blog dedicated to PR people who pitch her poorly. For a great laugh, see www.thebloggess.com/heres-a-picture-of-wil-wheaton-collating-papers.

- ✔ **You get what you pay for.** The less you're willing to invest in your influencer marketing program, the less successful it will be. The best talent doesn't work for free, so what level of talent are you engaging?

- ✔ **Air and traffic don't pay the bills.** Brands sometimes promise that they'll pay influencers by featuring them on their website or Facebook page, explaining to the influencers that this will benefit them — it will boost their visibility and increase their traffic. Unfortunately, that is a rare outcome for the influencer, and almost never worth the amount of work the influencer put in.

Avoiding compensation pitfalls

Several brands and agencies just entering the world of influencer marketing start off with this question: "How do I calculate what to pay influencers?" It's a tough question. And it's also the wrong one.

Bloggers and marketers have been struggling to come up with a formula for calculating how much a blog post is worth for over a decade. The trouble is, formulas are necessarily dependent on numbers alone, such as how much traffic a post is likely to receive, how many comments it generates, or how much revenue it drives. But what you're *really* asking influencers for is to create quality content — almost (but not completely) irrespective of numbers.

How can you create and apply a single formula based on subjective, qualitative requirements? You can't. The best way to figure out what to pay influencers is to understand what the going rates are in the influencer marketplace. That way, you avoid the two likely-to-fail approaches in the following sections.

Calculating influencer payments with traffic and engagement metrics

We've seen some marketers try to quantify the success of a program (and associated influencer payments) using formulas based on an influencer's reach and engagement, where engagement includes likes, comments, and shares of that influencer's sponsored content. They do this by placing a dollar value on these things — deciding, for example, that a Facebook "like" is worth $100 and a comment left on a blog post is worth $250.

At best, these numbers are arbitrary. At worst, they're absurd. For one thing, these numbers suggest that all content and engagement is created equal. But we know that some influencers have better content and more genuinely engaged fans. Someone who likes a brand's Facebook page in order to enter a contest is not as valuable as someone who likes a brand's Facebook page because they're genuine fans of that brand.

More important, if these numbers are used to calculate the value of an influencer program *without* taking into account the actual, measurable success of the program on the whole, the numbers are useless! How much money was invested in the program? What were the program's main objectives? To what extent were the objectives met? Did an increase in sales revenue occur? Only when taking those factors into account can you truly know the value of your influencer marketing. Otherwise, your calculations are being done in a vacuum and the numbers aren't tied to anything.

Tying influencer payments to click performance or revenue

Some brands prefer to pay influencers on a performance basis, such as how many clicks their posts generate, how many coupons someone downloads, how many sales are generated directly as a results of an influencer's post. This is an unfair and impractical approach for several reasons:

- ✓ **It devalues the work the influencer is doing.** Sometimes a product, brand, or service is simply not very compelling to readers and doesn't get traction through social media. But the influencer who has spent time, energy, and talent building good content for your brand should still be compensated for it.

✔ **Performance metrics don't tell the whole story.** Influencer marketing is primarily about building brand awareness, not delivering immediate conversions to sales. Paying influencers based solely on the sales they generate is called affiliate marketing, not influencer marketing.

Affiliate marketing is when a publisher (like someone who writes a blog or produces a website, not necessarily an "influencer") gets a portion of a sale that is generated from her site. For example, if a blogger has a link to Amazon.com on her sidebar, and you click it and then make a purchase, the blogger will be paid a portion of that sale (essentially a commission). The upside for affiliate advertisers like Amazon is that they only have to pay their publishers if and when a sale is made, so there's no risk for them. The upside for publishers or influencers is that they can make a fee simply for passively posting something on their site — they don't have to create sponsored content. The downside for affiliate advertisers is that very few people click the links and purchase something. The downside for publishers/affiliates is that the fees they make are a tiny, tiny fraction of sales they generate, which are usually small to begin with.

✔ **Performance metrics set influencers up for bad behavior**. Over the years, we've seen too many brands offer influencers payment based on the number of clicks they drive (pay per click, pay per performance, and so on). This sets up influencers to try to "stuff the ballots" and find unscrupulous ways to inflate their numbers. The best influencers know better and shy away from these arrangements.

Looking at the going rates for influencers

You'll only be able to engage and contract with the best influencers out there if you're willing to compensate them fairly based on market rates. The rates we list in this section are based on 2015 data, but you can make calculations based on an assumption that going rates increase 35 percent to 40 percent each year (as influencers become more and more in demand).

You don't have to pay your influencers in cash. You may offer to compensate influencers with product in addition to or in lieu of cash payments. However, the value of the product should be equivalent to what an influencer would command in cash. Of course, "value" may be calculated by retail value or by other intrinsic qualities of the offer: opportunities to meet celebrities, receive an in-demand product before it's available to the public, and so on.

Just be reasonable. Don't offer an influencer a coupon for $30 worth of shoes if she can command $300 for her work. And remember, nothing says, "I love your work" more than cash.

Here are the going rates for influencers as of 2015:

- ✔ **Blogs:** Influencers can expect anywhere from $175 to $5,000 or more. Factors that affect how much you should pay include the following:

  - Monthly page views ($175 for an average of 20,000 monthly page views is a baseline)

  - How much the bloggers are being asked to do

  - Quality of the content being produced

  - Level of amplification across other channels

  - Popularity of the market (for example, beauty bloggers are currently more in demand than pet bloggers)

  Celebrity bloggers can command more than $10,000 for a single post.

- ✔ **Instagram:** Influencers can expect $75 to $3,000 per image. Factors that affect how much you should pay include the following:

  - Number of followers ($75 for a baseline of 5,000 to 10,000 followers)

  - Focus of images

  A lifestyle Instagrammer with 20,000 followers may require $250 per image. A fashion Instagrammer with 20,000 followers may require $600 per image.

- ✔ **Facebook:** Influencers can expect $40 to $300 per single post. Factors that affect how much you should pay include the following:

  - Number of followers

  - What you're asking the influencer to post

  If you're asking them to share content that is easily shareable, payments may be lower. If you're asking them to promote something in their own language using their own content, payments will be higher.

- ✔ **Twitter:** Influencers can expect $5 to $5,000 per tweet. Factors that affect how much you should pay include the following:

  - Number and quality of followers (someone on Twitter may have 30,000 followers but demonstrate almost no engagement on any tweet, whereas a semi-known athlete may have 3,000 followers and draw tons of interactions with a single tweet)

  - How often the influencer tweets. Will your message be lost in a barrage of daily messages, or does the influencer post only occasionally with more attention given to each message? Given how short and sweet Twitter messages must be, you may consider bundling payments — offering a flat fee for a certain number of tweets rather than paying for each tweet.

✔ **Pinterest:** Pinterest doesn't allow influencers to be paid specifically for pinning things. In order to incorporate Pinterest into your influencer marketing plan, brands must work with influencers on larger, integrated programs. See Chapter 10 for more information on how to do this effectively.

✔ **Video:** Influencers can expect $500 to $5,000 or more per video. Factors that affect how much you should pay include the following:

- Quality of video production (working with influencers who don't specialize in video creation is not a good idea)

- Number of followers

Many agencies that specialize in video compensate on a pay-per-view model, which we don't recommend because if the video underperforms, the vlogger still put in time and effort and deserves some compensation. Plus, if the video over-performs and gets serious traction — or even goes viral — the brand could be on the hook for potentially hundreds of thousands of dollars.

Chapter 5

Outsourcing Influencer Marketing

In This Chapter

▶ Hiring a social influencer agency

▶ Deciding which kind of agency to hire

▶ Doing one big campaign versus multiple activations

*T*here comes a day in every marketer's career when you realize you need help. When the program is bigger than your internal resources or expertise can handle, you're smart enough to bring in the cavalry. Especially when you're working on something as specialized and dynamic as influencer marketing, it helps to have an experienced guide on the inside to help you navigate. In this chapter, we walk you through the process of finding and hiring the right agency for your needs.

So, You Want to Hire an Influencer Marketing Agency

The fact that influencer marketing is a developing industry, with rapidly evolving practices, can make it hard to evaluate and pick one agency over another. Like any other kind of outsourcing, it helps to start by understanding your budget, and what you want to accomplish, including the following:

✔ Who you want to reach.

✔ Where and how they already interact on social media channels, so you know which type of specialist to hire. You don't go to a Twitter agency if your target is active on YouTube.

✔ What type of message you want to share and have the influencers share in turn.

Having a clear picture of what you want your program to be will help you set specific and actionable goals for your agency partner, and make it easier to measure the success of your program. You want to be sure that any and all activity supports your business goals. Because if it doesn't, you're wasting your time and money!

May I borrow your relationships?

Managing relationships with influencers is hard work. Coming up with a concept, theme, and hashtag is just the beginning! Someone also has to manage the communication and administrative tasks, including identifying and recruiting the right people, setting up a contractual agreement, administering payment, and even dealing with typos. Setting up this infrastructure with each individual influencer at any kind of scale is costly and time-consuming, and around every corner is another opportunity to get it wrong and offend the very people you're trying to convince.

Perhaps most important, very few brands (Disney is the exception that proves the rule) have enough content or interesting reasons to interact with any one influencer more than two or three times a year. Influencers don't want to write about a brand more than that, and their audiences certainly don't want to read that much content about any one brand! Unless you can come up with diverse, creative angles from which to approach your brand's messaging (for example, a recipe one month, a post about a vacation the next, favorite pets the next, and so on), while still somehow staying relevant, content will get repetitive and boring.

This is where outsourcing to an agency, especially one with a network of influencers, is so valuable. A capable agency will have a comprehensive database with information that helps identify and vet the best candidates to work on your project. They'll have processes in place for quality control, systems to pay the influencers, and measurement and reporting methodologies. A great agency will even offer first-hand qualitative data about its influencers as well — that is, who is reliable, whose posts produce consistent engagement, who creates the most original/creative content, and which influencers can't be counted on to meet a deadline! This knowledge can't be found in a database or by simply looking at statistics.

An agency that works on behalf of multiple brands has multiple reasons to contact influencers, building credibility and a relationship over time. In practical terms, this means they have already weeded out the crazies and earned the respect of the good ones.

Consider the value of the influencers' desire to stay in the good graces of an agency that provides them with multiple opportunities to work on prestigious programs — they have more at stake than a single gig paying $150, which means they're motivated to behave professionally.

A strong relationship with an influencer is *extra* valuable when they hate your product. The influencer will be more likely to reach out privately with negative feedback, and less likely to take cheap — and brand damaging — shots on a public forum if she sees a long-term value to the relationship.

How it works: Self-service versus full-service

Approaches to managing influencer marketing programs range from fully automated and self-service, to highly personalized, high-touch, custom solutions. Most agencies skew more one way than the other. Each approach has value, and it's smart to let your needs, rather than a philosophical preference, dictate your selection.

Think of it as a choice between an all-you-can-eat buffet in a casino in Las Vegas, or having a personal chef come to your home and make a perfectly designed three-course meal for an intimate dinner date. They both can be delicious, but when you're in the mood for one, the other choice definitely won't satisfy you!

I <3 control: When self-service platforms rock

Often considered the "technology solution," self-service, automated platforms put the bulk of the control — and responsibility — in your hands. You log in to the vendor's system and have access to a variety of program components.

Many systems let you go in and sort their influencer database according to a set of desired characteristics. This can include demographic factors like household income, education, gender, and number of children, as well as information about their social channel presence like number of followers or monthly blog page views.

Automated solutions are usually a cost-effective way to get a general message to a broad audience at scale. Some platforms allow you to review posts before they're published, which is appealing to brands that are in highly regulated industries like financial services or have a desire to tightly control the messaging. However, the quality of the content tends to be fairly generic, and the engagement of the influencers audiences is often low. Also, there are usually few vetting or validating processes to join these automated platforms, so anyone with an email address can sign up.

This approach is fine if you can reach your goals with the lowest common denominator. For example, if you're trying to sell gift-wrapping supplies during the December holiday season, you can afford to be very general in your targeting and selection of influencers. It's a safe bet that pretty much every influencer out there has someone in their community of followers who needs a gift bag.

Automated solutions also make control freaks happy. Do you want, or even have a pressing business need, to check your results daily or even hourly? Great! Log on and watch the impressions roll in.

Just remember that most platform solutions don't provide very much customer service, so you need to have internal staffing resources, who are trained and available to do most or even all of the program setup, project management, and reporting.

Just make it happen: Getting someone else to do the heavy lifting

At the other end of the continuum is the full-service influencer agency that manually (or mostly manually — everyone uses some kind of contact management system, even if they don't give clients access to it!) sets up the program. This gives you great flexibility, starting by allowing you to be very specific in your influencer selection.

Need military moms in Florida, with three kids and a family history of diabetes? They can be found and recruited! But it'll be expensive, it'll take time, and your program size will be limited by the actual number of people who match your requirements and are also willing to participate in the program.

Speaking of participants, the members of this type of network usually meet minimum membership requirements and consequently are of a higher caliber, with better content and higher audience numbers, as well as being more reliable.

These more expensive services come with a full suite of benefits for you the marketer, including an expert project manager, who runs the programs, manages influencer communications, and provides you with reporting that can be highly customized.

This type of service is great when you really just want to outsource it all. If you want to hand over your list of requirements and goals, and go take care of something else, you'll be happier with a full-service agency.

Deciding Which Type of Agency Is Right for You

Realistically, your program probably needs a little bit of both. And few agencies are purely one or the other, although their pricing and standard service models will start at one point or the other. See Table 5-1 for a helpful chart on when to use a self-service agency versus a full-service agency.

Table 5-1	When to Use a Self-Service Agency versus a Full-Service Agency	
	Self-Service	*Full-Service*
You have a small budget.	X	
You have a bigger budget.		X
You have few demographic requirements.	X	
You have very specific demographic requirements.		X
You have a highly engaged, skilled, and/or dedicated internal staff.	X	
You have limited internal resources to manage the project.		X
You need real-time, frequent reporting.	X	
You have a broad topic that is applicable to most of the population.	X	
You have a very specific or sensitive topic.		X

One-Off Events versus Continuity Campaigns

As part of a broad marketing plan, influencer marketing activations can be a powerful tactic to get a spike in awareness or generate buzz around a specific event or launch.

On the other hand, influencer marketing can be a powerful ongoing tool to engage with your customers over the lifecycle of a product, supporting market research and customer service, as well as contributing to overall branding efforts.

Matching your program goals to the bigger business goals helps you decide which kind of program to design.

Making a big splash for maximum effect

Sometimes marketing goals are time sensitive. You need to get everyone's attention at the same time, for a product launch, a fundraising deadline, or a special event, like the Grammys or the #Batkid day we cover in Chapter 16.

In these situations, you want to use tactics and channels that are effective real-time and in the moment, such as Twitter. Using attention-getting techniques, like bringing in a celebrity or high-profile influencer, can help you generate a spike in attention and awareness.

Although they aren't sustainable over a longer timeframe, these high-intensity activations can be a spark that gets a fire burning for your brand.

Putting in the hours for a long-term relationship

We'd all love to have those big awareness spikes on a daily basis, but that's simply not feasible. And it's not even desirable — people get sick of seeing the same thing every day, and that's a good way to generate a backlash.

Taking the approach of multiple activations, over time, with modest but increasing goals, allows you to test and learn as you go. You can modify program elements to add more of what works, and eliminate problematic elements. This approach is great if you're in beta with a product, are doing regional rollout, or have any kind of phased program to support.

In these cases, activations with more evergreen content, such as blog posts or Pinterest boards, can be very effective. By creating content that is discoverable over time, you can gradually build up your library in a more organic and authentic-feeling manner.

Long-term programs may have the same overall budget, but because they happen over an extended period, they may also be more cost-effective if you're budget sensitive.

Part III
The Main Platforms for Influencer Marketing

M&M'S® Crispy "Sweet Summer" Twitter Party RSVP

Presented by Clever Girls, www.clevergirlscollective.com

* Required

First Name *

Last Name *

Email Address *

Twitter Handle *

Street Address *
If you win a prize, we need to know where to send it.

City *

State *

Postal Code *

Source: http://member.clevergirlscollective.com/node/1130

Get a year's worth of themes for engaging social content in an article at www.dummies.com/extras/influencermarketing.

In this part . . .

- ✔ Learn how to find the best influencers on each of the primary influencer platforms.

- ✔ Discover how to commission authentic sponsored content for your brand.

- ✔ Discover why Instagram influencers are the best visual story-tellers for your brand.

- ✔ See why Twitter chats are basically an online cocktail party (with prizes!).

- ✔ Learn about the most popular types of Facebook contests and how to make them successful.

- ✔ Find out how to create Pinterest content that lives on forever.

- ✔ Get the lay of the land on the latest video platforms for influencer marketing.

Chapter 6

Blog Influencers

· ·

· ·

*B*logs today play a huge role in the new media landscape and remain a pillar of digital content. Although mainstream media and journalism have also gone digital, there are currently more than 400 million blogs on the Internet covering every niche under the sun — from fashion, food, lifestyle, and entertainment to more obscure hobbies and interests such as model train collecting, geocaching, and beekeeping.

In this chapter, we explain how you can identify your target bloggers and where to find them. Then we show you how to commission custom editorial content for your brand and leverage it across your brand-owned social channels to maximize the value.

Recognizing the Role Bloggers Play Today

Blogs are truly the new magazine medium. Bloggers have become influential arbiters of taste, editors of their own aspirational lifestyle, and everyday experts imparting knowledge to loyal readers. They deliver trusted word-of-mouth recommendations and reviews of the products and services that they find valuable.

The primary difference between blogs and editorial content produced by traditional media is that personal blogs speak to the reader authentically in the voice of the content creator and allow for social interactivity with their audience. The best blogs feature magazine-quality visuals — from beautiful, artfully staged photos to engaging video content.

There are single-author blogs (one primary content creator), as well as multi-author blogs (those with many contributors). And like traditional media outlets, the most dedicated bloggers curate an editorial calendar of topics that they intend to cover on a daily or weekly basis, depending on how often they update their site content. Typically, brand-sponsored content is interspersed with non-sponsored content to ensure that there is editorial balance.

Finding the Bloggers Who Are Right for Your Brand

There is an enormous pool of blogging talent just waiting to be discovered. And you're in luck, because many, if not all, of them are open to working with brands if the sponsored opportunity is aligned with their mission and editorial content, and if they're compensated fairly.

So, how do you go about finding the right bloggers for your brand? The great news is that you're likely already reading them! Forty-six percent of people read blogs more than once a day, according to the 2010 HubSpot Science of Blogging Report 2010. Can you think of the top five blogs that you follow? Where do *you* go for fashion advice, recipe inspiration, or crafting/DIY tutorials? Who do you trust for product recommendations and lifestyle advice?

According to the 2013 Digital Influence Report by Technorati Media, 86 percent of online influencers blog, and 52 percent of bloggers operate two to five blogs, while 43 percent run just one. If you find a blog that looks interesting, take the time to check whether that content creator operates any other affiliated blogs or websites.

The blogger community may be vast, but it's fairly tight knit, and many influencers within the same vertical will frequently share and interact with each other's content online. They do guest posts and collaborations together. You can think of it as an online cocktail party where interesting guests rotate in and out.

Check out who is already talking about your brand online. Do you have fans who have reached out to praise your product or service on Twitter, Facebook, or Instagram? Do they have blogs?

Make a wish list of the top ten bloggers you would like to work with. But don't get too attached just yet — you still have to determine your budget! (See Chapter 4 for more information on fair compensation.) Once you have that top-ten list,

- ✔ Review their content and try to determine if your top bloggers have collaborated with any other online influencers.

- ✔ Evaluate the ratio of original nonsponsored content to brand-sponsored content. How many times per week is the blogger posting brand-sponsored content?

- ✔ Determine if they're part of a blogger community such as Bloglovin,' which is an excellent tool for finding other influencers within the same category/industry (for example, fashion, parenting, lifestyle, food, and so on).

- ✔ Check to see who they follow and socialize with on online channels. Who are they tagging on Twitter, Instagram, and Facebook? What online conversations are they a part of and engaged in?

- ✔ Find out whether they own other online properties. Maybe their primary site is a general lifestyle blog, but they also have a separate blog dedicated to celebrity gossip or parenting advice.

The best and most successful bloggers typically offer a tightly curated, voyeuristic view into their lifestyle, habits, and homes. They share their joys, challenges, and everyday adventures with a captive online audience. It's this human element that engages readers and keeps them coming back for more — think of it as a form of reality-based entertainment. You wouldn't want to read a blog that wasn't entertaining, informative, and relatable, would you?

That said, the issue of brand safety is a valid concern. Take time to get familiar with a blogger's content by reviewing a selection of current and archived posts. Search for past sponsored posts to gauge how they write about brands and the language that they use. Don't engage a blogger to write about your brand if she doesn't align with your brand's core values and mission.

Here are some red flags to watch out for:

- ✔ Excessive use of profanity

- ✔ Promotion of illicit activities (gambling, drug use, and so on)

- ✔ Coverage of controversial or potentially obscene topics (religion, politics, and so on)

WARNING!

Impressions: They don't tell the whole story

Impressions (the number of times users have viewed or accessed a piece of web content/ blog page) are the largest elephant in the room. Most marketers tend to make the common mistake of evaluating bloggers solely on the basis of their impressions and social followings. Monthly page views and impressions do matter, but it's also important to keep in mind that they aren't the be all and end all when it comes time to consider your influencer marketing mix. You also have to consider the overall quality of their content and engagement level of their audience.

Carefully evaluate the overall quality of a blog and whether it could be the right fit for a potential brand partnership by looking at a variety of factors:

✔ **Editorial voice and audience:** Who exactly is the blogger? What's her life story, age, and background? Is she an individual contributor, or are there other content creators involved with the blog? What's the editorial voice like? Is it playful, humorous, educational, authoritative, or sarcastic? Who is the target audience? Parents, millennials, young professionals, fashionistas, crafters, foodies?

✔ **Editorial content mix:** What topics are typically covered on the blog? What is the blogger passionate about? Does it skew heavily toward one vertical or is it evenly distributed (for example, food, fashion/style, DIY/home decor, parenting)? What other

sponsored posts/partnerships has the blogger worked on? Are these other brands competitive with yours?

✔ **Timeliness:** How frequently does the blog get updated? Is it consistent and daily, weekly, or monthly? Is the content evergreen? Will it stand the test of time?

✔ **Photography and visuals:** What is the overall esthetic of the blog? Is it in line with your brand identity and esthetic? What is the style and quality of the photography? Does the blogger also shoot video? If so, is it short- or long-form video?

✔ **Impressions and engagement:** What are the monthly blog impressions? What social channels are they active on? How many followers does the blogger have on each channel (Twitter, Facebook, Pinterest, Instagram, and so on)? Sometimes unethical influencers will buy followers to inflate their numbers. This is why it's important to look at engagement as well. What's the engagement level on each social channel? On average, how many comments, likes, tweets, repins, and shares are there on the blogger's social shares?

If these social media stats and audience metrics aren't readily available at a glance or on the website, ask the blogger for her PR/ media kit.

Looking at the Details: Content Is King

The best and most successful influencers care deeply about the quality of their content. They strive to maintain an authentic, relatable voice to engage their readership, and it's imperative that they never compromise on their personal values when they evaluate a potential brand partnership. Keep this in mind once you've identified the bloggers that you want to reach out to with product pitch for your brand. The most common frustration for bloggers is that the outreach is done in a way that's not relevant or authentic to their audience. (See Chapter 4 for more information on best practices for approaching influencers.)

Authenticity is key to any blogger's success. They need some degree of creative freedom to execute sponsored content in a way that will resonate best with their audience.

When you've decided which bloggers you want to approach for your influencer marketing campaign, it's time to consider what your dream editorial content looks like. Sponsored content should strive to fit seamlessly into the blogger's current editorial mix, so it's important to determine what kind of content you think will resonate best with their audience and the call to action that you'd like to inspire their readers to take once they've read the content.

Have clear campaign objectives in mind before you approach bloggers to work with you. The following questions are designed to help you structure the most effective calls-to-action for your sponsored post:

- ✔ Are you launching a new product/service or product line extension?
- ✔ Are you interested in inspiring creative, new uses for an existing product?
- ✔ Are you promoting a special, limited-time offer or sweepstakes/giveaway?
- ✔ Are you driving product trial and purchase? Will you offer a coupon?
- ✔ Are you interested in reaching social followers on the bloggers' other channels such as Twitter, Facebook, Pinterest, Instagram, and YouTube?

In the following sections, we walk you through the major types of editorial content, how to make sure your brand is included in the blog posts being written, and guidelines for transparency (so you're always in compliance with the law).

Identifying the major types of editorial content

There are several major types of content. Before you commission content from influencers, carefully consider how your product or service can organically fit into each theme, depending on what objective you're trying to achieve. In this section, we break it down based on genre — general/lifestyle, beauty/fashion, craft/home, health/fitness, and food.

General/lifestyle

In the general/lifestyle category, here are the major types of blog posts you may want to commission:

- ✔ **Product trial and review:** Bloggers share their authentic experience using your product or service, including key benefits.

- ✔ **Seasonal/celebration/holiday themes (for example, Christmas, New Year, Valentine's Day, summer, back to school):** Seasonal themes are timely and appropriate for highlighting special promotions or inspiring different usage occasions throughout the year.

- ✔ **Top ten tips or lists:** Lists are particularly effective for sharing a lot of information in easily digestible parts.

- ✔ **How-to/tutorial:** Tutorials are ideal for showing how to re-create a project or recipe in multiple steps with detailed instructions and photos.

- ✔ **Personal experience or favorite memories:** Draw on the blogger's life experience to relate to your brand. This is great for building emotional impact.

Beauty/fashion

In the beauty/fashion category, here are the major types of blog posts you may want to commission:

- ✔ **Top beauty/fashion picks:** Your brand is featured as part of a round-up of other related products.

- ✔ **Makeup/beauty tutorial:** This educational post highlights how your product works in conjunction with others to create a specific, desired look.

- ✔ **Fashion styling:** Your product is styled and paired with other fashion items to create an outfit of the day (OOTD) look or inspire different wearable combinations.

Craft/home

In the craft/home category, here are the major types of blog posts you may want to commission:

- ✔ **DIY/project tutorial:** Bloggers use your product to create a tutorial that is both educational and useful.

- ✔ **Home/room tour:** This type of post is highly visual and showcases how your product fits into the home environment. It's ideal for aspirational lifestyle products.

- ✔ **Problem solving:** Bloggers use your product or service to solve a common household problem.

Health/fitness

In the health/fitness category, here are the major types of blog posts you may want to commission:

- ✔ **Workout routines:** Bloggers highlight how your product fits into their regular workout routine.

- ✔ **Fitspiration:** Bloggers offer motivational tips for working out and staying healthy. Product mentions in this type of post are generally more subtle.

- ✔ **New Year's resolutions:** Bloggers offer advice for how to jumpstart or achieve new health goals for the year.

Food

In the food category, here are the major types of blog posts you may want to commission:

- ✔ **Recipe generation:** Bloggers use your product to create an original recipe, or a new twist on an old favorite. This type of post also pairs well with a seasonal or entertaining theme.

- ✔ **Pairings:** Your product is featured alongside complementary products to inspire delicious, unique, or unusual pairings.

- ✔ **Entertaining tablescape:** Your product is styled (similar to a still life) in a table/meal setting to inspire entertaining or usage occasions.

Setting clear guidelines for bloggers

After you've decided on the type of blog post, you need to offer bloggers a detailed contract outlining your requirements for the sponsored post or partnership you're seeking.

Set realistic expectations, keeping in mind that sponsored content should *not* read as an ad. Aim to be as specific as possible about non-negotiable items. Don't neglect to include any important brand restrictions with respect to competitive mentions, acceptable product usage, and geographic availability.

The ideal blog post should include the following four key elements (covered in the following sections in greater detail):

✔ Proper disclosure following the guidelines set by the Federal Trade Commission (FTC)

✔ Brand-provided key messages, including product or service benefits

✔ A clear call to action, including brand or product URLs

✔ High-quality photos

Prior to the start of your engagement, ensure that the blogger fully understands all the requirements set forth in the contract and is aligned with your campaign objectives.

Making sure bloggers make the proper disclosures for transparency

Influencer marketing is only effective when it's transparent and the content remains authentic. This is because transparency improves overall consumer trust. Influencers would lose readers and social followers if they didn't disclose potential conflicts of interest and paid relationships. Wouldn't you feel deceived if you read a sponsored post without any context for whether the blogger received compensation or product in exchange for sharing her opinion?

Don't jeopardize consumer goodwill by neglecting to disclose sponsored relationships. It will erode consumer confidence. Clear, conspicuous, and meaningful disclosures benefit both advertisers *and* consumers.

Full disclosure of paid relationships is required by the FTC to ensure that consumers are aware that they're viewing sponsored content. The FTC states that the disclosure must be written in a clear and conspicuous manner that can be understood by the average reader. The disclosure must also be placed directly next to (or as close as possible to) the sponsored content. Typically, this is addressed with a simple disclosure statement at the top of each sponsored blog post. Repeat disclosures, as needed, on lengthy blog posts (for example, it may be reiterated at the end of the post).

According to the FTC, required disclosures must be clear and conspicuous. In evaluating whether a disclosure is likely to be clear and conspicuous, advertisers should consider its placement in the ad and its proximity to the relevant claim. Here are some sample disclosure statements:

✔ "Thank you [brand name] for sponsoring this post!

✔ "This post was sponsored by [brand name]."

✔ [Brand], provided me with a free supply of [product] in exchange for my review of [product]. The opinions in this post are my own."

Check out the Appendix for the full FTC guidelines related to influencer marketing. If you don't adhere to these guidelines, you're liable to be fined by the FTC.

Telling bloggers the message you want communicated about your brand

You should make it as easy as possible for bloggers to understand your brand, product or service benefits, and use cases by providing brand-approved assets. Give bloggers five or six key messages that they can select from to craft their blog posts. You may also want to share press releases as an FYI — but keep in mind that dry documents filled with marketing buzz-words are not appealing to a general audience.

Here are some do's and don'ts for leveraging brand-provided assets:

- ✔ **Use bullet points to convey key messages.** They're more easily digestible than lengthy paragraphs or tedious press releases.

- ✔ **Don't send bloggers your press release and expect them to pull out the key points on their own.**

- ✔ **Ask bloggers to incorporate at least two or three of your key messages in their blog posts.**

- ✔ **Don't expect bloggers to use key messages verbatim.** Your message will come across more effectively if you allow bloggers to use their own voices to organically convey key messages to their audience.

- ✔ **Direct bloggers to useful URLs on your brand website.** For example, you might steer them to your product/store locator, a microsite for a specific product, or a promotional landing page.

- ✔ **Share direct links to your brand-owned social channels (for example, Twitter, Facebook, Pinterest, Instagram, YouTube, and so on).** Don't make bloggers hunt for key information and links.

- ✔ **Share brand-provided images or infographics only if they add value and useful context for your product or service.**

- ✔ **Provide a dedicated hashtag for sharing sponsored content.** Using a unique/branded hashtag will help readers find your content across social channels once it's shared.

Highly regulated industries such as healthcare and financial services often have stricter guidelines for brand-approved messaging. Always defer to your legal team and industry guidelines for best practices in this case.

Driving engagement with calls to action

Simply put, clear calls to action drive engagement because they give readers a next step to act upon once they've read the sponsored post. Sticking with one or two actionable steps is typically most effective — more than that, and the post could become muddled. You may also ask the blogger to repeat the call to action in his social amplifications for further emphasis.

Here are some sample calls to action:

- **Educational:** "Click here to learn more about the new [product name]."

- **Product trial and purchase:** "Click here to download a coupon to try [product name]."

- **Promotional/limited-time offer:** "Now through [date], visit [location] to buy/try [product name]."

- **Sweepstakes/giveaway entry:** "Click here to enter the [brand] sweepstakes for a chance to win amazing prizes!"

- **Expanding social reach:** "Click here to follow [brand] on [social channel]."

Providing photo guidelines

A picture is worth more than a thousand words, and considering that most blog posts will average anywhere from 300 to 500 words, you'll want exceptional photography to showcase your product in its best light. All text and no photos make for a very dull blog post, indeed.

An ideal blog post should include at least three to five original, high-quality photos. You may want to provide a brand-approved image, but original photos are typically better for the sake of authenticity. If feasible, encourage bloggers to style your product within their own environment in a manner that will help to enhance and illustrate your chosen theme.

Being explicit about guidelines for photography will save you (and the blogger!) a lot of time and frustration when it's time for the blog post to go live. After all, it does take time to properly style the product and stage and edit photos.

Not all bloggers are professional photographers, so err on the side of providing detailed technical specs and product shooting tips whenever possible.

Photo guidelines should include guidance on the following:

- **Product visibility:** Should photos feature product packaging and/or a front-facing logo?

- ✔ **Product styling:** How should the product be presented or staged? Is it an action shot or still life? If it's a food product, should it be shown as a finished recipe or part of a meal? If the product is decorative, how should it be styled in the desired environment (outdoors, indoors, in a specific room or setting)? If it's a fashion product, should it be styled as an outfit of the day (OOTD) or part of a "curated lookbook"? Alternatively, would a photo collage or Polyvore-style board be an acceptable option?

- ✔ **Competitive products:** Are there any restrictions on showcasing your product along with competitive brands or products in the background?

- ✔ **Compatibility with other social channels:** Consider where else the photo may potentially be shared (for example, Pinterest or Instagram) and ask bloggers to consider styling or cropping the photo accordingly. On Pinterest, recipe photos are most appealing when they showcase the finished product (see Chapter 10). On Instagram, close-ups and action shots are most appealing (see Chapter 7).

Sharing Is Caring: Repurposing Content

When a sponsored blog post is live, there are many creative and effective ways to leverage the content to support your overarching marketing goals. First, decide where else you'd like to see the sponsored content shared. Do you want to reach social followers on the bloggers' other channels, such as Twitter, Facebook, Pinterest, and Instagram?

Your blogger contract should stipulate exactly how many social amplifications the influencer is required to execute once the blog post is live. Ask the blogger to share her blog post with a direct link across the social channels that are a top priority for your campaign or brand. Resist the temptation to blanket *all* the social channels — there's no point if they're irrelevant to your campaign.

Consider prioritizing sharing of food, beauty/fashion, and travel posts on the highly visual, image-driven social channels such as Pinterest and Instagram. Text-heavy and sweepstakes/contest-driven sponsored posts are most effectively shared on Facebook and Twitter.

Selecting the proper hashtag

Hashtags are important because they help readers find your content across social channels, especially on Twitter and Instagram. Select a hashtag that is short, unique, and memorable, and don't forget to double-check the spelling!

Search Twitter to check if anyone else is already using the hashtag you have in mind. You don't want readers to confuse your product/campaign with that of another competitor!

Hashtags for sponsored content should be

- **Short:** You'll want a concise hashtag to leave room for the rest of your message (for example, Twitter has a 140-character limit).

- **Unique:** A unique hashtag will enable you to better track metrics from the campaign.

- **Easy:** Your hashtag should be easy to spell. Be aware of potential misspellings or weird abbreviations when shortening words.

- **Memorable:** Funny, tongue-in-cheek hashtags are great, but make sure it's still brand safe and aligned with your marketing objectives for brand awareness.

Leveraging commissioned content as sponsored advertising on Facebook

If you've partnered with a blogger who has created an amazing blog post featuring your product, consider sharing it far and wide with the Facebook community! According to the Hubspot 2012 State of Inbound Marketing report, 77 percent of business-to-consumer (whereby merchants sell products to consumers) companies acquired customers from Facebook, compared to 43 percent of business-to-business (whereby businesses sell products/services to other businesses) companies. Additionally, 80 percent of U.S. social network users prefer to connect to brands through Facebook. What does this mean for marketers? Facebook ads can be an effective vehicle for targeting new and existing customers, especially if you sell a B-to-C product/service!

Using influencer-created sponsored content, you can create your own brand-approved Facebook ads and target them to a set demographic of your choosing. Posts you should promote include the following

- Evergreen content that will get long-term views or shares, and will provide consumers with useful information they can re-share

- Special offers and coupons that provide immediate value to the consumer

If your influencer marketing campaign is going well, you should have a wealth of content to leverage as a sponsored Facebook ad. Ideally, you should select a blog post that is already gaining traction on social channels. If an influencer has created a sponsored blog post that has been shared on Facebook with her audience and it's already racking up a significant volume of like, shares, and overall engagement, consider turning that content into a sponsored Facebook ad for your brand.

An effective Facebook ad is

- ✔ **Visual:** Pick a beautiful picture that will grab the consumer's eye! People are naturally drawn to images over text.

  Ask the influencer for the right to use her image(s) in your sponsored ad, if you haven't already outlined this stipulation in your blogger contract. Select the most beautiful image and pair it with compelling text to create your perfect ad.

- ✔ **Relevant:** Target your ad to the right audience. Play with the Facebook Ad Manager settings to tweak your "relevance score." If you're showing ads that aren't relevant to your target audience, you're simply wasting your time and money. Facebook Ad Manager also allows you to create custom audiences using email addresses or phone numbers from existing customer data. This can dramatically increase your ad's impact and return on investment (ROI) through better targeting, in addition to tracking conversions.

- ✔ **Enticing:** Make your value proposition and call to action compelling, timely and clear. By adding a sense of urgency, you'll encourage readers to take action now to buy, save, learn more, or enter to win.

For example, Coffee-mate leveraged a sponsored blog post by The Rebel Chick, featuring a recipe that uses Coffee-mate creamer to create its own Facebook ad. The original blog post (`http://therebelchick.com/sweet-banana-pudding-recipe-coffee-mate-extra-sweet-creamy-coffee-creamer`), created in March 2014, was shared more than 6,500 times across social channels, and racked up 115 blog comments. In May 2014, Coffee-mate decided to leverage The Rebel Chick's image in a sponsored Facebook ad (`www.facebook.com/CoffeemateUSA/photos/a.130052849238.103991.120251049238/10152649756939239/?type=1`), which generated more than 90,000 likes and 55,000 shares!

Always give proper attribution to the original content creator. This can be done by tagging the influencer on Facebook and/or linking back to the original sponsored blog post.

Looking at Examples of Great Blogs

In this section, we offer examples of blog influencers in the following categories: food, lifestyle, and parenting. We walk you through specific campaigns they participated in, tell you what they did, and explain why it worked.

These are just examples of influencers in various categories. These aren't the only bloggers worth your time — not even close! Use these profiles as examples of what to look for when you're searching for influencers for your own campaign.

A food blogger: Life Made Simple

Blog name: Life Made Simple (www.lifemadesimplebakes.com)

Brand sponsor: Ghirardelli

Blog post theme: Valentine-themed recipe for chocolate cupcakes using Ghirardelli baking products

Highlights: Blog post was shared over 1,000 times, primarily on Pinterest.

Hashtags: #GhirardelliVday #CG

Link: www.lifemadesimplebakes.com/2015/02/chocolate-sweetheart-cupcakes

Natalie, who blogs at Life Made Simple, is a self-taught baker who features recipes that are quick and easy, using ingredients that you'd most likely have stocked in your pantry or fridge. Her desserts are typically unique, approachable, and budget friendly.

Ghirardelli asked food bloggers to create a custom Valentine's Day dessert recipe using Ghirardelli products, including 60% Cacao Baking Chips and/or Candy Making & Melting Wafers.

Natalie crafted a decadent chocolate cupcake recipe topped with chocolate buttercream and decorated with Ghirardelli Valentine's Day Impressions for an extra festive touch. Her recipe is easy to follow and takes the reader through a step-by-step process of creating the dessert, illustrated with mouthwatering photos. As a result, her blog post was shared over 1,000 times, primarily on Pinterest.

A lifestyle blogger: Bubby and Bean

Blog name: Bubby and Bean (`www.bubbyandbean.com`)

Brand sponsor: Dremel

Blog post theme: A step-by-step tutorial for how to create a DIY lamp shade using the Dremel Micro 8050 tool

Highlights: Blog post was pinned 143 times and generated 16 blog post comments.

Hashtag: #MyBrilliantIdea

Link: `www.bubbyandbean.com/2014/09/diy-tutorial-personalized-dotted-name.html`

Melissa is a design enthusiast who chronicles her life with her husband and young children on her blog, Bubby and Bean. Her blog and editorial aesthetic is modern bohemian — a combination of free-spirited playfulness and minimalist simplicity. She also features a variety of contributor content across food, fashion/style, home, and craft categories.

Dremel engaged craft and DIY bloggers to review the Dremel Micro 8050 multipurpose cordless tool and write about their experiences using the product on a creative home project.

Melissa shared a comprehensive tutorial teaching readers how to craft a personalized table lamp using the Dremel Micro 8050. Her clear-cut instructions were accompanied by photos illustrating each step. She also promoted the Dremel #MyBrilliantIdeaSweeps and encouraged readers to share their own projects for the chance to win weekly prizes.

Her blog post was shared nearly 150 times and generated 16 blog post comments.

A parenting blogger: A Semi-Delicate Balance

Blog name: A Semi-Delicate Balance

Brand sponsor: Western Union

Blog post theme: A personal post inspired by the brand-provided Western Union video; sharing stories about being away from home/family and the memories that bring you back to your culture

Highlights: Blog post embedded the Western Union video and was shared over 294 times, primarily on Pinterest.

Hashtags: #WUHomecooked #Paid

Link: www.semidelicatebalance.com/2015/01/03/5-ways-families-can-connect-long-distance-loved-ones

JD is a working mom and military spouse. Her blog, A Semi-Delicate Balance, offers useful tips, advice, and humor for other parents and military spouses who are working hard to balance motherhood and family life with career and household responsibilities.

Western Union sought out bloggers who understand what it's like to live in a different part of the country — or world — from their families. These bloggers shared stories of family connections, as well as a touching Western Union video, where real customers are surprised with unexpected "home cooking."

JD was selected to write a very personal blog post highlighting five ways that families can connect with long-distance loved ones. She shared her own family history and struggle with frequent moves due to her husband's military deployments, and how she stays in touch with extended family members all over the world. Her post also embedded the Western Union video. As a result, her content was shared nearly 300 times, primarily on Pinterest.

Chapter 7

Instagram Influencers

*I*nstagram is the number-one social photo platform. It launched in 2010 and scaled rapidly to one million users in just two months. As of July 2015, Instagram had 300 million active users sharing 30 billion photos, generating an average of 70 million photos per day. This visual platform is ideal for brand storytelling and showcasing your product or service through amazing imagery.

Instagram is a unique social platform because it can stand alone as a vehicle for visual storytelling. The influencer's content can exist solely on the Instagram channel, and it doesn't necessarily have to tie back to a blog or another social platform for additional context.

Instagram influencers are passionate about beautiful photography, sharing intimate vignettes of their lives, the products they love, and of course, selfies. Most Instagrammers post their own original content, although some channels aggregate existing content, reposting photos from other Instagram feeds.

The best Instagram feeds capture snapshots of everyday life or an aspirational lifestyle using clever composition, skilled photo editing, and tightly curated thematic content. In fact, these influencers make it look easy. But don't be fooled — Instagram may be a simple tool to use, but it takes work to make photos look so good!

In this chapter, we help you leverage Instagram for your brand and tell you how to identify your target Instagrammers. We also show you how to commission custom editorial content for your brand and leverage it across your brand-owned social channels to maximize the value.

Finding Instagrammers to Share Your Brand Story

As with nearly any online channel, you'll find that Instagrammers typically fall across the spectrum of varying levels of influence and engagement. There are three primary influencer groups:

- ✔ **Everyday influencers:** Up to 1,000 followers

- ✔ **Premium influencers:** Thousands of followers

- ✔ **A-list influencers:** Hundreds of thousands to millions of followers

Unless you're a Fortune 500 brand with a correspondingly large budget, engaging A-list influencers is probably a shot in the dark. A single sponsored photo posted by a user with more than 100,000 followers can command upwards of $3,000 to $5,000. Compensation will vary depending on the brand requirements and influencer's overall reach (see www.dummies.com/cheatsheet/influencermarketing for specifics). So, you'll likely want to review your marketing goals and focus the majority of your Instagram recruiting efforts on everyday or premium influencers who can help elevate your brand through organic storytelling within your budget.

There are a few ways to recruit Instagrammers who are receptive to telling your brand story. The most direct avenue is to search for existing content on Instagram, see what's trending, and observe the conversation. For example, if your brand name is Jojo's Ice Cream Shop, try these tips:

- ✔ **Check to see who has already tagged your brand in a photo.** You can do this by going directly to your Instagram account profile. Click the tab on the far right that shows the person icon.

- ✔ **Search by your hashtagged brand name (for example, #jojosicecream).**

- ✔ **Check relevant hashtags related to your brand or product (for example, #icecream, #sundae #sweettooth, or #dessert).**

- ✔ **If you have a physical location or retail store, enter your store name or address and search using the Places filter.**

A secondary method for Instagrammer recruiting is to review your favorite blogs, including bloggers who have covered your brand in the past. Check to see if they're on Instagram.

As you're filtering through these Instagram feeds at a glance, take note of their photography skills, total number of followers, and whether they have a dedicated theme. We call this the 4R model:

- ✔ **Reach:** How many followers do they reach?

- ✔ **Relevance:** What subjects or themes does their photos cover? Is the Instagram feed cohesive and tightly curated, or all over the place?

- ✔ **Resonance:** Is the content resonating with their audience? What is the average engagement level on each photo (volume of likes and comments)? Read the comments for sentiment analysis.

- ✔ **Relationship:** How do they currently relate to brands? Do they have a mix of sponsored content in their feed? Does the content feel organic, authentic, or forced? Would your brand look out of place in their Instagram feed?

This is just the first step to recruiting. You still need to vet Instagrammers for authenticity, engagement, and brand safety in the next stage (see Chapter 6 for tips).

Commissioning Custom Editorial Content

The Instagram platform supports both photos and video (with a 15-second time limit), which allows influencers a certain amount of creative freedom to share creative content. Take advantage of this!

Whether to use photos, videos, or both

Consider whether the content you want influencers to create would be better shared as a short video or static image. Instagram as a whole is focused on quickly capturing individual moments. Not everyone wants to stop and spend even 15 seconds to watch a video when they're quickly scrolling through their Instagram feed, so plan your content judiciously. But if sound and movement is critical to or enhances your content, then definitely go with video!

When to use photos
We recommend using photos when the story can be

- ✔ Told effectively in a single shot

- ✔ Staged beautifully (ideal for still life or portraits)

- ✔ Effectively shared as a series of multiple photos over a period of time

When to use videos

We recommend using videos for the following situations:

- ✔ Before and after, or show and tell (for example, makeovers and makeup/shopping hauls)
- ✔ Short, step-by-step tutorials (how-to, DIY, meal prep)
- ✔ Location walk-throughs (mini travelogues)
- ✔ Shout-outs and short testimonials (fan messages)

When to use hybrid photo-video content

You don't have to stick with just photos or videos. Would you prefer your influencers to share many images quickly? A third-party app called Flipagram (www.flipagram.com) allows users to quickly combine photos, videos, links, text, and music into short, edited video clips. Essentially, they're short photo-video stories paired with music.

Flipagram is also great for memorializing live events — like a launch party, or celebration — or making a self-expressive collage to be saved and shared across Instagram, or other social channels such as Facebook, Twitter, Pinterest, Vine, YouTube, and Tumblr.

In addition, Instagram now supports the use of cinemagraphs, which are `still photographs` in which a minor and repeated movement occurs (similar to a GIF animation). You can create this animated effect using a free iOS app such as Cinemagraph Pro and then upload the looped video to Instagram for sharing.

How to write captivating captions

There's really only one key rule for Instagram captions: Keep it short and sweet.

The Instagram audience is most interested in engaging with beautiful photography and inspirational images. They aren't interested in lengthy blocks of text, so it's best to keep the captions concise, simple, and direct. Witty, punny hashtags can be effective as well (see the next section), but avoid muddling your message with extraneous links and directives unless you're sharing a contest or other promotional effort that requires certain rules and regulations required by your legal counsel.

How to choose the right campaign hashtags

A campaign-specific hashtag is critical to your promotional campaign. It allows other users to find your content and provides a point of reference for the promotion.

We highly recommended using a hashtag that is unique to your campaign for the most accurate metrics tracking. For example, consider using your brand/business name with "contest" or your contest theme (for example, #JojosIceCreamContest or #JojosSummerScoops). By using a unique tag for your campaign, you're also instantly building a community for your entrants — everyone who enters can see the other campaign photos via Instagram search.

Your hashtag should also be easy to spell, memorable, and not too long or complicated. Keep in mind that mobile users may get frustrated with a hashtag that is too long to autocomplete.

Don't forget to double-check the usage of your campaign hashtag to ensure it's not already in use or too similar to an existing hashtag.

Disclosures for transparency

As discussed in Chapter 6, sponsored content must be disclosed. The Federal Trade Commission (FTC) states that the disclosure must be written in a clear and conspicuous manner that can be understood by the average reader. The disclosure must also be placed directly next to (or as close as possible to) the sponsored content. On Instagram, this can be addressed using a simple hashtag such as #sponsored or #ad.

There is no character limit on Instagram captions, so influencers are able to combine a dedicated campaign hashtag with #sponsored for proper disclosure, in addition to other relevant subject hashtags as appropriate.

Arranging an Influencer Channel Takeover

Influencer channel takeovers are a very direct and effective way to attract new followers to your brand's account. A channel takeover involves an influencer posting on her own account, telling her followers that she's going to "take over" your brand's account for a certain period of time (typically for

24 hours or less), during which she'll post pictures and sometimes answer questions. A takeover is also an ideal tactic for celebrating a holiday, live event, launch party, or other special occasion that your brand is promoting.

This type of partnership is mutually beneficial because the brand gains access to the influencer's following, and the influencer is promoted through the brand's channel. It's an opportunity to showcase your brand through the lens of a tastemaker, borrowing her aesthetic for just a limited time. For example, Zappos partnered with Instagrammer @ASideofSweet on a takeover during the 2015 Bay to Breakers race, sponsored by Zappos: www. instagram.com/p/2y4LsKqJ9H. Another example: BarkBox partnered with Instagrammer @Weenteam on a takeover to celebrate National Hot Dog Day (www.instagram.com/p/5ghNZaICEm).

Apply the lessons learned in Chapter 6 to ensure that the influencer advocate you've selected is brand safe and a worthy evangelist for your brand.

We don't advise a literal "takeover" of your brand channel. It may be stating the obvious, but in the interest of protecting your brand, you don't actually want to hand over your social channel log-in/account info to even the most well-respected influencer. This should not be a free pass to post anything they please.

Instead, we recommend outlining a process by which the influencer takes photos in advance for brand approval and posting. Whether this is hours or days in advance will depend on the nature of the takeover (if it's a live or scheduled event, you won't be able to have as much lead time). After the photos are taken (and edited if necessary), they should be routed directly to the brand to manage the schedule for posting.

As discussed in Chapter 4, we cannot overstate the importance of having an iron-clad contract that outlines in detail what the influencer's responsibilities are in the partnership, including the exact number of deliverables (typically both photo and text captions), duration of the engagement, any other cross-promotional efforts, and compensation or payment terms. Influencer compensation can vary depending on whether you're paying per photo (fees typically range from a few hundred to thousands of dollars) or per engagement on the photo (likes and/or comments).

Organizing an Instagram Flash Mob

Another method of taking over Instagram feeds with a flood of original, organic content is to organize a flash mob of influencers who are coordinated to post at the same time on a particular day for maximum reach.

Case study: Montagne Jeunesse #AhhSleepSpa

In this flash mob program, 102 millennial influencers shared before and "ahhhfter" photos of their experience using the Montagne Jeunesse Sleep Spa masks. The brand sent product to all the influencers, and each participant was required to share two photos. Photo captions included the campaign hashtag and a short brand-approved message:

"Montagne Jeunesse Renew You Sleep Spa Mask is available now at Ulta stores and online at Ulta.com!" The campaign hashtag was #AhhSleepSpa. The campaign generated more than 13,000 likes and hundreds of comments across the sponsored posts. You can see a gallery of the images at `http://clvr.li/mjtakeover`.

This tactic is most effective when you have a simple call to action for influencers that doesn't require a lot of setup time. You're working with a greater volume of influencers instead of one for a brand channel takeover, so keep the actions simple. That way there is less room for error in the coordination.

Be sure to get everyone to sign contracts to ensure that you're aligned with deliverables and deadlines.

As with any marketing effort, have a plan B in place in case anything goes awry during your Instagram takeover or flash mob. Make sure you have a solid crisis communications plan in place to deal with any questions or technical glitches during the takeover event. The social media winds are fickle and change happens quickly, so knowing the plan is only half the battle. Be prepared to pivot and change tactics quickly depending on how the situation unfolds.

Putting Together Contests, Giveaways, and Promotions

Instagram is an excellent platform for driving user engagement on contests and giveaways because the engagement actions are simple. It's quick and easy to tag a friend or a brand and comment on a photo.

First, you need to decide the method of contest entry — what users need to do to qualify for an eligible entry. Do they have to submit or upload their own photo using the contest hashtag, or just follow your brand on Instagram?

As a general rule of thumb, the lower the barrier to entry, the greater the volume of entries!

What you ask for at the time of entry depends on your marketing goals. Are you trying to gain new followers, increase your brand channel's social engagement, drive more sales?

Don't forget to include a shortened link in your caption to the official rules and regulations! However, keep in mind that links in the photo description/caption aren't active. You can only have a clickable link in the Instagram account profile/bio URL.

Here are five standard entry methods to consider:

- ✔ **Submit photo to win:** The user must upload and share a photo on Instagram with the dedicated contest hashtag(s) and tag the brand with an @mention to be entered into the contest. This method works well for Instagram photo challenges that offer a different prompt each day to encourage both frequency and variety of entries (see "Hosting an Instagram Photo Challenge," later in this chapter).

- ✔ **Regram to win:** User must regram/share the brand image on their own Instagram channel with the dedicated contest hashtag(s) to count as a valid entry.

- ✔ **Like to win:** This is the simplest entry method, with the lowest barrier to entry. All a user needs to do to enter is to like one of your photos on Instagram.

- ✔ **Follow to win:** This can be used as the only required entry method or in conjunction with like to win and/or regram to win.

- ✔ **Comment and/or tag a friend to win:** This requires a user to comment and/or tag another friend on Instagram to be entered, which is great for increasing brand awareness, engagement, and adding new followers. We don't recommend tagging more than one friend — tagging more than one person may be considered spammy by users who are tagged without permission.

Offering prizes

It's no secret that enticing prizes will encourage a greater number of entries, but make sure that your incentives are aligned with your brand. Here are some tips to keep in mind:

- ✔ **Prizes should ideally spur consumer action or be related to your business.** For example, you might offer a gift card to your store or a new product you're promoting.

- ✔ **Prize value should be proportionate to the ask from entrants.** If you're asking for one photo, that's an easy task and your incentive can be of a lower value. If you're asking for a creative video or requiring multiple steps for entry, you'll want to give away a bigger, more valuable prize.

- ✔ **Offer duplicate prizing for tag a friend to win.** This further incentivizes entrants to share your contest with friends to increase the reach of your contest!

- ✔ **Consider frequency of prizing.** Daily or weekly prizes tend to work best, because social content turns over quickly. You want your contest to stay top-of-mind for the duration of the campaign! Frequent prizing also typically translates to more chances to win, which is incentivizing.

Setting eligibility requirements

Contest eligibility requirements should be simple and clearly spelled out in the rules and regulations. Typically, we recommend the following actions to qualify eligible entries for an Instagram contest:

- ✔ Follow @BrandHandle on Instagram

- ✔ Complete the contest entry form (include shortened URL or micro-site link).

- ✔ Post to Instagram during the contest period using the photo prompts for inspiration, and the hashtags #CampaignHashtag.

- ✔ Adhere to demographic restrictions (for example, age requirements or geographic limitations).

Measuring your contest success

Be sure to identify and set up your analytics tools *prior* to the start of your campaign/promotion. This gives you a baseline to measure your achievements. Instagram currently doesn't offer built-in analytics features, so you'll need to set up third-party monitoring of your key performance indicators. You may set up a Google Analytics campaign, use Facebook Insights (if you're running in conjunction with Facebook), or use a third-party monitoring app such as Hashtracking or Union Metrics that offers in-depth analytics.

Hosting an Instagram Photo Challenge

An Instagram photo challenge with a set number of daily prompts is yet another option for driving user-generated content to promote your brand. Done successfully, you'll generate an organic groundswell of new images surfacing daily, promoting your brand by extension.

There are five key components to executing an effective photo challenge:

- **Choose a theme and prompt.** Keep the photo challenge theme and prompts general enough so that anyone participating can easily find something to photograph during their daily routine each day of the challenge. Obscure references are not recommended.

- **Create a landing page.** Create a campaign landing page or microsite that houses both your rules and your entry form. Third-party services like ShortStack (`www.shortstack.com`), HubSpot (`www.hubspot.com`), or Lander (`www.landerapp.com`) are all good choices for this. You may also host your photo challenge via a platform such as Offerpop (`www.offerpop.com`), which integrates easily with Facebook for cross-promotion.

- **Plan and promote.** Have a plan in place to schedule your promotional posts and don't forget to use the photo challenge hashtag to build buzz! Choose a memorable hashtag that will entice followers to click through.

- **Engage.** Review your photo challenge entries daily in real-time to engage with followers who have entered. Regram and share their photos across your social channels outside of Instagram to extend the reach of your campaign.

- **Award daily or weekly prizes to keep the momentum going throughout the photo challenge period.** And don't forget to congratulate the winners publicly on your brand channels!

Seven-day challenges are typically easier to manage than 30-day challenges!

Case study: Sutter Home Wines #MYMiniMoments

Sutter Home Wines launched a 30-day photo challenge in April 2014 to promote its mini bottles. The daily prompts were seasonally focused and celebrated the little moments in life that bring you joy. Hundreds of participants posted their Instagram photos using the hashtag #MyMiniMoments for a chance to win fabulous prizes (six $100 Visa gift cards and two iPad Mini grand prizes). You can check out the rules and regulations at `http://clvr.li/11h07DV`.

The campaign generated more than 22,000 likes across the contest photos. The brand also saw an 86 percent increase in @SutterHomeWines Instagram followers after the campaign. You can visit the contest microsite at `http://clvr.li/minimoments` to see more.

Know your meme

Need more ideas for keeping your Instagram feed fresh? Check out these popular Instagram memes:

- **#FromWhereIStand:** Footwear selfies and other interesting flooring/carpeting/ground details shot from one's point of view looking down. Rebecca Finch (@bexfinch) a Brooklyn-based photographer and Instagram user is credited with originating the hashtag #FromWhereIStand. Naturally, she's collaborated with footwear brands such as Tretorn and Keds. @GoJane shared a chic #FromWhereIStand by fahion blogger @ProFresh Style at `www.instagram.com/p/5fMy8sCD1M`.

- **#MCM/#ManCrushMonday:** Hot men. 'Nuff said! @tartecosmetics shared a #ManCrushMonday featuring Aussie actor Chris Hemsworth at `www.instagram.com/p/5XoisgvpAS`.

- **#TBT (Throwback Thursday):** Nostalgia reigns supreme. Photos celebrate decades or even days, weeks and months in the recent past, reminiscing on good times.

Fashionista @9to5chic shared a #TBT featuring fellow style maven @Wendyslookbook promoting the @BananaRepublic Fall Presentation at `www.instagram.com/p/zT8rL3rr8L`.

- **#NoMakeupSelfie:** Originally created to raise cancer awareness in the UK, this hashtag gained a resurgence in popularity to combat cyberbullying after an incident involving teen beauty pageant queen Isabella Gaines (@Bellagainess). The hashtag has been adopted by influencers everywhere to showcase "everyday beauty." Beauty vlogger @shamelessfripperies bared all in a #nomakeup selfie at `www.instagram.com/p/4W6jHAIDwU`.

- **#OOTD (Outfit of the Day):** Fashionistas show off their stylish outfits — head to toe or via a style board layout. Strike a pose! Fashion blogger @JuliaHengel shared her Parisian #OOTD inspiration at `www.instagram.com/p/47dq_gvsry`.

Taking Inspiration from Great Instagrammers

In this section, we offer examples of Instagram influencers in the following categories: food, fashion, and beauty. We walk you through specific campaigns they participated in, tell you what they did, and explain why it worked.

These are just examples of influencers in various categories. These aren't the only Instagram influencers worth your time — not even close! Use these profiles as examples of what to look for when you're searching for influencers for your own campaign.

A food Instagrammer: What Jew Wanna Eat

Instagram handle: @WhatJewWannaEat

Brand sponsor: M&M'S Crispy

Photo theme: Promote M&M'S Crispy relaunch and highlight enjoyment of the candy as a sweet summer treat

Highlights: The Instagram post generated 510 likes and 42 comments.

Hashtags: #CrispyMMSummerCG #Sponsored

Link: `www.instagram.com/p/57LA7MHQBU`

Amy is a humorous food blogger who proudly shares her Jewish culinary roots through homemade, (sometimes) kosher recipes handed down from her Bubbe. She attended culinary school at Le Cordon Bleu in Austin and now spends her time teaching cooking classes, developing recipes, and working as a personal chef and blogger. Her modern interpretation of classic Jewish recipes have been featured in *Cosmopolitan* and `Bon Appétit` and on `The Today Show`.

M&M'S Crispy engaged influencers to share an engaging Instagram post featuring the candy to promote its relaunch and availability in stores nationwide. Instagrammers channeled their enthusiasm for the brand in colorful and fun photos, showcasing how they enjoy M&M'S Crispy candies as a sweet treat.

Amy chose to highlight M&M'S Crispy sprinkled on top of a bagel. Her Instagram post generated 510 likes and 42 comments.

A fashion Instagrammer: Carrie Bradshaw Lied

Instagram handle: @CarrieBradshawLied

Brand sponsor: Gloria Ferrer Winery

Photo theme: Promote Gloria Ferrer sparkling wine and inspire entertaining occasions

Highlights: 1,022 likes

Hashtags: #BeGloriousContest #CleverGirls

Link: www.instagram.com/p/21C103C-QF

Kathleen is budget-friendly fashionista and ex-beauty queen who curates a lifestyle blog from her home base of Southern California. Her Instagram feed catalogs her daily outfits and style inspiration.

Gloria Ferrer Winery selected lifestyle bloggers (ages 21 and over) to sample their wines and write a blog post that authentically reflected their experiences tasting and serving the product. They also wanted to promote the Gloria Ferrer Spring Photo Contest and encourage readers to enter for a chance to win fun weekly prizes.

Kathleen chose to showcase the wine as the perfect sparkly pairing for a light al fresco summer dinner on her patio. Vivid photography accompanied her beautiful blog post, highlighting casually glam touches and a fashionable outfit that evoked key elements of the Gloria Ferrer brand. She also included her favorite bruschetta recipe to accompany the wine.

Her Instagram photo amplified the blog post and garnered more than 1,000 likes!

A beauty Instagrammer: Money Can Buy Lipstick

Instagram handle: @TeresaLaucar

Brand sponsor: RESCUE

Photo theme: Promote RESCUE Remedy products to inspire usage for stress relief

Highlights: 670 likes, 24 comments

Hashtags: #StressLess2BmyBest #CleverGirls #sponsored

Link: www.instagram.com/p/0EQhKDCXwe

Teresa is an NYC-based beauty blogger who shares her makeup hauls, tutorials, and style inspiration on her tongue-in-cheek Instagram feed.

RESCUE selected bloggers to sample a selection of RESCUE products and write a blog post sharing their daily stresses. Bloggers shared personal wellness tips and relaxation methods to destress, as well as a link to download a RESCUE product coupon.

Teresa offered tips for finding balance and relieving stress, which included a suggestion for using RESCUE Sleep Liquid Melts as part of her bedtime routine. This blog post was accompanied by pretty photos of her nightstand and relaxation rituals. Her Instagram post generated 670 likes and 24 comments.

Chapter 8

Twitter Influencers

*T*witter was founded in 2006 and, according to InternetLiveStats.com, the platform grew from 5,000 tweets per day in 2007 to 500,000,000 tweets per day in 2013, which represents a six orders of magnitude increase. Today, every second, around 6,000 tweets are posted on Twitter, which corresponds to more than 350,000 tweets sent per minute, 500 million tweets per day, and around 200 billion tweets per year. That is a *lot* of content in 140-character bursts!

In this chapter, we explain how you can leverage Twitter for your brand and how to identify your target Twitter influencers. We also show you how to connect those influencers with your brand and get them talking about your products and services.

Seeing What Twitter Has to Offer

Twitter is an incredibly powerful platform for timely information distribution, but the key is to target the right people. According to a 2014 study by the Pew Research Center, 19 percent of American adults over age 18 use Twitter. Compared with late 2013, Twitter has seen significant increase in users from the following demographic groups: men, whites, those ages 65 and older, those who live in households with an annual household income of $50,000 or more, college graduates, and urbanites.

But did you know that the average Twitter user has just 208 followers? In comparison, the average business has 14,709 followers. When done right, it's clear that Twitter is a useful channel for a two-way brand-to-customer dialog.

So what does it take to be influential on Twitter? Mainly, just a willingness to share opinions publicly and frequently. It helps to be witty, funny, smart, and/or useful, too.

When experiencing positive events, people prefer to share via texting and Twitter according to a 2014 study by researchers at the University of Wisconsin at Madison. That's largely because both media are easily accessible from smartphones and are nonintrusive — communication partners don't have to reply immediately.

More than any other social platform, Twitter is the best and most rapid distribution channel for sharing breaking news, live event updates, and timely promotions.

Don't hop on social media memes, or use trending hashtags on Twitter, without doing research first to understand the context. Brands can easily get themselves in hot water by using a hashtag without sensitivity.

Influence can clearly extend across many spheres and communities online. Besides social and political activism, what else are people talking about? According to GO-Gulf (www.go-gulf.ae), more than 285 million Twitter users are using the platform to post comments about daily activities, 223 million are sharing links to blogs, and 322 million are uploading and sharing photos. Evidently Twitter is an excellent platform for influencer marketing because it's quick and easy to share links, images, and promotional offers in addition to maintaining a dialog with your target audience.

Finding Twitter Influencers to Start the Conversation

The process of finding Twitter influencers is similar to that of finding bloggers (see Chapter 6). Start with a list of all the blogs you read, particularly those that cover your industry, and check to see if they have an active Twitter presence. To expand that list, look at who those influencers are following and engaging with online. Begin to build relationships with your target influencers on Twitter; engage them in conversations to develop rapport.

We can't overemphasize the importance of maintaining authenticity! Once you've established rapport, you'll have a greater chance of your brand content getting noticed and shared.

There are three primary types of influencers on Twitter:

- **Industry influencers:** These are the people, companies, and brands that carry weight in your industry and have the most followers (hundreds of thousands to millions) and the greatest credibility. They consistently share valuable content that generates exceptional engagement with their audience.

- **Amplifiers:** As Twitter power users, amplifiers generally have thousands of followers (hundreds of thousands to millions) and are heavy content consumers and creators. According to a 2013 survey by Twitter and Compete.com, amplifiers are twice as likely to follow more than 20 brands, 86 percent more likely to send tweets, and 102 percent more likely to favorite tweets. They're also highly visual and more likely to share photos and videos.

- **General audience:** Basically everybody else. This group consists primarily of casual users who may not tweet daily but still use Twitter to check the news, join Twitter chats and parties, enter sweepstakes, and so on. Their follower count may be low (hundreds to low thousands), but connecting with your target audience comes down to knowing their interests and what they like to do and identifying the content they like to share.

Hosting the Best Ever Online Cocktail Party

A sponsored Twitter party is a dynamic, real-time conversation hosted by a brand that engages online influencers through a series of prescripted questions. This public chat takes place at a certain date and time set by the brand. To encourage attendance, prizes are offered. The party is also promoted by the brand through its various social channels to encourage RSVPs in advance. Influencers who RSVP to attend the party and show up at the appointed date and time to participate in the chat are eligible to win a prize.

Twitter parties and chats are the online equivalent of a really fascinating cocktail party. You never know who might show up (the more the merrier, of course), but you hope that the guests are interesting and will have a good time!

Deciding on the goal of your party

When deciding your goal for the party, consider how it will map back to your marketing objectives and how you aim to measure success. What are the key takeaways you'd like to impart to attendees, and what actions would you like influencers to take either during or after the party?

For example, you may want to raise brand awareness for a new product launch or educate consumers on a particularly timely topic. What's the next actionable step? Will you drive influencers to watch a video, download a product coupon, visit a dedicated landing page/microsite, or enter a contest? Consider these various actions when you write your scripted Twitter party questions and sponsored brand messages.

You can also measure overall party attendance and engagement using a third-party analytics tool such as Simply Measured (www.simplymeasured. com) to track usage of the party hashtag, including any promotional activities leading up to the party. After the party has concluded, consider the ratio of total RSVPs to actual participants during the chat.

Choosing a theme for your party

We recommend selecting a theme that is general and broad enough that the average Twitter user will be able to jump in to participate without any special knowledge. The exception is if you're trying to target a niche group or special demographic for a particular business reason. Themes should inspire engaging open-ended questions (not yes/no responses) and dynamic conversation among participating influencers.

Here are some popular themes to consider:

- How do you celebrate [holiday of choice]?
- Share seasonal fashion trends or beauty/makeup tips.
- Share helpful entertaining tips or favorite recipes using [ingredient/ product of choice].
- How do you make time for health and wellness or care for family, children, and/or pets?
- Discuss your favorite award shows or TV series.

Setting a date and time for your party

Are you timing your party to coincide with a live event or holiday? If so, the timing is largely chosen for you. Even so, the exact time of day is an important consideration because you'll want to target when your audience is going to be most active. Do you know if it's during the middle of the day (lunch break/coffee break) or evening (happy hour)?

If you're not timing your party to any holiday or event, you have a bit more leeway, but timing is still important. Weekdays are ideal and one-hour chats are most common. Generally the most popular times for a party on any given weekday or time zone are noon, 3p.m., and 6p.m. An afternoon option like 12p.m. Pacific/3p.m. Eastern can be appealing because it's neither too early nor late for either coast. Evenings can be extremely competitive.

Consider the time zone based on who your core audience is and where they're primarily located. If you're targeting parents, school drop-off and pickup times can be challenging for scheduled events. If you're targeting working professionals, consider hosting your Twitter party in the early evening.

Coming up with a party script

Like any good host, you should be prepared to engage your party guests with interesting questions to draw them out of their shell, encourage mingling, and foster conversation with other guests.

Once you've determined your theme, you'll want to draft six to eight relevant questions to engage participants and generate a lively dialog. Here are some tips on generating the right kinds of questions:

- ✔ Remind participants to RSVP early and often if you're offering prizes. (See the next section for more on RSVPs).

- ✔ Leave room in your script for casual, off-the-cuff banter and commentary.

- ✔ Keep the party to a firm timetable — keep the questions moving along. One-hour chats tend to be the most effective (maximum 2 hours if you're live-tweeting an event).

- ✔ Check the word count for each tweet to make sure you're within 140 characters, including any photos, links, or hashtags. Leave at least 23 characters remaining in your tweet text if you plan to attach a photo.

✔ Set your analytics tool to start tracking the campaign hashtag before you start to promote it. Retroactively pulling archived hashtag activity can be limiting and costly depending on the metrics software you're using.

✔ Use your campaign hashtag in every tweet. Pick a hashtag that's unique to your event, but descriptive and memorable enough that people will click on it.

✔ Ask users to mention you (with @yourusername) in their response so you can see all the eligible participating tweets. Remind users *not* to start their tweets with @ (unless they put a period before it, like so: .@) because starting with just an @ will limit the visibility of the tweet.

✔ Don't ask yes-or-no questions. Make sure your questions are open ended to encourage conversation.

Here's a sample Twitter party script to give you an idea of what yours might look like. Each paragraph is a separate tweet, and this is just the start of a script:

12:00p.m. PST

Hi! It's @Clever_Network leading the Summer Celebrations Party! #CleverSummer

We're talking about your favorite summer activities today! #CleverSummer

Want to win great prizes? RSVP `http://clvr.li/rsvp1` & tag replies w/ #CleverSummer! Fun!

See the official rules and regulations: `http://clvr.li/rulesreg`. #CleverSummer

Let's get this party started! #CleverSummer

12:07p.m. PST

Q1: What are your favorite outdoor summer activities? #CleverSummer

RSVP & answer Qs for a chance 2 win $50–$150 gift cards! `http://clvr.li/rsvp1` #CleverSummer

Enter our Summer Sweepstakes at `www.clevercontest.com` for a chance to win a dream vacay! #CleverSummer

This is your opportunity to play up key messages relevant to your campaign and the purpose of the party. You may include a link that drives back to your website or other online content. Sponsored brand messages are typically woven into the script, alternating with party questions. The number of brand messages should correspond to the total number of questions — don't have more brand messaging than you do questions.

Creating an RSVP form

Like any proper party, you'll need to keep track of attendees. RSVPs are essential not only for determining prize eligibility, but also for collecting valuable contact information for future marketing outreach.

We recommend creating a simple RSVP form via Google Docs (`www.google.com/forms/about`) to collect party participants' contact info, including:

- ✔ Name
- ✔ Address (for prize fulfillment if shipping product)
- ✔ Email
- ✔ Twitter handle
- ✔ How they heard about your Twitter party
- ✔ Age verification (if necessary for participation or eligibility to win)
- ✔ Link to the Twitter party rules and regulations
- ✔ Any other information they'd like to share (for example, comments/feedback)
- ✔ An opt-in question verifying that the party participant will allow the brand/agency to contact them in the future to potentially verify winner's information and reach out with marketing/promotional offers (This is an email marketing best practice to avoid being seen or reported as spam.)

Figure 8-1 shows an example of an RSVP form for the M&M's Crispy "Sweet Summer" Twitter Party.

Offering prizes

Cash is king, but product prize packs are also a great option to consider if the product carries a minimum of $50 retail value. E-gift cards make prize fulfillment a cinch.

In addition to (but not in lieu of) prizes, you may also consider offering a discount code for your product or service. Not everyone can be a prize winner, but all participants can benefit from a discount code!

As a general rule of thumb, it's ideal to award one prize per question asked during the party. A one-hour Twitter party can generally accommodate six to eight questions, so plan on six to eight prizes per hour as well.

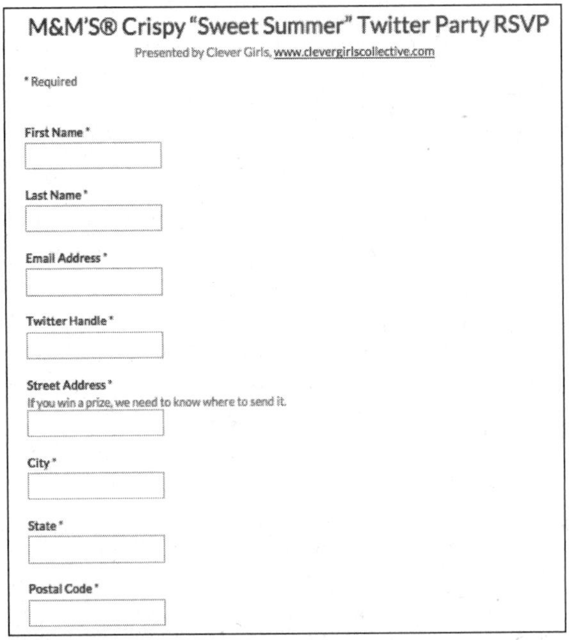

M&M'S® Crispy "Sweet Summer" Twitter Party RSVP

Presented by Clever Girls, www.clevergirlscollective.com

* Required

First Name *

Last Name *

Email Address *

Twitter Handle *

Street Address *

If you win a prize, we need to know where to send it.

City *

State *

Postal Code *

Figure 8-1: A sample RSVP form.

Source: `http://member.clevergirlscollective.com/node/1130`

Laying down the rules and regulations

Similar to an online contest, you'll want to provide an easily accessible link to the rules and regulations that govern your Twitter party. Check with your legal team to make sure all your bases are covered.

Inviting influencers to your party

If you have an existing marketing list or newsletter, you may want to promote your Twitter party with an invitation. This is often done in conjunction with sharing the event information across social channels with a link back to the Twitter Party RSVP.

Here's a sample invitation you might send out to influencers or other interested audiences via email:

> Calling all Feline Fans: Join our Cat Chat!
>
> Share your love for kittens and tell us how you care for your favorite felines. We want to hear all about your grooming, feeding, and playtime routines. Get those curious cat photos ready!

Who: Cat lovers, cat owners, and animal lovers

What: The Feline Fans Twitter Party

When: Tuesday, October 13 at 12p.m. PT/3p.m. ET

Follow: Hashtag #CatChat+@Brand and @Clever_Network on Twitter!

Prizes: Six $50 gift cards to your favorite pet store, one Grand Prize $100 gift card+a year's supply of cat food

Rules and Regulations: <Insert link to party rules>

Click **here** to share on Twitter!

Promoting the party

One to three weeks before the party, you'll want to start promoting it across your social channels and any other method of communication you have with your target audience, including e-newsletters. Promote the party via daily tweets and weekly Facebook posts to drive RSVPs.

On the day of the party, your promotions will consist of the following:

- Leading the Twitter conversation based on your prewritten script
- Engaging directly in conversation with your fans and potential customers with off-script responses in real time
- Responding to participants where appropriate, and retweeting your favorite responses
- Requesting that the conversation be taken offline via email or direct message (DM) on Twitter if a participant asks a question that you can't answer in 140 characters.
- Selecting prize winners during the party and collecting their contact info via the RSVP form
- Monitoring the trending hashtags box to see if your hashtag is trending during your party hour

Following up after the party

After the party, reach out to prize winners shortly after the party ends to complete prize fulfillment. Don't forget to secure prize affidavits where required by law.

Be sure to measure the results of your party's success. See "Measuring Your Engagement with Twitter Analytics" for more information.

Twitter Contests, Giveaways, and Promotions

Twitter is a popular platform for promoting contests and giveaways because the engagement actions are simple and it's easy to retweet to share content. The three most popular types of Twitter contests are

- **Photo contests:** Users must upload a photo with the campaign hashtag to count as a valid entry. Photos may be shared across Twitter, Facebook, or Instagram for cross-channel promotion.

- **Caption contests:** Users must tweet a funny or witty caption for a brand-provided photo using the campaign hashtag.

- **Follow and retweet to win contests:** Users must follow your brand handle and retweet a specific message with the campaign hashtag for a chance to win.

Contest eligibility requirements should be simple and clearly spelled out in the rules and regulations. Typically, we recommend the following actions to qualify eligible entries for an Twitter photo challenge:

1. Follow @BrandHandle on Twitter.

2. Complete the contest entry form (include shortened URL or micro-site link).

3. Post to Twitter and/or complete the call to action during the contest period using the required hashtag.

Prizes should ideally spur consumer action or be related to your business — for example, you might offer a gift card to your store or a prize pack that includes the new product you're promoting.

You may also choose to amplify an existing contest and ask influencers to share a pre-approved tweet with proper FTC disclosure, which requires the use of either #ad or #sponsored. The benefit of this tactic is increasing the reach of your content to new audiences. Make sure that your call to action is direct and consider using a trackable shortened URL to measure click-throughs.

Attaching a photo or video is also recommended because tweets with images tend to be shared and favorited more than text-only tweets. In 2014, Twitter analyzed the content of over 2 million tweets sent by thousands of users over the course of a month and results showed that adding a photo to your tweet can boost retweets by an impressive 35 percent! Adding video generated a 28 percent boost.

Measuring Your Engagement with Twitter Analytics

We can't overemphasize how important it is to measure the results of your social campaigns, and luckily, Twitter offers one of the most robust analytics dashboards of all the social platforms out there. Simply log into `http://analytics.twitter.com` to access Twitter's free analytics. With just a few clicks, you can find out what's working well and what can be improved. Your account home provides a quick overview of your Twitter statistics, including monthly averages for engagement rates, replies, and more.

Visit the tweet activity dashboard to see in-depth metrics for individual tweets, including impressions and total engagements.

 Twitter impressions are the potential number of times a particular hashtag could be viewed, as calculated by number of tweets multiplied by number of followers. Twitter reach is the combined number of followers of people who used a particular hashtag.

 Another great tool for measuring Twitter engagement is SimplyMeasured (`www.simplymeasured.com`). They offer several basic free tools, but the paid service is a worthwhile investment if you're tracking multiple hashtags for various campaigns. For more information on metrics measurement, refer to Part IV.

Taking a Look at Some Top Twitter Influencers and What They Do Right

In this section, we offer examples of influencers in the following categories: food, lifestyle, beauty, and entertainment. We walk you through specific campaigns they participated in, tell you what they did, and explain why it worked.

 These are just examples of influencers in various categories. These aren't the only Twitter influencers worth your time — not even close! Use these profiles as examples of what to look for when you're searching for influencers for your own campaign.

A foodie influencer: Krystal's Kitsch

Twitter handle: @KrystalS

Brand sponsor: DIGIORNO Pizza

Followers: 12,500

Hashtag: #YouBeTheJudge

Link: www.twitter.com/KrystalS/status/614285484701974528

Krystal is a food and lifestyle influencer who shares on her blog her favorite recipes, family activities, and tips to stay organized and save money. She's a full-time writer and blogger based in Florida.

DIGIORNO engaged lifestyle bloggers to try the new DIGIORNO pizzeria! thin pizzas and write an engaging blog post sharing the experience of baking and eating the pizza at home.

Krystal chose to pair her pizza with a refreshing recipe for strawberry mint lemonade. Her blog post (www.krystalskitsch.com/2015/06/strawberry-mint-lemonade.html) was shared more than 150 times, primarily on Twitter. Krystal also has more than 12,500 followers on Twitter, and her tweet amplifying the blog post was retweeted 17 times and favorited 23 times.

A lifestyle influencer: Official PR Girl

Twitter handle: @OfficialPRgirl

Brand sponsor: M&M'S Crispy

Followers: 33,000

Hashtag: #CrispyMMSummerCG

Link: www.twitter.com/officialPRgirl/status/628798932798169089

Angela is a passionate fashion, beauty, and style influencer. She blogs full-time at AngelaRicardo.com and manages multiple sites. As a savvy bargain hunter, she happily shares her thrifty finds with thousands of social followers.

M&M'S Crispy engaged influencers to share an engaging tweet featuring the candy to promote its relaunch and availability in stores nationwide. Influencers channeled their enthusiasm for the brand in colorful and fun photos, showcasing how they enjoy M&M'S Crispy candies as a sweet treat.

Angela's Twitter account has more than 33,000 followers. Her tweet promoting M&M'S Crispy was retweeted 86 times and favorited 10 times.

A beauty influencer: Blushing Noir

Twitter handle: @BlushingNoir

Brand sponsor: Q-Tips

Followers: 14,500

Hashtags: #BeautyQTips

Link: www.twitter.com/blushingnoir/status/570689679529549824

Brooke is a Pittsburgh-based beauty blogger who is self-admittedly obsessed with makeup, nail polish, hair care, and skincare. She also frequently writes about lifestyle and fashion.

Q-tips engaged beauty influencers to celebrate award season by re-creating their favorite red-carpet-worthy makeup looks using Q-tips Precision Tips.

Brooke crafted a step-by-step tutorial for completing a perfect at-home manicure. Each step was meticulously illustrated with a photo. Her blog post was shared 74 times across social channels, and amplified on Twitter to more than 14,500 followers. It was also retweeted 36 times and favorite 32 times.

An entertainment influencer: Kathy King

Twitter handle: @MrsKathyKing

Brand sponsor: Lenovo

Followers: 26,900

Hashtags: #CleverYoga #Sponsored

Link: www.twitter.com/MrsKathyKing/status/591232236243918848

Kathy is a social media strategist and full-time blogger at MrsKathyKing.com. Her site focuses on family-friendly entertainment and travel and product reviews. Kathy is passionate about providing creative editorial content and resourceful tips for parents.

Lenovo engaged Twitter influencers to promote and amplify the Lenovo YOGA Tastemakers Trend Hub. Readers were encouraged to enter the brand-sponsored sweepstakes for a chance to win a Lenovo YOGA 3 Pro.

Kathy has more than 26,900 Twitter followers, and her tweet about the sweepstakes generated 53 retweets and 3 favorites.

Chapter 9

Facebook Influencers

*F*acebook launched in 2004 and, as of June 2015, there were 1.49 billion monthly active users. In fact, 65 percent of monthly Facebook users are on the platform daily, and according to comScore data, users spend an average of 20+ minutes per day on the social network, liking, commenting, and scrolling through status updates. Most consumer-facing brands have a presence on Facebook (whether it's active or not is an entirely different matter) because the platform has proven longevity and offers robust metrics for measuring engagement and advertising performance.

In this chapter, we cover best practices for leveraging Facebook for your brand and tell you how to identify your target Facebook influencers. We also show you how to connect your influencers with your brand and get them talking about your products and services.

Seeing What Facebook Has to Offer

According to a 2014 study by the Pew Research Center, 71 percent of online American adults use Facebook. Women are more active on Facebook than men, and users ages 18 to 29 make up 87 percent of active users. According to a 2013 survey conducted by SheKnows and Harris Interactive, American women have, on average, 250 friends on Facebook.

So, why the broad appeal despite new social networks launching every year? Well, for starters, Facebook was originally created to replace the college yearbook, so most users are connected to their friends and families on Facebook in a way that they may not be on other newer social channels.

Although Facebook has arguably lost its hip and cool cachet with the tween and young adult demographic (ages 13 to 25), it's still a useful platform for connecting with friends, families, co-workers, social and political communities, and of course, brands that you love and admire.

Like Twitter, Facebook users may post multiple times a day, sharing life updates, photos, funny memes, and news stories. Although Facebook may not necessarily break the news as fast as Twitter, Facebook's unlimited character count allows users to provide greater detail and context in their updates, as well as offers a platform for ongoing discussion. You can follow a conversation on Facebook more easily than you can on Twitter, because all the comments are grouped in a timeline under each post.

From a brand perspective, Facebook is a veritable goldmine for targeting customers and their extended network. It's also an opportunity to create an authentic two-way conversation channel.

Consistently posting compelling content is the best way to engage your customers and fans. But you don't want to overdo it either, by inundating their Facebook newsfeeds with brand updates. In a survey conducted by BuzzStream and Fractl, respondents indicated that they prefer brands to post on all social networks between two to five times per day. For Facebook in particular, 68 percent of respondents said that they would want a brand to post one or two times per day; 19 percent said they would want a brand to post three to five times per day.

Of course, you don't just have to post content yourself — you can drive brand conversations through influencer engagement. That way, you can increase the frequency of online dialogue about your brand without initiating the conversation yourself. This type of word-of-mouth marketing is excellent — nothing is worse than a party where the host is talking nonstop about herself. In other words, let your influencer advocates start the fire, and you can simply fan the flames.

Working with Influencers on Facebook

The process of finding Facebook influencers is similar to that of finding bloggers (see Chapter 6). Start with a list of all the blogs you read, those that cover your industry, and check to see if those bloggers have an active Facebook presence.

If you haven't already read it, check out Chapter 5 for information on self-service platforms and how to find influencers yourself versus hiring an influencer marketing agency.

Review your target influencer's Facebook newsfeed to check how frequently she updates, what types of content she shares, and the level of follower engagement (number of likes and shares).

When it comes to Facebook influencers, you're looking for:

- **Frequency of posting:** Do they post multiple times a day, once a day, a couple times a week? How often are they sharing new content?

- **Number of followers:** This will tell you how many people are interested in the content the influencer is sharing.

- **Level of engagement (number of likes, shares, and comments):** In addition to number of followers, engagement is important for gauging whether the content is actually resonating with the influencer's audience. Does the influencer's audience feel compelled to comment and share the content they're viewing?

- **Quality of photos:** Beautiful, visually stunning images will always attract more attention and engagement than low-resolution, poorly staged ones.

- **Frequency of sponsored content/posts:** If the influencer is posting too much brand-sponsored content on a daily basis, readers may be fatigued or lose interest quickly.

Once you've chosen your Facebook influencers, you're ready to get them working for you. Oftentimes, it's far easier and more cost-effective to have influencers amplify existing content than asking them to create content on their own — and Facebook is well suited to just this kind of amplification. You can provide the content for influencers to share with their audiences on Facebook. This content doesn't have to be content you created yourself — for example, if you've worked with bloggers on sponsored blog posts (see Chapter 6), you can have them share that content on their Facebook pages. (You should share those blog posts on your brand's Facebook page as well!)

Keep the call to action simple and ensure that the content is compelling, fresh, and appealing to a broad audience. When directing influencers to amplify content, follow these steps:

1. **Decide what you want to amplify.**

   This can be an existing blog post, a video, a brand-provided infographic, a contest, or something similar. If you prefer, you can provide a selection of preapproved Facebook messages written by your company, that influencers may choose to share verbatim.

2. **Provide the influencers with a link to the content and include a photo if you can (visual posts get higher engagement).**

3. **Provide concise guidance on appropriate brand messaging.**

   This will help influencers craft an authentic Facebook post to share your content.

4. **Provide your campaign hashtag as well as the proper FTC disclosure (which requires the use of either #ad or #sponsored as a hashtag).**

Creating contests, giveaways, and promotions on Facebook

Facebook offers an easy solution for hosting giveaways via its built-in contests tool (`https://apps.facebook.com/my-contests`). There are predesigned contest templates and robust analytics, and it's already optimized for sharing on desktop, mobile, and tablets. The contest entry landing page also provides easy access to calls to action, such as liking the page, sharing on Facebook, or tweeting — each of which extends the reach of your contest. Facebook also integrates well with third-party applications such as Wishpond (`www.wishpond.com`) if you wish to use an external tool for your contest.

The three most popular types of Facebook contests are the following:

- **Photo contests:** Users must upload a photo to count as a valid entry. You can share the photo across Twitter or Instagram with the campaign hashtag for cross-channel promotion.

- **Submit to win:** Users must submit original content (recipes, videos, and so on). This content can also be combined with an open voting mechanism to extend the reach and engagement, while also narrowing the submissions pool for final winners.

- **Follow and share to win:** Users must follow your brand page and share a post about the contest with a friend for a chance to win.

Contest eligibility requirements should be simple and clearly spelled out in the rules and regulations. The following actions are typically used to qualify eligible entries for a Facebook contest:

- Follow/like your brand page on Facebook.

- Complete the contest entry form and call to action for a chance to win.

- Share contest details with their friends on Facebook, or across social channels such as Twitter and Instagram using the campaign hashtag.

Prizes should ideally spur consumer action or be related to your business. For example, offer a gift card to your store or a prize pack that includes the new product you're promoting. Frequency of prizing is another consideration — daily and weekly prizes will encourage more sharing and engagement among fans.

Remember: The value of the prize should be commensurate with the level of effort required to enter. If the entry requires the submission of user-generated content (a photo, video, or recipe, for example), you should offer a higher-value prize.

Super-charge your influencer marketing campaign with concurrent efforts. First, contract bloggers to create sponsored content (see Chapter 6). Then pair that content with a second set of influencers to provide additional amplification and increase reach by sharing the original sponsored content across social channels like Facebook.

Influencer-created sponsored content can also be leveraged as a Facebook ad and targeted to a set demographic of your choosing. Refer to Chapter 6 for best practices on how to select the appropriate content and create the perfect ad.

Measuring Your Engagement on Facebook

Facebook Insights offers a wealth of data to measure interactions with your own brand page. These metrics are easily accessed in your Facebook account. The brand engagement metric can be found at the top of your page (under your page name). Review this metric to determine how engaged Facebook members are with your brand — it tracks mentions, likes, shares, comments, and links to your brand's page.

Another great tool for measuring Facebook engagement on your brand page is SimplyMeasured (www.simplymeasured.com). Use it to run a report that provides in-depth analysis of your Facebook fan page with amplification, reach, content performance, and engagement trends.

For more information on metrics measurement, refer to Part IV.

Measuring secondary influencer engagement requires a more manual process because there are currently no third-party tools that can track shares and engagement on an influencer's sponsored posts, or even a dedicated campaign hashtag across Facebook.

The best way to assess the success of your Facebook campaign is to benchmark results. When your influencers' sponsored Facebook amplifications are complete, allow the content time to circulate for a certain period of time before recording the total number of likes, comments, and shares on sponsored posts. Rinse and repeat campaigns to benchmark results.

Taking a Look at Some Top Facebook Influencers and What They Do Right

In this section, we offer examples of influencers in the following categories: lifestyle, food, parenting, fashion, and DIY. We walk you through specific campaigns they participated in, tell you what they did, and explain why it worked.

These are just examples of influencers in various categories. These aren't the only Facebook influencers worth your time — not even close! Use these profiles as examples of what to look for when you're searching for influencers for your own campaign.

A lifestyle influencer: Homemaking Hacks

Facebook page: www.facebook.com/HomemakingHacks

Brand sponsor: Mellow

Followers: 47,728

Hashtags: #CookMellow #Sponsored

Link: www.facebook.com/HomemakingHacks/posts/872210576147844

Dawn is a Central Florida–based lifestyle influencer who enjoys experimenting in the kitchen, finding awesome shortcuts, taking road trips, and sharing her favorite tips and products with her readers. She also frequently hosts Twitter parties.

Mellow engaged influencers who enjoy cooking and entertaining and whose readers are interested in tech to promote the U.S. launch and pre-order of its new sous vide machine for home chefs.

Dawn's post encouraged readers to learn more about Mellow and the benefits of sous-vide cooking at home. Her Facebook post included a link to the Mellow site for pre-orders, generated 37 likes, and reached more than 47,000 followers.

A food influencer: Self Proclaimed Foodie

Facebook page: https://www.facebook.com/SelfProclaimedFoodie

Brand sponsor: Ghirardelli

Followers: 8,676

Hashtags: #GhirardelliVday #CG

Link: www.facebook.com/SelfProclaimedFoodie/photos/
a.1549950738562353.1073741828.1517784071779020/
1624311887792904

Krissy is, as her blog title suggests, a self-proclaimed foodie. She has a full-time job in the high-tech industry, does photography on the side, and manages to produce a popular food blog because she simply enjoys sharing delicious eats and recipes with her followers.

Ghirardelli asked food bloggers to create and share a custom Valentine's Day dessert recipe using Ghirardelli products.

Krissy's Facebook post teases a recipe for a rich and decadent chocolate raspberry pot de crème. She directs readers to her blog post to read more, or to pin the recipe for later. Her sweet Facebook post generated 65 likes and 17 shares and reached 8,676 followers.

A parenting influencer: Mom on the Side

Facebook page: www.facebook.com/momontheside

Brand sponsor: Method

Followers: 49,870

Hashtags: #StyleByMethod #Sponsored

Link: www.facebook.com/momontheside/posts/915546075174136

Lisa is a parenting and lifestyle influencer whose blog is filled with adventures in parenting twins, a tween, and a teen. She shares her love for entertainment and traveling, and her attempts at creating recipes that her family approves of, with her readers.

Method engaged fashion, parenting, and crafting influencers to promote the new method laundry detergent with a variety of engaging content.

Lisa's Facebook post shared details of the method X ASOS Collaboration, a Method product coupon code, and useful information about the new laundry detergent. Her post reached nearly 50,000 followers and generated 81 likes.

A fashion influencer: April Golightly

Facebook page: www.facebook.com/aprilgolightly

Brand sponsor: Sunrun

Followers: 5,619

Hashtags: #SunrunSolar #Sponsored

Link: www.facebook.com/aprilgolightly/posts/889307661128164

April is a fashion and lifestyle influencer based in South Florida. She loves sharing ideas and inspiration for living a life of style with her readers, covering a variety of topics including fashion, beauty, DIY, entertainment, and food.

Sunrun engaged homeowners and influencers to promote the benefits of solar energy and share the Sunrun sweepstakes with readers for a chance to win a Nest Learning Thermostat.

April's post encouraged followers to learn more about Sunrun and the benefits of solar power, as well as enter the Sunrun Sweepstakes. Her post reached 5,619 followers and generated 76 likes.

A DIY influencer: Inspiration for Moms

Facebook page: www.facebook.com/inspirationformoms

Brand sponsor: American Greetings

Followers: 12,296

Hashtags: #ThankList #Ad

Link: www.facebook.com/inspirationformoms/posts/
1088259557854079

Laura is a DIY/craft influencer and stay-at-home mom. She was inspired to start a blog to help parents like herself connect, learn, and empower their families to live better lives. Her blog Inspiration for Moms is filled with DIY tutorials, room makeovers, recipes, advice, and tips that make life as a mom easier and more fun.

American Greetings engaged influencers to promote the ThankList by American Greetings campaign by creating their your own #ThankList video and sharing it across Twitter and Facebook.

Laura shared a custom #ThankList video on Facebook, along with a message of gratitude for her best friend. She encouraged her readers to create their own #ThankList videos with a link to the American Greeting site. Her touching post reached 12,296 followers and generated 75 likes.

Chapter 10

Pinterest Influencers

*P*interest launched in 2010, around the same time as Instagram, and in just five years it has fundamentally changed the way that people curate, save, and share visual content online. It introduced users to the concept of pin boards, which function as both a visual bookmarking tool and an inspirational outlet for sharing content.

To date, Pinterest users have created 50 billion pins across 1 billion pin boards. Data from comScore showed that from March 2014 to March 2015, Pinterest's user base climbed 25 percent year-over-year to 72.8 million monthly active users. This visual platform is ideal for aspirational brand storytelling and showcasing your product or service through dynamic content, such as recipes, tutorials, infographics, and more.

In this chapter, we cover best practices for leveraging Pinterest for your brand, how to identify your target Pinterest influencers, and where to find them. Finally, we show you how to commission custom editorial content for your brand and leverage it across your brand-owned social channels to maximize the value.

Seeing What Pinterest Is About

The beauty of Pinterest lies in its simplicity. With just a few clicks, users can easily create pin boards; pin and share favorite products, images, and articles; and curate them for future reference. Pin boards are essentially vision boards full of beautiful, eye-catching content. Users can spend hours pinning aspirational items to their ever-growing collection, search for recipes they want to make for dinner and collect ideas for their kitchen remodel or DIY crafting project.

According to Ahalogy's 2015 Pinterest Media Consumption Study, Pinterest inspires action. Almost two-thirds of *active pinners* (those who use Pinterest least once a month) and 84 percent of *daily pinners* (those who use Pinterest at least once a day) are inspired by Pinterest to try something new once a week or more often. In addition, 73 percent of active pinners and 89 percent of daily pinners have bought something new they discovered on Pinterest.

As reported in *VentureBeat* in March 2015, the top content categories on Pinterest are as follows:

- ✔ **Recipes:** Pinterest boasts more than 1.7 billion recipe pins.
- ✔ **Shopping:** Nearly 2 million people pin product-rich pins daily.
- ✔ **Articles**: More than 14 million articles are pinned daily.

Two-thirds of all pinned content is from a business's website, so keep your website fresh!

The rapid ascent of Pinterest and its origin story is an interesting one. Pinterest co-founder Ben Silbermann has said that he built the platform to help people "discover things they didn't know they wanted," that seem "handpicked" for them and serve as a repository for aggregating vast collections of interesting content. As reported in *The Wall Street Journal,* the company now bills itself as a "visual search engine for people to use in the course of things like wedding planning and decorating a new home."

And unlike most of the social networking sites we've covered in this book, Pinterest's earliest adopters were from outside the Silicon Valley bubble — moms, mostly residing in the Midwest, and between the age of 25 and 54.

Huffington Post tech reporter Biana Bosker largely attributes Pinterest's popularity to the way it redirects people's attention to who they aspire to be and the life they dream of living: "What sets Pinterest apart and makes it so appealing is its focus on who we want to be — not on what we're doing, where we've gone, how important we are or how beloved. While much of the content shared on existing social networking sites like Facebook, Twitter, and Foursquare screams, 'Look at me,' Pinterest posts urge, 'Look at this.'"

Women are still the primary users of Pinterest (80 percent), but the ratio of male users is also shifting and growing. *Mashable* reported that men are its fastest-growing user demographic, with the number of men pinning and repinning doubling in 2014.

Evan Sharp, Pinterest's cofounder and chief creative officer, claims that more men began logging onto Pinterest regularly around the time its recommendations began getting smarter. Pinterest serves more than 1.5 trillion recommendations annually. And in April 2015, Pinterest rolled out a "smart board picker" for iOS and Android mobile users that predicts which boards users will repin something to.

According to TechCrunch, over 80 percent of pins are actually repins rather than brand-new content, which speaks to the power of shareable, evergreen content and the way it continues to live on indefinitely. In addition, Pinterest referrals spend 70 percent more than visitors referred from nonsocial channels, including search, according to industry reports.

The best and most popular "pinfluencers" offer a variety of tightly curated thematic content. Users are also predominantly "makers" who are passionate about beautiful photography and sharing DIY tutorials, recipes, life hacks, and other useful content for improving your life.

Finding Pinfluencers to Share Your Brand Content

So how do you go about finding influential people on Pinterest? Well, first let's start with a simple benchmark: The average Pinterest user has 229 followers and gets about 4.2 repins per pin. But when it comes to influencers, there are different levels:

- **Low-average:** 1,000 to 10,000 followers
- **Intermediate:** 10,000 to 50,000 followers
- **High:** More than 50,000 followers
- **Celebrity status:** 1 million+ followers

As it turns out, finding Pinterest influencers is quite similar to scouting for Instagrammers (see Chapter 7). Review your favorite blogs, including bloggers who have covered your brand in the past. Check to see if they have an active Pinterest account and review their pin boards. As you're reviewing pin boards, take note of what general themes they cover, whether they pin mostly original content or repins, their photography skill level, and total number of followers.

You can outsource this research to an agency that specializes in networks of influencers across social platforms (see Chapter 5).

Commissioning Pinnable Content

It's great to have influencers pinning original content that they've created for their blog posts, but what if your brand needs fresh content to pin on *your* Pinterest boards? How do you keep the content on your brand-owned channels interesting and evergreen without overextending your in-house team? Again, influencers to the rescue!

If you don't have resources in-house to work with an on-staff photographer to create specialized product content for your marketing needs, consider contracting the job (or at least parts of it) to a professional influencer who can work on more budget-friendly terms. The right influencers will happily work with you to shoot a set of commissioned photos that can then be pinned on your brand's Pinterest account or used in other marketing materials.

Chapter 4 has more information on how to contract influencers, but you can manage expectations on execution and increase your chances for success by following these four best practices for commissioning pinnable photography:

- **Provide plenty of product.** This is especially true if you can't provide the highest level of cash compensation to the influencer. Err on the side of providing more product than you think the influencer will need. Having a variety of product to work with often fuels greater creativity for different styling options during the shoot.

- **Set clear styling guidelines.** You know better than anyone how your brand should be represented visually. Be clear about whether you want a label or packaging to be visible. Specify how many photos you need and whether they should be close-cropped or wide angle. Are there any restrictions regarding placement next to competitive products or brands? Be explicit about do's and don'ts, and offer helpful tips for how to style your product in the best light.

- **Allow creative license.** Although you want to set clear guidelines, keep in mind that you've selected this influencer specifically for their photography skill and aesthetic, so let them shine by showcasing a unique perspective on your product. Allow a healthy amount of creative license. This will also serve to demonstrate to them that you respect their craft and it will result in the best, most authentic content.

- **Give specific image file guidelines.** Make sure to request high-resolution, original files without watermarks. Photos should also be shot to optimize for mobile, so go vertical. Pinterest organizes images vertically, stacked one on top of another in a grid, so pins with a vertical aspect ratio flow better on the platform. Also, most people use Pinterest on their mobile phones, and vertical pins look better than horizontal ones.

✔ **Amplify your boards.** When appropriate, ask influencers to share your boards with their audience as well in an amplification on Facebook, Twitter, and so on. Of course, this sponsored messaging should also be disclosed per Federal Trade Commission (FTC) guidelines.

Pinterest search doesn't support hashtags, so they don't track what's trending, and hashtags are only clickable in a pin description.

In the following sections, we offer more tips on working with influencers for commissioned content on Pinterest.

Making the proper disclosures for transparency

Sponsored content must be disclosed (see Chapter 6). The FTC states that the disclosure must be written in a clear and conspicuous manner that can be understood by the average reader. The disclosure must also be placed directly next to (or as close as possible to) the sponsored content. On Pinterest, this can be addressed using a simple hashtag such as #sponsored or #ad.

There is no character limit on Pinterest captions, so influencers are able to combine a dedicated campaign hashtag with #sponsored for proper disclosure, in addition to other relevant subject hashtags as appropriate.

Check out Pinterest's Terms of Service and Acceptable Use policy for more information about promoted pins and guidelines for advertising on Pinterest: `https://about.pinterest.com/en/advertising-rules`.

You may also want to review the Pinterest contest and promotion guidelines at `https://about.pinterest.com/en/acceptable-use-policy`.

Optimizing content pins

After the content is created, you'll want to ensure that it's seen, right? Eighty percent of Pinterest's traffic now comes from mobile devices. Ahalogy reports that 28 percent of active users say they have pulled up pins on their mobile devices to guide in-store purchases. It's clear that advances in mobile have fundamentally changed the way people search for and consume content online.

Optimize pins for both mobile and desktop viewing. This means the text in the image should be clear and easy to read.

According to a study by Pinerly, a call-to-action pin description sees an 80 percent increase in engagement, pins related to trending topics see an average of 94 percent increase in click-throughs, and the best time to pin during the day is between 2p.m. and 4p.m. Eastern time.

The best Pinterest content is evergreen and engages users far longer than content on Twitter or Facebook. According to Wisemetrics, the half-life of a tweet — the time in which you earn 50 percent of all clicks and views — is approximately 24 minutes. On Facebook, posts only have about a 90-minute half-life. By comparison, the half-life of a pin is three and a half months! In Internet time (similar to dog years), that's practically forever.

Promoted pins + influencer pins = #winning

In 2014, Pinterest launched its first ad product, Promoted Pins, allowing brands to pay for a sponsored pin on a cost-per-click basis. And yet savvy marketers at brands such as Staples, Clinique, and Nordstrom have taken the influencer route over purchasing Pinterest ads.

Case study: Nordstrom's online-to-offline Pinterest strategy

Pinterest is so integral to Nordstrom's overall marketing strategy that Nordstrom has even used it as an in-store promotional tool. *Business Insider* reports that the store highlights its most popular pins by "pinning" them in the stores with signage next to the product.

"Our customers are on Pinterest, so we want to be there, too," Bryan Galipeau, social media manager at Nordstrom, told *Business Insider*. "Pinterest is in many ways the world's biggest wish list — and so it also fits well with our goal of having our merchandise show up in our customer's wish lists."

Nordstrom has approximately 4.5 million followers on Pinterest, so when those followers see the hottest, most-pinned items in-store, it can drive an increase in sales. The most popular categories on Nordstrom's Pinterest account include women's fashion, home, wedding, gifts, beauty, and kids. Customers are literally voting with their pins and directly feeding valuable real-time data to the brand's marketing team, which then decides which items to promote in-store. To aid their salespeople, Nordstrom also created an in-store app that matches popular Pinterest items with current department inventory on a store-by-store basis.

This is the perfect example of a brand doing it right with a full-circle marketing strategy that smartly leverages both paid social placements and influencer marketing to drive in-store sales.

In January 2015, *The Wall Street Journal* reported that Sean Ryan, director of social and mobile marketing for J.C. Penney Co. said that while the retailer has purchased some ads on Pinterest, "We often see twice the lift in engagement on a product when we use an influencer on Pinterest."

This is hugely significant in terms of calibrating marketing strategy to include a mix of both paid ads and sponsored influencer posts. Authentic engagement on a product pinned by an influencer is that much more valuable to the brand than a paid placement.

Having your influencers create Pinterest storyboards

Although the Pinterest Terms of Service prohibits brands from paying influencers to pin specific content to their own boards (you can't dictate what someone chooses to pin via a paid relationship), you *can* contract influencers to create Pinterest "storyboards" by pinning items of their own choosing inspired by your brand and a designated theme.

For example, if your company sells a line of house paint, you could enlist lifestyle and shelter or DIY bloggers to create their own pin boards inspired by this season's hottest Pantone colors. The idea is to collect and curate pins that your brand's target audience would love to build, make, or decorate. For example, lifestyle blogger To the Motherhood created a "Tech Savvy Traveler" Pinterest storyboard inspired by Lenovo products (`www.pinterest.com/pin/436075176396358021`).

Another great way to leverage storyboards is to utilize the Mapping Place pins to create a custom travel itinerary or adventure bucket list. Think of it as a visual mash-up of maps and pins to showcase favorite destinations and local hot spots. For example, parenting blogger Being MVP curated a Maps pin board sponsored by the California Association of REALTORS to share her favorite neighborhood spots (`www.pinterest.com/beingmvp/champions-of-home-my-amazing-neighborhood`).

Users go to Pinterest for inspiration, so create content that is irresistible and aspirational! Inspire them to travel, make, and create! Avoid the hard sell.

When it comes to storyboarding on Pinterest, here are some best practices to keep in mind:

✔ Select fun themes that are general enough to allow for curation of authentic content.

✔ Request that influencers populate their boards with at least 15 to 20 pins.

✔ Remind influencers to include a disclosure statement in their board description. For example:

  • Thank you Clever Paints Co. for sponsoring this board. For more inspiration, follow #CleverPaints on Pinterest: www.url.com. #sponsored

We recommend that you also provide influencers with very specific guidelines on do's and don'ts for creating a successful Pinterest storyboard that adhere to the Terms of Service. Here are some suggestions of what you might tell your influencers:

✔ Your pins can be created from images you take or can be pulled from anywhere. Using brand products in your pins is highly encouraged.

✔ Do not include any images that contain products of or made specifically for brand competitors.

✔ If you're repinning from the brand Pinterest page, please do not leave the copy as is — write your own description.

✔ Each pin must have language stating that it is sponsored by the brand, ideally with hashtags #brandname and #sponsored.

Leveraging Guest Influencers on Your Brand Pin Boards or Group Boards

Another creative way to leverage influencers is to contract them to "guest pin" to your brand boards or group boards. This allows you to curate influencer-selected content without violating Pinterest Terms of Service.

Influencer channel takeovers are mutually beneficial because they're an opportunity to showcase your brand through the lens of a tastemaker, borrowing her aesthetic to curate content. And the influencer is promoted through your brand's channel while adding an element of novelty. It's an easy win-win for all parties! For example, Etsy leveraged a guest pinner's vibrant picks in a custom pin board by lifestyle blogger A Subtle Revelry, hosted on the Etsy account (www.pinterest.com/etsy/guest-pinner-a-subtle-revelry).

To ensure that the influencer advocate you've selected is brand safe and a worthy evangelist for your brand, follow our suggestions in Chapter 6.

Group boards are a wonderfully collaborative way for brands to connect directly with consumers and influencers. By tying into an engaging common theme, brands can generate goodwill and authentic engagement.

In a recent #Pintermission campaign, Honda gave some avid pinners $500 to take a break from aspirational pinning to do an activity inspired by something they pinned before. Then these avid pinners were invited to document their adventure on a group board on Honda's Pinterest account. See an example here: www.pinterest.com/caitlin_cawley/caitlin-s-pintermission. Caitlin's #Pintermission board had 10 pins and reached 613,000 followers.

Group boards can also be leveraged effectively by brands with overlapping audiences or similar consumer demographics. One brilliant example is the Etsy/Random House group board: www.pinterest.com/etsy/guest-pinner-random-house. Inspired by a mutual love of literature, Etsy invited Random House to share their favorite literary finds as their Guest Pinner. Random House then shared its favorite literary-themed Etsy products on the group board, which has 29 pins and reaches more than 475,000 followers!

Measuring the Success of Your Pinterest Efforts

Your analytics dashboard on Pinterest will provide you with a wealth of information about the performance of your brand's pins and pin boards, but currently there is no analytics platform that allows you to track the performance of pins outside of your own account. So, it can be a bit challenging to get a comprehensive read on how well your Pinterest influencer marketing efforts are doing.

For more helpful information on Pinterest analytics, watch the Pinterest video at www.youtube.com/watch?v=bt_aw6Q9Fb8.

Although it can be very manual, these are the concrete metrics you *can* measure from influencer marketing:

- Total number of Pinterest followers
- Total number of repins and likes
- Total number of comments

You may also use third-party tools such as Ahalogy (www.ahalogy.com) to measure the success of your Pinterest marketing/content campaigns and optimize the performance of your brand pins and boards. If you're interested in Pinterest contests and sweepstakes, we recommend using the Piqora platform (www.piqora.com) for hosting — they offer robust campaign metrics.

Learning from the Most Creative and Inspirational Pinfluencers

In this section, we offer examples of influencers in the following categories: food, craft/DIY, lifestyle, and travel. We walk you through specific campaigns they participated in, tell you what they did, and explain why it worked.

These are just examples of influencers in various categories. These aren't the only Pinterest influencers worth your time — not even close! Use these profiles as examples of what to look for when you're searching for influencers for your own campaign.

A foodie pinfluencer: Fake Ginger

Pinterest handle: FakeGinger

Brand sponsor: Kraft

Theme: Recipe using Kraft Barbecue Sauce

Highlights: 202 repins, 31 likes

Hashtags: #EverGrillers #CleverGirls

Link: www.pinterest.com/pin/242068548697292157

Amanda is a Colorado-based food blogger, Army wife, and mother of three young boys. She has been blogging since 2007 and enjoys creating delicious, new recipes to share with her readers.

Kraft engaged barbecue-enthusiasts and food bloggers with strong photography skills to creating a recipe with the newly update Kraft Barbecue Sauce!

Amanda posted a step-by-step recipe for Orange Barbecued ribs using the Kraft Barbecue Sauce. She also shared information about the Kraft-sponsored giveaway, encouraging readers to enter for a chance to win their own Grill 'N' Flip Mitt and a year's supply of Kraft Barbecue Sauce. Her pin amplifying the blog post was repinned 202 times and generated 31 likes.

A craft/DIY pinfluencer: Happiness Is Homemade

Pinterest handle: Hihomemadeblog

Brand sponsor: Coffee-mate

Theme: Recipe using Coffee-mate product

Highlights: 2,617 repins and 249 likes

Hashtags: #CMInspires #CGC

Link: www.pinterest.com/pin/255579347579512165

Heidi is a craft/DIY influencer, Northern California mom, and homeschool teacher to three energetic boys. She started her blog in 2010 as a place to document the arts-and-craft projects that she was doing with her children, and expanded it to include recipe ideas, homeschooling advice, and holiday crafting/party-planning tips.

Coffee-mate engaged lifestyle, craft, and entertainment bloggers to show off their true Coffee-mate fan love by trying the new, limited edition David Bromstad–designed bottles, sharing how Coffee-mate inspires their lives, and promoting a brand-sponsored sweepstakes.

Heidi's blog post shared a delicious recipe for a Creamy Blended Frozen Mocha Coffee Drink, promoted the #CMInspires sweepstakes, and hosted a giveaway for a fun Coffee-mate prize pack. Her pin amplifying the blog post was repinned 2,617 times and generated 249 likes.

A lifestyle pinfluencer: My Life Well Loved

Pinterest handle: MyLifeWellLoved

Brand sponsor: Lenovo

Theme: Pinterest story board inspired by fun summer activities, recipes, and products

Highlights: 21 pins reaching 15,100 followers

Hashtags: #Lenovo #Sponsored

Link: www.pinterest.com/mylifewellloved/endless-summer

Heather is a 20-something lifestyle blogger and new mom chronicling her entry into motherhood. Her blog also covers fashion, beauty, family life, and recipes. In her day job, she works as the social media and blogger network director at eMeals.

Lenovo engaged influential Pinterest-savvy moms and millennials with an eye for tech, travel, and lifestyle to create Pinterest story boards inspired by Lenovo products.

Heather created a fun Endless Summer Pinterest board featuring 21 pins and reaching more than 15,000 followers. It includes light and refreshing recipes, warm weather fashion, tech-friendly accessories, and useful travel tips.

A travel pinfluencer: Surf and Sunshine

Pinterest handle: Jeanabeena

Brand sponsor: California Association of REALTORS

Theme: Favorite local hangouts in Redondo Beach, California

Highlights: 19 pins reaching 5,700 followers

Hashtags: #ChampionsofHome #CleverGirls

Link: www.pinterest.com/jeanabeena/champions-of-home

Jeana is a prolific travel photographer and lifestyle blogger. Her site covers a variety of topics, including family life, travel, beauty, recipes, DIY/crafts, and entertainment. Jeana's passion for people, cultures, and food has led her to 22 countries in 4 years. She was recently named by *Social Media Week* as one of eight people who have more social influence than some large travel brands. You can also find her sharing her jetsetting adventures at the *Los Angeles International Travel Examiner* and the *LA Family Travel Examiner*.

California Association of REALTORS engaged active Pinterest influencers to share their favorite hometown restaurants, shops, hangouts, and California day trips to inspire local homeowners and consumers in the market for their first homes in the Golden State.

Jeana's blog post shared her favorite family-friendly activities in Redondo Beach, California. Her California Association of REALTORS–sponsored "Champions of Home" Pinterest board features 19 pins and reaches 5,700 followers. She includes curated recommendations for local beaches and parks and delicious eats.

Chapter 11

Video Influencers

*N*umerous video platforms have sprouted in the past several years, fundamentally changing the way people consume media online and across devices. According to the Pew Research Center, a national survey conducted in July 2013 showed that the percent of American adult Internet users who upload or post videos online doubled in the previous four years, from 14 percent in 2009 to 31 percent in 2013. As such, video influencer marketing will continue to grow in popularity as savvy brands leverage content creators to drive views and engage audiences through creative video channels.

In this chapter, we cover best practices for leveraging video for your brand, how to identify your target video influencers, and where to find them. We also show you how to commission custom video content for your brand and leverage it across your brand-owned social channels to maximize the value.

Looking at the Major Players in Video Sharing

ComScore reports that 188.6 million Americans watched online content videos via desktop computer in February 2015. Google Sites ranked as the top video content property, driven primarily by activity on YouTube.com, reaching 144.6 million unique viewers. In fact, YouTube influencers are more popular among U.S. teens than mainstream celebrities.

According to a study by the IAB Mobile Marketing Center of Excellence, mobile video usage is also on the rise. Thirty-five percent of respondents report watching more video on their smartphone than last year. Sixty-eight percent share the videos they watch on their smartphones, and 42 percent say social media is a way they often find smartphone videos they watch. Short-form content platforms such as Vine and Instagram video have experienced explosive growth since launching in 2013. There are also new platforms like Periscope and Meerkat for live broadcasting when you want to share an event in real-time.

In the following section, we'll review the six major video platforms in greater detail and share how influencers are using these social media channels to reach their unique audiences.

YouTube

Online video consumption has exploded ever since YouTube came on the scene in 2005. Today, YouTube boasts more than one billion users, reaching 81.2 percent of Internet users in the United States, according to comScore data. Three hundred hours of video are uploaded to the channel every minute, and half of YouTube views are on mobile devices. Content can be short or long, including comedic outtakes, music videos, movie trailers, product reviews, tutorials and more.

Although YouTube attracts an even split of female and male users, the platform is still fairly male dominated. *Digiday* reports that men spend 44 percent more time on the site per month. Of 51 categories of YouTube content measured by OpenSlate, men made up the majority of viewers in 90 percent of them. Unsurprisingly, women are more interested in watching beauty reviews and tutorials, while men are into sports and gaming.

Age-wise, YouTube has a broad demographic reach. According to comScore data, released in March 2015, YouTube drew 31.8 million users ages 18 to 24 (98.3 percent of U.S. Internet users in that age bracket) who spent an average of a little over ten hours on the site (per month). Meanwhile, the platform attracted 19.4 million visitors 65 and older (74.4 percent of Internet users in that age bracket) who spent an average of nearly four hours using the video-streaming service in the month of February 2015.

Vine

Vine was founded in June 2012, quickly acquired by Twitter in October 2012, and officially launched in 2013 as a free iOS app. The platform uniquely enables users to share short-form video that loops in six-second increments. Like Twitter, Vine lowered the bar for the average user to create and publish content quickly on the go. Vine's cofounder Dom Hofmann introduced it this way: "With Vine, capturing life in motion is fun and easy. . . . They're little windows into the people, settings, ideas, and objects that make up your life."

Vine was hailed as the "Instagram of video" for a hot minute before it quietly pivoted. Today, the platform has emerged as a bite-size entertainment factory of programmed content — rapidly minting new stars and nurturing them as a collective. *Fast Company* reports that the product's focus has changed to "support content creators who intend to entertain rather than share, and viewers who participate by interacting with content rather than necessarily posting it themselves."

Vine users skew much younger than YouTube users. On Vine, it's primarily teens, which is a key demographic that many brands are eager to reach. According to social media agency Tamba, about six in ten Vine users are women, with 18- to 20 year-olds the top demographic. Polling by NuVoodoo reports that 31.8 percent of U.S. Internet users ages 14 to 17 use Vine.

Teens are notoriously fickle media consumers, so in order to be successful on Vine, you'll need to create content that teens want to watch and re-Vine, racking up the loops to go viral. Content is predominantly centered around users competing to be as funny as possible in only six seconds — think outtakes, parodies, pranks, and other comedic memes.

Amazingly, branded content accounts for 4 percent of the top 100 tracked Vines, and branded Vines generate 400 percent more shares than other branded video.

More than 100 million people are watching Vines online each month, resulting in more than 1 billion "loops" a day. Vine is positioned as the go-to network for quick laughs and just about everything else you can fit into six seconds.

Instagram video

In 2013, Instagram launched the ability to share 15-second video, which has competed directly with Vine's capabilities. Of course, Instagram and Vine are still two distinct platforms. Key features offered on Instagram that aren't available on Vine include multiple filters, video editing, and image stabilization tools. Because Facebook owns Instagram, video content on the latter platform cross-promotes into Facebook news feeds.

Instagram video is a great brand channel to engage consumers if your Facebook following is already actively engaged. Nine out of ten Instagram video shares occurred on Facebook. According to a recent study from Unruly Media, 40 percent of the Top 1,000 most-shared Instagram videos came from iconic social-savvy brands, including MTV, NBA, and GoPro. The most popular verticals in the top 1,000 were Entertainment and Clothing and Apparel.

For more information about working with Instagram influencers, turn to Chapter 7.

Snapchat

Snapchat pioneered the magic hat trick of "disappearing, self-destructing video" in 2011. It uniquely offers an instantaneous way for users to share photos free from the constraints of permanence — or at least it the *illusion of impermanence* (Snapchat data privacy concerns continue to generate hot debate).

TechCrunch reports that Snapchat is quickly approaching 200 million active users. In May 2014, Snapchat reported 700 million photos sent per day on the app, with 500 million Snapchat Stories. With the launch of Snapchat Stories in 2013, the platform allowed users and brands to go beyond the "one-to-one" limitation that came from Snapchat's origins, where one individual would send a message to another. Snapchat Stories allows content creators to add Snaps together to create a continuous narrative. When you add a snap to your story it lives for 24 hours before disappearing, making room for new content. Your story plays forward, allowing users to share moments in the order they experience them. This added feature — the "one-to-many" broadcast mechanism — is more familiar to brands who reach out to thousands of followers at once across social platforms such as Facebook, Twitter, and Instagram.

Even more so than Vine, Snapchat's audience skews young. According to July 2014 polling by NuVoodoo, teens are the platform's biggest fans. Among 14- to 17-year-old U.S. Internet users surveyed, 36.8 percent said they used Snapchat at least weekly.

Snapchat has garnered its fair share of controversial press and remains somewhat of a novelty platform for brands, given that it doesn't provide robust metrics for measuring the success of video marketing efforts. However, that doesn't deter forward-thinking brands such as Taco Bell, Acura, and Rebecca Minkoff from being wildly successful with innovative video marketing campaigns.

Meerkat

Meerkat is a live video-streaming app that launched in a splashy debut in February 2015 to great acclaim by early adopters. It made waves at the South by Southwest (SxSW) conference in Austin, Texas, where it was used in conjunction with live sessions.

As of May 2015, TechCrunch reported that the app had approximately two million users. Unfortunately, its early growth was quickly eclipsed by Twitter's "me-too" launch and acquisition of Periscope (more about the latter platform in the next section). With the advent of these two new platforms, however, the ability to broadcast yourself in real time is becoming easier than ever and more mainstream.

Ben Rubin, Meerkat's founder, has said that he intends to differentiate in the live-streaming space by "pulling many to one," as opposed to "pushing one to many" — a la rival products like Periscope and Twitter. Two-way participation and collaboration will be key to Meerkat's future.

There are many similarities between Meerkat and Periscope — both offer their own way for viewers to like the videos, have options to save the broadcast streams to your phone when you finish, and allow public chats within the videos.

It's still too early to parse demographics closely because neither app has gained mainstream adoption just yet. Just over one-fifth of U.S. Internet users polled by Horizon Media in April 2015 had used or were interested in using Periscope or Meerkat. Unsurprisingly, millennials are leading the pack in adoption with half of 18- to 34-year-old respondents saying they used or would use Periscope or Meerkat. This dropped to one-quarter for 35- to 49-year-olds.

Despite Meerkat's early lead on user adoption, Twitter has endeavored to keep Periscope on top by disabling some of Meerkat's Twitter integration features. Originally Meerkat relied on Twitter for distribution — that is, until Twitter pulled the plug on Meerkat's access to its social graph, citing competitive concerns.

In response, Meerkat cozied up to Facebook and opened up the ability for brands to post a link to their Meerkat live streams on their Facebook pages using Facebook Connect instead of Twitter. This new functionality will also help those already on the Meerkat platform find their Facebook friends' streams. Cross-platform video content sharing at its best!

In July 2015, Meerkat also added a new feature called Cameo, which enables the host of a live stream to invite anyone watching to take control of the stream. During a live stream, you may tap the profile of a viewer to invite him to take over. If the viewer accepts, then everyone on the stream will see that person make a cameo appearance on your stream for up to 60 seconds. This feature opens up some potentially exciting new avenues for brand-sponsored promotion!

Meerkat rolled out Cameo with a number of participating partners lined up for the launch, including The Weather Channel, TMZ, Fox, the CW, Champions League Cup, Above Average, and MasterCard.

Periscope

Periscope, which was acquired and launched by Twitter in March 2015, is another social platform that specializes in broadcasting live video, allowing users to easily stream footage from their devices to followers. Viewers can then engage through comments and send "hearts" to the streamer in real time. The footage can also be replayed later — a key difference from Meerkat, where the footage is gone for good once the stream is over (similar to how content disappears in Snapchat).

The novelty lies in the ability to broadcast and share instantaneously in real time. According to a Periscope blog post on Medium (`www.medium.com/@ periscope/up-periscope-f0b0a4d2e486`), the founders "always imagined Periscope as a visual pulse of what's happening *right now.*"

As of August 2015, TechCrunch reported that Periscope may have hit the impressive milestone of 10 million registered users after just four months. The sheer volume of video content that its users are streaming is astounding — amounting to nearly 40 years of watch time (or just over 350,000 hours of video streamed) per day from its iOS and Android apps.

Like Meerkat, Periscope provides brands with new opportunities to interact with their audiences in real time. According to a recent blog post by Twitter, "Brands can forge a more personal relationship with consumers by using Periscope to give them real-time access to moments that matter, from big announcements to fashion shows to sponsored events." In April 2015, `Target` used Periscope to tease its Lilly Pulitzer line, which helped to fuel huge consumer demand — 90 percent of the collection sold out in a few days.

Check out Social Media Examiner for a helpful comparison primer on how to broadcast live video on Meerkat and Periscope: `www.socialmediaexaminer. com/meerkat-or-periscope-how-to-broadcast-video-via-mobile`.

Finding Video Influencers to Create and Share Branded Content

According to the Pew Research Center, 18 percent of online adults share videos online that they have recorded or created themselves. For this group, the most common subject matter is friends and family doing everyday things (58 percent), followed closely by videos of themselves or others doing funny things (56 percent) and videos of events attended (54 percent).

Brands are quickly recognizing the advantages of leveraging video influencers and their immense marketing power. TechCrunch reported that in 2014, Activision, a major video game publisher, worked with YouTube influencers and gained outstanding results. Influencers' videos featuring "Call of Duty" have been viewed 9.7 billion times to date, which is nearly 20 times the number of views for videos on the brand's own media platforms.

Working with established video platforms

For brands, there's established value in working with YouTube content creators. Unlike some of the newer emerging platforms like Snapchat, Periscope, and Meerkat, YouTube can provide robust analytics to benchmark total number of video views, engagement, and shares. Experimentation on the more ephemeral video platforms is fun for big brands with multi-million-dollar marketing budgets, but if you have more limited funds, we recommend starting your video influencer marketing journey with the tried-and-true influencers on YouTube.

The first step is to develop a video content plan. Here are the four key questions to ask yourself:

- ✔ **What's your goal?** Is your goal to achieve greater brand awareness, promote product trial/purchase, or grow brand loyalty by adding new users to your video channel?

- ✔ **Who are you trying to reach?** You likely know the target demographic you're trying to reach, but you'll also need to research how they're using YouTube. A handy tool for this is the YouTube Trends Dashboard (`www.youtube.com/trendsdashboard`).

- ✔ **What does your brand stand for on YouTube?** What type of existing brand content is resonating with viewers? Check your analytics to find out!

- ✔ **What does success looks like?** If you had already created the perfect piece of video content, how would you describe its success? What metrics can you track to measure this success?

The second step is sourcing the right video influencers to work with. YouTube is so established that there are numerous talent management agencies — including Maker Studios (www.makerstudios.com), Fullscreen (www.fullscreen.com), and Machinima (www.machinima.com) — that will help recruit YouTube influencers and set up a brand campaign for you. These companies reach out to their network of YouTube channels, find available talent, target the best influencers for your brand, and contract them on your behalf.

The next sourcing tier consists of influencer exchange networks such as Reelio (www.reelio.com) and Famebit (www.famebit.com), which act as virtual marketplaces to connect brands to video content creators. They're very similar to other outsourcing platforms like Elance (www.elance.com) or Upwork (www.upwork.com), where people can submit projects and get proposals from freelancers.

Commissioning sponsored video content

If you're interested in connecting with content creators directly, take the time to research the creator landscape, do exhaustive YouTube searches for the type of content you're most interested in leveraging, and review the contracting guidelines outlined in Chapter 4. Most YouTube talents publish their business email and contact info in the channel's About section.

Be sure to vet the influencers' overall qualifications and ability to meet your marketing objectives, especially if the video influencer is not quite a celebrity but an undiscovered talent.

Here are some questions to ask video bloggers (vloggers) you're thinking of working with:

- ✔ **Do you have a sponsored video sample?** Ideally, ask for a sample that is similar in terms of quality and style to the one they'll do for your campaign.

- ✔ **What program do you use to edit your videos?** If they don't use one, it could be a red flag — they may only know how to shoot with their phone and then upload to YouTube (which is not ideal).

- ✔ **What equipment do you use?** iPhones *can* produce fabulous material if someone doesn't have a professional camera setup. But vloggers need to prove that they can do it with an iPhone if that's all they have.

- ✔ **Do you have any creative suggestions for fulfilling the brand objective?** This is a great way to gauge whether they're excited about and understand your brand. Does their video idea sound like it would be entertaining, useful, or cool?

✔ **Can you meet the video deadline?** Don't forget to build in extra time for your internal brand review and any potential edits before the video is set to go live!

✔ **How many revisions/edits do you allow?** Video can be a fickle platform and many variables — such as sound quality, staging, and lighting — can affect the finished reel. It's not a static medium the way photography is. Are they able to be flexible about accommodating brand edits? Are they willing to reshoot their videos if needed?

Offer something valuable to the influencer (besides cash compensation) in exchange for their commitment to your brand. Depending on the stage and focus of their YouTube channel, video creators may be open to any of the following arrangements:

✔ Developing exclusive content with your brand

✔ Increasing exposure outside their own channel (for example, cross-promotion on your brand's channels)

✔ Co-developing an ongoing video series, which can lead to a mutually beneficial long-term partnership

✔ Offering value-added audience engagement through interactive campaigns, contests, and giveaways

Depending on the number of channel subscribers, video influencers can charge anywhere from $300 to $5,000+ per video. For more information, check out the Cheat Sheet at www.dummies.com/cheatsheet/influencermarketing.

When you work with an influencer to create sponsored content, it should be shared as widely as possible on the channels that are most effective for your marketing goals. Make sure your video influencers are cross-promoting and sharing their content with your campaign hashtag across all their active social channels, including blogs, Twitter, Facebook, and Instagram, if applicable.

Remembering to make the proper disclosures

Sponsored content must be disclosed (see Chapter 6). The Federal Trade Commission (FTC) states that the disclosure must be written in a clear and conspicuous manner that can be understood by the average reader. The disclosure must also be placed directly next to (or as close as possible to) the sponsored content.

Case study: Dove

Dove worked with video influencers to promote its Dove Pure Care Dry Oil product line. Video influencers received Dove Pure Care Dry Oil products to trial, and created a hairdo inspired by the latest in-season trends. The YouTube videos took viewers through a step-by-step process outlining how to re-create the look at home using Dove hair-care products. They also explained the benefits of using Dove and encouraged viewers to try it out! Additional amplification took place on Twitter, Facebook, and Instagram. For example, Spanish-language YouTube vlogger DanielaBBH demonstrated a mod hairstyling tutorial featuring Dove hair-care products (`www.youtube.com/watch?v=B9X9Fn51UCQ`), generating nearly 16,000 views.

On YouTube, there are no limits on the length of the video description, so we recommend asking the influencer to include one to two lines of short text disclosure, in addition to verbally stating sponsorship in their video. For example:

> Thank you [BRAND] for sponsoring this video. Visit [URL] for more information about [BRAND PRODUCT].

Across the short-form video platforms, disclosure can be addressed using a simple hashtag such as #sponsored or #ad in the description and/or caption.

Measuring Results

When you find the right video influencers and determine the content type, don't forget to set key performance indicators and put tracking in place to measure your campaign results. Here are some tips on which metrics you should you be measuring and how:

- ✔ **Campaign cost per action (CPA) and cost per click (CPC):** Generate tracking links to measure clicks and conversions. Ask the influencer to use your tracking link within their video descriptions and any other cross-channel social amplifications. Use short branded links that can be generated with Bitly (`www.bitly.com`).

- ✔ **Views and share rate:** In addition to capturing the number of YouTube views, tools like Tubular (`www.tubularlabs.com`) or Unmetric (`www.unmetric.com`) can provide metrics to quantify how popular a video is outside of YouTube itself and provide real-time data on top performing videos.

✔ **Velocity:** You can gain more insight about video performance on a YouTube video page by clicking More – Statistics beneath the video. Stats include data about the video's popularity and trending, how many times the video was shared, and how many viewers subscribed to the channel.

In total, these metrics will help you understand how strongly your brand resonates with the channel's audience and whether you should run more campaigns with your selected influencers. Being strategic in your outreach will lead to success in reaching an engaged fan base.

Case study: Vine vignettes

Tech Insider reports that Vine celebrity Logan Paul's first branded Vine netted him $2,000 in 2014. He currently has more than 8 million followers and charges in the high five figures for branded content. A sponsored Vine looks no different from any other six-second Vine, but it's tagged #sp (for sponsored) per FTC required disclosure. A recent brand collaboration by Logan Paul with Hefty products (#HeftyCupChallenge) took hours to film despite it being edited down to mere seconds. But the effort paid off — it resonated with followers, generating 162,000 likes, 30,000+ re-Vines, and 1,000+ comments! Here's the Vine he produced: `https://vine.co/v/eZg6w0v2agB.`

In July 2013, to promote its annual Summer Clearance Sales Event, Honda asked fans to tweet to @Honda about why they need a new car, and Honda would tweet back with a custom Vine video response that incorporates each person's specific reason and why they should make theirs a Honda. According to Socialbakers, the first day of Honda's #WantNewCar Vine campaign brought the brand more than 1,000 new followers (compared to its six-month average of 242 new followers) and 2,292 mentions.

Case study: Snapchat superstars

Taco Bell was among the earliest group of brands to embrace Snapchat. *AdWeek* reports that its 200,000 followers are "crazy engaged" and when the brand sends a snap, 80 percent of followers open its snaps (90 percent of whom view them in their entirety). This is astonishing engagement — some snaps are up to five-minute-long digital photo-video collages. Taco Bell has successfully promoted its new $1 menu with a campaign on Snapchat, dovetailing with similar cross-promotional efforts on Facebook and YouTube.

Checking Out the Most Creative Video Influencers

In this section, we offer examples of video influencers in the following categories: teen, millennial, craft/DIY, and parenting. We walk you through specific campaigns they participated in, tell you what they did, and explain why it worked.

These are just examples of influencers in various categories. These aren't the only video influencers worth your time — not even close! Use these profiles as examples of what to look for when you're searching for influencers for your own campaign.

Teen vlogger: Lauren Giraldo

Video handle: LGlaurenn

Platform: Vine

Brand sponsor: Coca-Cola

Theme: Share A Coke

Highlights: 21,400 likes; 1,954 revines, and 214 comments

Link: https://vine.co/v/ebI6MrzOxMX

Lauren Giraldo is a 17-year-old musical theater enthusiast and Vine star reaching more than 3.3 million followers. Her hilarious Vines poke fun at pop culture and bizarre millennial tendencies. She also enjoys embarrassing strangers by bombarding them with awkward questions and commentary while recording.

Coca-Cola promoted the Share a Coke tour at DigiFest NYC by offering guests the ability to personalize Coke products.

In her Vine video, Lauren promoted #ShareACoke by holding a custom Coke bottle emblazoned with her name and accosted an apparent stranger on the street. Her kooky antics generated 21,400 likes, 1,954 revines, and 214 comments.

Millennial vlogger: Cody Johns

Video handle: CodyJohns

Platform: Vine

Brand sponsor: Axe

Theme: New York Fashion Week: Men's 2015, featuring AXE product

Highlights: 52,900 likes, 6,962 revines, 277 comments

Link: `https://vine.co/v/erO25uKFIDq`

Cody Johns is a 24-year-old aspiring actor who has acquired more than 3.5 million followers on Vine. He is also one of the founders of Niche, a company that connects social media stars to companies who want to take their advertising to the next level.

AXE was the Official Grooming Sponsor of the inaugural New York Fashion Week: Men's 2015. AXE grooming products were stocked backstage and the brand engaged millennial influencers to create humorous Vine videos, incorporating AXE products. Fans were encouraged to visit AXE social channels for exclusive behind-the-scenes access to New York Fashion Week: Men's 2015.

Cody Johns's funny Vine loop on smelling like a model generated nearly 53,000 likes, 7,000 revines, and 277 comments.

Craft/DIY vlogger: The Kim Six Fix

Video handle: TheKimSix Fix

Platform: YouTube

Brand sponsor: Dremel

Theme: Holiday themed-craft tutorial featuring Dremel product

Highlights: 23,480 views

Link: `https://youtu.be/6wL4ZPhE2u0`

Kim is a homemaker and craft/DIY influencer. She shares her successful home improvement projects and the trials and tribulations of motherhood on her blog and various social channels, including YouTube.

Dremel engaged craft and DIY bloggers to review the Dremel Micro 8050 multipurpose cordless tool and write about their experience using the product on a creative home project.

Kim created a creative video tutorial and blog post, with step-by-step instructions on how to craft engraved and illuminated holiday ornaments using the Dremel Micro 8050 (`www.thekimsixfix.com/2014/09/engraved-and-illuminated-ornaments.html`). Her extremely popular YouTube video generated 23,480 views.

A parenting vlogger: Brett Martin

Video handle: Brett Martin

Platform: YouTube

Brand sponsor: Ubisoft

Theme: Just Dance Kids 2014 video game review

Highlights: 520 views

Link: `https://youtu.be/zsrAcEg6RRo`

Brett is a Connecticut-based parenting influencer who blogs on her site This Mama Loves (`www.thismamaloves.com`). She and her editorial contributors share content about family life, house and home, recipes, and travel. Brett also frequently hosts brand-sponsored Twitter parties.

Ubisoft engaged parenting influencers with game-loving children to review and write about their experience playing with the Just Dance Kids 2014 video game.

Brett's blog post (`www.thismamaloves.com/just-dance-kids-2014-fun-ages-justdancekids2014-cgc`) shared her children's genuine enthusiasm for the Just Dance Kids 2014 video game illustrated with a series of action shots. She also embedded a short YouTube video of her dancing kids, which generated 520 views.

Part IV
Measuring Your Success

Find out how to get influencers to advocate for your brand in a free article at www.dummies.com/extras/influencermarketing.

In this part . . .

- ✔ Understand how influencer marketing directly ties back to your business goals.

- ✔ Discover the sales/marketing lifecycle and how influencer marketing fits in.

- ✔ Learn how to measure your influencer marketing activity with concrete metrics (and why it's important!).

- ✔ Learn how to get the most out of your influencer marketing programs.

Chapter 12

Meeting Metrics

- -

In This Chapter

▶ Seeing what metrics can do for you

▶ Understanding the importance of metrics

- -

*I*n order to know if your campaign is successful, you have to measure the results against your stated program goals. Your goals and the campaign metrics must align. Only then can you set benchmarks, adjust as you grow, and prove your program's return on investment (ROI).

In this chapter, we cover how to measure the success of your influencer marketing campaigns. We outline best practices and common pitfalls, tell you why many industry standards are becoming outdated, and show you how setting the right metrics milestones will make or break your influencer marketing programs.

How Influencer Marketing Can Help Your Business

Ever since the very first "artsy" folks started doing marketing, "business" folks have been asking them to create cool stuff with questionable value — other than satisfying their urge to be like other companies whose marketing materials they've come across out in the wild. Influencer marketing is no different. In fact, in many ways, it's even more subject to the desire to keep up with the Joneses because the best activations tend to be on the cutting edge of social media — and totally fun!

As soon as your Facebook feed is jammed with the latest BuzzFeed quiz results sponsored by Food Brand A, you know the sales teams at Food Brands B, C, and D are scrambling to come up with a "Me, too!" activation. It's human nature (or marketing nature).

Here's the problem: Activity that's "fun" isn't necessarily productive. In fact, all too often, it's actually *different* from activity that accomplishes a goal — specifically a business goal. In this section, we yank your feet back down to earth and make sure you've set realistic goals that you can measure. That's what metrics are all about!

Setting goals: No, really, what are you trying to do here?

The only reason to do influencer marketing is if it will help you achieve your business goals. Activity that fails to help you meet your business goals is a waste of time, money, and brainpower. Even worse, an activation that is "just fun" puts you at risk of wasting a rare and valuable opportunity to get in front of your target market and convince them to do something useful. Sure, it may be entertaining for your audience, but unless your goal is to *be* entertaining (and sometimes it is!), you're missing a chance to convert that audience from a prospect to a customer, or from a first-time customer to a repeat buyer.

If your marketing plan is a rocket ship, your messaging is the flight plan and social media is the rocket fuel that sends it to outer space, or at least somewhere amazing (see Chapter 16). Without a plan, without that ship, you just have a bunch of liquid sitting in your garage that can catch fire and burn down your house.

You'd be surprised by how many marketers forget to start with these very basic questions:

- What job does the program need to do?
- How does it fit into our business plan to help us reach our business goals?

To answer these questions, you need a business plan. We assume that if you're here, you *do* have a clear understanding of your organization's strategic business goals. Maybe your goal is to be the go-to website for teen athletes to buy sports equipment, the best subscription service for gluten-free snacks, or the leading financial services provider for retirees.

When you have a clear understanding of the big-picture goal, you can start to build a road map of the tactics that will help you get there.

If you're scratching your head thinking, "A business plan? What's that?," check out *Creating a Business Plan For Dummies,* by Veechi Curtis (John Wiley & Sons, Inc.). Then come back to this book to find out how to use influencer marketing to reach your business goals.

Matching your program goals to your business goals

Defining your business goals takes a lot of work, but it's worth it because it makes all your other choices easier. Here are some of the things you need to define:

- ✔ To whom do you want to talk?
- ✔ Where are they? (For example, are they on Twitter, Facebook, Instagram, or Pinterest?)
- ✔ Are they okay with hearing from a brand, product, or service in those channels?

You want to ask people to do one, clear, specific task. Common influencer marketing calls to action (CTAs) include the following:

- ✔ Click here.
- ✔ Share with your friends.
- ✔ Retweet.
- ✔ Tag a friend.

Your goal will tell you who is included in your ideal target audience. For example, if you are trying to reach fashion-forward millennials and get them to help raise awareness of your shoe brand by sharing pictures of themselves wearing the shoes, market research will tell you that Instagram, with its visual content and high interaction, is a good place to engage with your audience.

Know where your audience lives. If no one is talking about fundraising on Instagram, you're wasting time doing programs there.

Market research uncovers facts about your target and how to reach them. It can also be extremely expensive. The nice thing about influencer marketing is that so much of it happens "in the clear" — the people you're trying to reach are behaving, talking, and oversharing out in public. Unlike traditional market research, which can be very costly to purchase or conduct, plus take quite a bit of time, with influencer marketing there is a whole library of "free" self-reported and observed behavior available at your fingertips. Just go to the different social networks and channels; do a search for yourself, your competitors, and logical keywords; and see the truth for yourself. Go to where your users are!

Are people posting pictures on Instagram of the amazing crafts they made with your product? But are there hardly any @mentions of your brand on Twitter? Then you should concentrate on Instagram. Continue to monitor Twitter but don't spend a lot of time or money there.

Maybe there isn't a lot of activity about your brand happening anywhere, but your biggest competitor has an active Pinterest board showcasing recipes of desserts created using their gluten-free flour. Now you've found a whole group of people you know are interested in gluten-free products, and you know where they like to congregate.

If you take it a step further, you can start to follow their Pinterest boards, like their pins, and pay attention to the things they post about *why* they like your competitor. It's literally your target customer telling you what they want to buy and why — all you need to do is tell them why your product meets exactly those needs.

In fact, once you figure out which channels are relevant for your users, you should be monitoring them *all* the time, even when you're not running a campaign. It will help you understand your audience better than any research, and give you authentic, organic reasons to interact with them — which is excellent and necessary for your success!

You Get What You Measure: Metrics Are Mandatory

In this section, we talk about how you can tell if your campaign is a success or a failure, and the measures, or *metrics,* that are the most commonly used to evaluate whether you achieved your goals. We also explore some of the most popular and helpful tools to help you do this evaluation.

Picking the right metrics

In order to measure the success of your influencer marketing campaign, you need to choose the right things to measure. So, how do you know what to measure? In general, influencer marketing campaigns measure the top of the funnel (see Chapter 13 for more information about the sales funnel) and how well you're raising awareness of your product or service.

The specifics of what you measure are related to the goals of your campaign. For example, if your goal is to drive traffic to your website, you might measure the adjusted click-through rate (CTR), which is the percentage of people who click on a link or ad to go visit another site.

Make your goals SMART

Every influencer marketing program must have a goal, and you must measure to find out if you achieved that goal. When you're setting goals for your influencer marketing campaign, make sure they're SMART:

✔ **Specific:** Decide *exactly* what you want to happen.

✔ **Measurable:** Pick a number, (almost) any number!

✔ **Attainable:** This where that "almost" comes in, as a reality check. You want to make sure your goal is something you can actually reach.

✔ **Relevant:** The goal of your influencer marketing program needs to be relevant to your business's goals.

✔ **Time-bound:** Give yourself a timeframe, including a deadline.

For example, say Company X wants 100 high-influence, fashion-forward millennial women to share photos of Company X shoes, mentioning them by brand name, on Instagram in late October, leading into holiday party outfit season. Here's why that goal is SMART:

✔ **It's specific.** Company X wants influencers to share photos of the shoes, and the Company X brand name, not just mention "Nude pumps go well with most dresses."

✔ **It's measurable.** Company X wants 100 women to share photos. Even if they miss their target, setting the number will get Company X close to it.

✔ **It's attainable.** Even the coolest, most desirable product has to start at the beginning. Getting 100 women to share photos is attainable for Company X because it has a large user-base they can contact and a well-known and popular product, or they have a big enough budget to hire an agency that can pay influencers to try the product and share the image.

✔ **It's relevant.** If your goal is make fashionistas aware of your brand, then you want fashion Instagrammers to post — not travel photographers. Match the activity to the goal.

✔ **It's time-bound.** Most industries and products experience seasonality in demand. If your highest activity and biggest sales goals are during the holiday season, it would be silly (and too darn late) to start your program in February.

If your goal is to generate awareness and reach lots of eyeballs, you might measure the following:

✔ **Monthly aggregate reach – impressions:** The combined total number of monthly visits to all other blogs of the influencers who wrote about your product in the program. Numbers reflect the bloggers' most recent 30 days of traffic.

✔ **Monthly aggregate reach – uniques:** The combined total number of unique blog visitors for all participating bloggers. Numbers reflect the bloggers' most recent 30 days of traffic.

✔ **Search engine marketing (SEM) and discoverability:** Methods for increasing the visibility of keywords in search engine results, and ultimately driving more traffic to your site, which you can measure by comparing traffic pre-, post- and during the campaign.

✔ **Social actions:** Someone interacting with online content. This can include measuring the number of

- Posts

- Tweets and retweets

- Pins

- Likes

- Social shares

- Comments

Although it's harder to quantify, marketers often find valuable information in *qualitative data* (information about the qualities of something that can't be counted or measured by numbers — for example, the color of your eyes), as opposed to *quantitative data* (which can be expressed in numbers, measurements, or quantities — for example, your weight or the number of people who score 100 percent on a test). For example, a conversation with influencers responding to comments can reveal brand sentiment or generate positive (or negative) mentions for your product. Whether positive or negative, it's all information that you can respond to — and act on!

What's the hashtag?

A *hashtag* is a specific, easily identifiable keyword, with the hash (#) symbol in front of it. You include a hashtag in social network posts (for example, on Instagram, Twitter, or Facebook), and people can click the hashtag to see all posts that include that hashtag. Many analytical tools track influencer marketing programs by measuring the frequency and location of hashtags.

Imagine that you have ten people in a building, and they're all on separate floors, yelling about the same topic. No one can really hear them, unless they're on the same floor, and it's just one person yelling. But if you put all ten people in the lobby of the building, and they're all yelling about the same thing, everyone who walks into the building hears them loud and clear. The people who walk into the building might even join in, and start yelling with them! This attracts more people, possibly even people from outside the building. Soon you could have a crowd of people overflowing from the lobby, onto the street, making a big noise, and people from up and down the street might be drawn in. A hashtag is what gets everyone into the same "virtual" lobby.

Nofollow links and when to use them

When you put a link on your blog to somewhere else, you're saying, "I trust this link — you should click it." This is how Google knows sites are worth attention — the more links there are to a site, the higher the Google page rank, which means it's easier for people to find that site.

Nofollow was developed for people who wanted to include links but didn't want them to be counted as "votes" for another site for whatever reason — maybe you were talking about how terrible a site was, or responding to a negative comment. You wouldn't want those sites to get more "votes" and be discoverable because of your activity.

In parallel, there were people who were misusing the way that you could improve a page rank by linking to it. They built *link farms,* spam sites that had nothing but links to other sites. People built businesses where they were paid to link to things. Think of blog commenters who leave nonsensical comments with links.

As a result of these spammers trying to game the system, Google came out with harsh language forbidding people to pay for links to sites. Some people took an extreme reaction to that, and applied it to linking to sponsor sites when they're being paid for promoted content. These bloggers are afraid of being dinged by Google for having this link, so they use nofollow links.

It's our professional opinion that if bloggers are thoughtful and selective in which sponsors they work with, and only include relevant links to sites that they can vouch are not spam, nofollow is not necessary and the bloggers won't be penalized by Google.

However, if they overuse links, get paid directly to link to other sites, or participate in keyword programs (like where they're paid to put tons of links in a post that they normally wouldn't), then using nofollow is a good idea.

If you're ever in doubt, it's better to default to using a nofollow link on a sponsored post. It's just not necessary in all sponsored cases.

Selecting your hashtag can be one of the most important decisions you'll make in designing any kind of social media campaign! You want to make sure that it's unique, descriptive, catchy, and as short as possible.

The unique part is important for data collection, as well as for brand association. If you're paying for a service to monitor a hashtag, you don't want your metrics to include posts that don't have anything to do with your program because it'll compromise the data.

Check your hashtag before using it to make sure that it's not already being used by a competitor and that it won't create negative brand associations. For example #playtime could be used for a daycare center . . . or a strip club. If you're a daycare center, you probably don't want posts about strippers muddying your waters. And if you're a strip club, pictures of little kids probably aren't the kinds of posts you want.

Tools of the trade

Marketing is an industry of data hounds. Numerous tools are available to help you analyze your campaign results, with new tools being launched all the time. Many of these tools are free, but some have paid features that are worth the investment, because they make your life, or at least the measuring part of it, so much easier.

Here are a few of the top tried-and-true free and paid analytics tools:

- **bit.ly** (`http://www.bitly.com`): This tool shortens URLs and allows you to see how many people clicked the link and whether they accessed your content from a desktop or mobile device.

- **Curalate** (`www.curalate.com`): User-generated content continues to grow in popularity and value for influencer marketing. Curalate special-izes in managing and measuring visual programs, and offers a variety of competitive and user analyses.

- **Facebook Insights** (`www.facebook.com`): Facebook is collecting *all of the data* about how we use the site. The good news is that Facebook is willing to share this information with users, in the form of Audience and Page Insights. You can see which posts perform well, figure out the best time to post, and gather information like audience geolocation. Of course, Facebook's master plan is to make you spend money advertising on the site, but the information is still useful!

- **Google Alerts** (`http://alerts.google.com`): It may seem simple, but a surprising number of companies forget to set Google Alerts to let them know when people are talking about them. Set up listening searches for your own brand, competitors, and hot topics for your industry.

- **Google Analytics** (`http://analytics.google.com`): Google Analytics tracks and reports on traffic to your website. It's useful when your goals include understanding where traffic comes from, and how people behave on your site. The dashboard is fairly intuitive and allows you to drill down into more granular data sets. It's nicely visual, and you can get a lot of useful data just from the free service, adding premium fea-tures if and when you need them.

- **Hashtracking** (`https://www.hashtracking.com`): This newer paid service offers a variety of service levels and lets you track hashtags over a period of time on Twitter and Instagram. It offers concise, easy-to-read reports and analytics.

- ✔ **Hootsuite** (`http://www.hootsuite.com`): Hootsuite is a paid service that allows you to manage up to 100 social accounts, across more than 35 different social networks, all on one dashboard. You can schedule updates to post later, and it offers a variety of analytics reports.

- ✔ **Klout** (`www.klout.com`): Klout uses an algorithm to calculate an individual's influence on social channels, generating a score from 1 to 100. It doesn't take into account qualitative data, but some users find it useful as a relative measure of value.

- ✔ **Little Bird** (`www.getlittlebird.com`): Little Bird helps you find influencers and track how they help your brand.

- ✔ **PinPuff** (`www.pinpuff.com`): Klout for Pinterest.

- ✔ **Simply Measured** (`www.simplymeasured.com`): This powerhouse tool allows you to track your program activity across almost every social channel — including Twitter, Facebook, Google+, Instagram, YouTube, LinkedIn, Tumblr, and Vine — by monitoring hashtags. It also can provide channel, use case, and industry analytics, as well as competitive analysis and benchmarking. You can set up a plan that aligns with the channels you're using for your programs. It also offers several free tools, including analysis of your social accounts.

- ✔ **Sprout Social** (`www.sproutsocial.com`): Sprout Social is a dashboard that allows you to look at programs across channels and track engagement. One helpful feature is that it analyzes both mentions and your responses, which allows you to evaluate and improve over time.

- ✔ **Tailwind** (`http://www.tailwindapp.com`): Pinterest is an important channel for influencer marketing, and this tool helps you manage Pinterest activity. You can schedule pins, measure performance of pins to analyze which ones are most popular, and measure follower growth. Best of all, Tailwind can provide competitive industry benchmark information! An additional sweet feature is that it easily integrates with Google Analytics.

Benchmarks: A study in patience

When you know the results of your influencer marketing campaign, you can calculate the value of the program relative to how similar programs have performed. Many influencer marketing programs are unique, or at least among the first of their kind. That means you have to build your own *benchmarks* (a standard point of reference that you measure your progress against) — and sometimes guess.

Benchmarking is a critical first step in understanding the value of influencer marketing campaigns for your business. There are two types of benchmarks you can develop:

- ✓ **Competitive benchmarks:** You look at industry data and measure your results against your competition. Competitive benchmarks are valuable, and often hard to come by because most companies want to keep that information private. The value of many paid analytic tools (see the list of options in the preceding section) is that, as a third party, they can get access to success metrics across multiple brands or service providers, and create competitive benchmarks for you.

- ✓ **Goal benchmarks:** Remember how we were *so* adamant that you have to define program goals that support the overarching business goals? This is where those goals come into play, especially if you don't have access to competitive benchmarks. When you're doing a brand-new type of program, you often set a goal based on what you hope and think you can logically expect to happen. (It's more of a hypothesis than a goal.) Over time, as you do more programs, you can refine the goal so that each subsequent program aims to improve performance.

Your experience will inform how much you aim to improve over time. In a large, mature market, an improvement of ½ percent may be cause for a three-day celebration. On the other hand, a new product with little or no track record may be able to see improvement of 100 percent or even 1,000 percent from one program to the next.

Sometimes you hit your goal, and sometimes you miss it by a lot. From a data perspective, both results are great because you get actionable information about what to adjust. Don't be disappointed if you don't get positive results immediately on the first campaign. You're still learning how to improve your product, user experience, or sales cycle!

Once more, with feeling! Adjusting goals and metrics for long-term success

When you conduct an influencer marketing campaign, you have lots of authentic, gritty, true-feeling content. It also means you probably found some surprises in your results. And let's hope so! If not, you might have been too conservative with your goals.

One of the many wonderful things about having metrics and interpreting your results is that it gives you very specific information about where you can improve.

When you hit your numbers, and then some, it means you're doing something right. Here are some ways you can capitalize on your success:

- ✔ You have room to grow, so push yourself to increase your goals.
- ✔ See if there are additional goals you can add to your future programs.
- ✔ Consider new or different programs that will build on the momentum or relationship you've started with the influencers.
- ✔ Ask how you can add to or expand the target market, possibly with new demographics.

In a way (okay, a super optimistic way, but stay with us here), it's almost better when you *miss* your goals because there are lots of things you can examine and adjust. Review the results, especially anecdotal information, to try to understand where you're coming up short. Here are some questions to ask yourself when you miss the target:

- ✔ Is it the product or service that's underperforming?
- ✔ Are you doing a bad job of fulfilling orders or providing customer service?
- ✔ Are you trying to connect to the wrong audience?
- ✔ Was your message or value proposition wrong for that audience?

Influencer marketing is about working with people and building relationships over time. It's a commitment to ongoing interactions, so you always have the next program, touch point, or conversation to look forward to — and to plan!

Interpreting the Data, and Deciding What to Do Next

Now you have your results. You know how much and what types of influencer activity you were able to produce, you know what the qualitative reactions were in their communities, and hopefully you have some metric on how much it helped your business (for example, increased traffic to your website during the campaign and a corresponding increase in sales).

If it's your first influencer marketing campaign, the next step is to do another one, and compare the results. If you've done this a few times, you'll want to compare, adjust, and optimize the program to get more of the results you want. The ideal is to have a campaign that worked so well that you can duplicate it, set a new and higher goal, and simply do it again — for more success.

For example, if you had ten influencers post a coupon code on their Facebook pages, each post was shared an average of 23 times, and you had an increase of 10 percent of average daily traffic from Facebook, and a whopping 27 percent increase in daily sales, it's a logical interpretation to decide to focus on finding Facebook influencers with similar demographics and audiences to help distribute coupon codes and drive traffic and sales.

Even when it's not this simple, you still have a lot of useful data from your SMART goals (see "Make your goals SMART," earlier in this chapter). You want to evaluate the results, how close to or far from the goal you were, and try to understand why something was successful. This tells you what to change, and what to keep the same.

For example, imagine that one of the goals of the Facebook coupon code program was to have an average of 30 shares per post. This program got an average of 23, but the data shows that Facebook influencers who posted in the morning had more than double the shares than the ones who posted at night. In your next campaign, you would encourage the influencers to post in the morning, and see if your average shares and overall results for site traffic and sales increase.

This is a "test and learn" discipline. You won't have perfect campaigns every time, and there aren't any magic answers. But by measuring *everything* against specific goals, you can understand which aspects of a campaign are successful, and which things you need to adjust or fix. Use the data to drive your decisions. Over time, you'll see improvements and watch your business grow!

Chapter 13

Integrating Influencer Marketing with Your Sales Funnel

....

In This Chapter

▶ Understanding the sales funnel

▶ Reaching the right audience

▶ Identifying where you can exercise control

....

*T*he ultimate goal of all marketing programs — the good ones anyway! — is to support the business by getting more people to buy your products. There are many steps in the consumer's journey — from finding out your product exists to handing over cold hard cash and taking it home.

Like the characters in an ensemble comedy, your marketing team and each of your marketing initiatives — including influencer marketing programs — has a role to play. Think of the product as your heroine, and your sales team as the sexy love interest. The marketing team is in charge of creating dazzling scenery and sumptuous costumes, writing witty dialogue, and enforcing continuity of the story. As the director, you make sure all the parts work together, with no one character upstaging another.

The influencer marketing program is the very important BFF supporting character. She's the one to whom the heroine tells everything, who cracks the funniest jokes at the perfect moment, and without whom you couldn't have a movie. As integral to the plot as she is, you would never expect that wisecracking best friend to carry the whole TV show by herself.

In this chapter, we look at the stages of the cycle (also known as the sales funnel). We also talk about getting the right prospects into the funnel and tracking that relationship through all the stages.

The Sales Funnel: A Funnel of Love

As much as we all wish that customer acquisition was a matter of love at first sight, even the smoothest sales cycle includes multiple steps. And it doesn't even end with a purchase! When you have a customer, you want to keep him, get more business from him, and have him help you reach even more customers.

There are lots of ways to slice and dice it, but most definitions of the customer acquisition life cycle, or "sales funnel," will include the following six stages (see Figure 13-1):

- ✔ **Stage 1: Awareness:** The first step is getting your target market to know you're on the scene.

- ✔ **Stage 2: Consideration:** Next you need to convince your target market that your brand, product, or service is worthy of them.

- ✔ **Stage 3: Preference:** When you aren't the only game in town — and really, when are you ever? — this is the stage when you need to hammer home your differentiator and value proposition.

- ✔ **Stage 4: Purchase:** That magic moment when someone agrees that she really *does* like your product best, or at least enough to give you money and take the product home.

- ✔ **Stage 5: Loyalty:** Every marketer's favorite thing: repeat business!

- ✔ **Stage 6: Advocacy:** Marketing is most cost effective when people start convincing friends, family members, and even complete strangers to share in the wonder and joy of your product.

Figure 13-1:
The sales
funnel.

AWARENESS

CONSIDERATION

PREFERENCE

PURCHASE

LOYALTY

ADVOCACY

© *John Wiley & Sons, Inc.*

Influencer marketing is especially effective at the top and bottom of the funnel, effectively turning the "funnel of love" into a circle of love, with brand advocates generating awareness on your behalf, filling up the top of the funnel with the best and brightest possible prospects through your funnel and turning them into customers for life.

Your sales cycle and the funnel

The sales cycle and the customer acquisition life cycle are the same thing, even though many organizations use different names or have different milestones for them.

The average conversion rate through each funnel stage, including timing and trigger for a move from one stage to the next, varies based on your market, the complexity of the product, pricing, the skill of your sales team, and even how good your marketing efforts are. That said, it always goes from big to small — you start with a big group of potential prospects, only a percentage of which will make it to the next stage. So it stands to reason that you want to start as big as you possibly can, to create the biggest possible potential endpoint.

Customer relationship management (CRM) is your friend! Tools like Salesforce (www.salesforce.com) and Zoho (www.zoho.com) create order and data. When you know about who is in your funnel at each stage, and why they moved from one stage to the next, you can easily create a simple to do list — more of what worked! — to get even more prospects.

When you have your target market's attention and consideration, you need to give them an offer they can't refuse, or a reason to say "Yes!" The same thing goes for programs that didn't work. If an activity didn't get any measurable success moving prospects through the cycle, you can stop doing that and spend your time and money on activations that *do* work.

Tell everyone — or at least the right people!

So, how do you get as many people as possible to enter your funnel? Start by defining who you want there in the first place. Even more important, identify who is mostly likely to convert all the way through the six stages — or at the very least to a sale?

In addition to all the smart business and marketing reasons for knowing as much as possible about your customer, this information will help you build influencer programs that attract more of the right prospects. And by the same token, it will help you avoid spending money attracting the wrong people.

You want to know who buys your product, why they buy it, what influences or informs their purchase, where they buy it, and if there are any seasonal considerations.

For example, imagine you're selling a children's toy that helps teach reading, targeted to preschool-age kids — a toy that pairs pictures with the first letter of the name of the object, like G for giraffe or T for train. By looking at previous buying patterns of your products, as well as of your competitors' products, you'll find out a lot of what you need to know about who you want to reach with influencer programs at the awareness and consideration stages, as well as the advocacy state. And, although influencer marketing programs usually don't have a direct conversion metric, you'll be able to see the correlation between getting more of the right people into the top of the funnel and getting more sales further down the process.

Using our example of the alphabet toy, you'll want to know the following:

- ✔ **Who buys similar educational toys?** Based on your research, maybe you find that the answer to that question is the following:

    - Mothers and fathers of 3- to 5-year old children

    - Educators

    - Grandparents

- ✔ **Why do they make this purchase?** After you identify who buys your product, you need to figure out why. For the alphabet toy, maybe it looks something like this:

    - *Mothers and fathers:* Parents buy the toy as an educational toy, as a gift, as well as because of impulse buying — the purchase wasn't something they planned.

    - *Educators:* Teachers buy the toy as an educational tool.

    - *Grandparents:* Grandparents buy the toy as a gift.

- ✔ **What influences the purchase?** When you know why your customers are buying your product, you need to figure out what's leading them to make that purchase. For example, for the alphabet toy, it may be something like the following:

    - *Mothers and fathers:* Parents buy the toy because their kids ask for it, as well as because a friend recommends it to them.

- *Educators:* Teachers buy the toy based on professional recommendations — recommendations from their fellow educators.

- *Grandparents:* Grandparents buy the toy because of the contextual information they find at the point of sale. They're in the store shopping for a gift for their grandchild, and they come upon a display with your toy, and the display convinces them to buy.

✔ **Where do they make the purchase?** Different shoppers have different shopping habits. Here's what you may find for your alphabet toy:

- *Mothers and fathers:* Parents tend to purchase your product online, especially when they're surfing the web late at night.

- *Educators:* Teachers tend to purchase your product online and in brick-and-mortar bookstores.

- *Grandparents:* Grandparents purchase your product predominantly in brick-and-mortar bookstores.

✔ **When do they make the purchase?** You want to identify whether there's a particular time of year when your customers are most likely to make the purchase. For the alphabet toy, maybe it's something like the following:

- *Mothers and fathers:* Parents buy your toy year-round. No particular time of year results in more sales than another.

- *Educators:* Teachers primarily buy your toy at back-to-school time.

- *Grandparents:* Grandparents primarily buy your toy at the holiday season, although they do also shop year-round for birthdays and other special occasions.

Every business needs to understand its own industry, its ideal customer, and what the competition is doing to reach those customers first. There are many ways to conduct qualitative and quantitative market research. If you have the budget, you can purchase packaged data from marketing research companies, or even conduct research on your customers and target market. A less expensive, although less precise, method is to gather intelligence by reading and analyzing everything you can find on industry trends and consumer behavior.

If you were doing awareness and consideration campaigns for the alphabet toy, you'd want to cast a broad net that would reach as many people as possible who

✔ Are parents, grandparents or educators

✔ Are researching purchases online and in stores

✔ Like to shop both online and in brick-and-mortar stores

The stages you can (and can't) control

In theory, you should control all of it, right? And wouldn't that be great? But in reality, the best you can do is influence how some of this plays out.

You have the most control over the earlier stages, when you can make choices about who you try to reach, what communication channels you use to reach them (the "where" of it),

and the messages in your communications, including your call to action.

It's much harder, at least in terms of influencer marketing programs, to control your target market's reactions and activities. There's a reason it's called "influencer marketing," and not "mind control marketing."

You'll want to design an influencer marketing program that

- ✔ Involves family and education-oriented themes
- ✔ Happens online and in bookstores where prospects are shopping
- ✔ Involves influencers with communities of parents and people who discuss educational themes
- ✔ Has year-round presence, with additional efforts during back-to-school and holiday seasons

You would probably *not* set up a program that

- ✔ Has a theme about motorcycle maintenance
- ✔ Is exclusively direct-mail
- ✔ Happens during January, right after holiday shopping has wrapped up

You'd probably reach some of your intended audience this way, but hyper-focusing your campaign increases your chances of reaching the optimal group of people because you're effectively doing the first level of screening for interest.

Integrating Influencer Marketing with the Rest of Your Sales Program

In the most effective scenarios, influencer marketing campaigns have a collaborative and cooperative relationship with your other sales and marketing activities. But influencer marketing doesn't stand alone.

Think of influencer marketing is as a terrific accessory, like a statement necklace. That necklace can take your outfit from boring to memorable, but you'd never dream of walking around wearing only the necklace! You need the whole outfit to work together.

Influencer marketing is especially good at amplifying your other marketing efforts — helping your other marketing activities reach a bigger and better audience (just like that statement necklace takes your entire outfit to the next level). In some cases, influencer marketing can even help your programs be more successful.

Influencer marketing is a great complement to new product rollouts. It's a terrific way to get new branding in front of people. It can help create awareness of a direct marketing campaign, which in turn can have a strong call to action that creates a sale.

Influencer marketing works well with direct marketing (see Chapter 14 for the similarities and differences between the two). An influencer marketing campaign for a baking chocolate brand may have a goal of producing 50 recipes that use their 87 percent cacao chips and posting them on Pinterest where avid bakers look for recommendations. This helps awareness ("Oh, they have 87 percent cacao chips!") and consideration ("I want to eat those cookies. I should see if they have that brand at my supermarket").

A companion direct marketing campaign could try to reach an overlapping market segment. Data on Pinterest users could show that they're predominantly women ages 25 to 38, who live in metropolitan areas that have a high concentration of average household incomes of more than $100,000 (so they can afford fancy chocolate) and are college-educated. Using this data, the brand could set up a coupon for stores in those neighborhoods, either at point of purchase or through direct mail to those zip codes.

A perfect campaign result would be a woman in a supermarket who recognizes the brand from a Pinterest posted recipe, and decides to make cookies with those chips because she can use the coupon attached to the packaging. An extra perfect campaign would have that woman becoming an advocate, Instagramming the cookies she made with the chocolate, tagging the brand, which in turn can share the Instagram post to all its followers, creating a whole new cycle of influence, awareness, and consideration.

Chapter 14

Using the Type of Marketing You Need: Influencer or Direct Marketing

In This Chapter

▶ Figuring out which marketing tactic works best for your goals

▶ Making sure you're measuring what you're actually doing

▶ Learning from your results

*N*ot all marketing tactics that speak to target customers — particularly ones that happen online — are the same. People often confuse *where* a marketing initiative happens with *what* that initiative is designed to do.

Influencer marketing is most often confused with direct marketing. Both are fantastic tactics that can have meaningful impact on your business. But they use very different tactics, accomplish very different goals, are connected to very different parts of the sales funnel, and are evaluated by very different metrics.

In this chapter, we help you determine whether influencer marketing or direct marketing will work best for your goals, and help you learn from the results of your campaign.

Influencer Marketing versus Direct Marketing: Similarities and Differences

As influencer marketing has become more popular, it has also sometimes been confused with direct marketing (also known as direct response). Direct marketing programs include display ads, text messages, ads in periodicals, email campaigns, and even *out-of-home advertising* (any kind of advertising that reaches you when you're not home, like billboards or ads on the sides of buses). Direct marketing has some similarities to influencer marketing:

✔ Both influencer marketing and direct marketing focus on understanding who and where you customers are.

✔ Analytics play an important role in both influencer marketing and direct marketing (although the analytics are different for each).

✔ In direct marketing, as in influencer marketing, there is always a very specific call to action. Except in direct marketing (unlike in influencer marketing), there's a call to convert to a sale.

The big difference between influencer marketing and direct marketing is that direct marketing is one message to many. It's the brand talking to the audience, with the intention of compelling that audience to become customers. Influencer marketing is many voices, with a variety of hopefully similar and consistent, but nonetheless individualized messages, to a very broad audience. Figure 14-1 shows how the two types of marketing differ. And Table 14-1 gives you a side-by-side overview of both.

Figure 14-1:
Influencer
marketing
versus
direct
marketing.

© John Wiley & Sons, Inc.

Table 14-1	Direct Marketing versus Influencer Marketing	
	Direct Marketing	*Influencer Marketing*
Goal	Conversion	Awareness, consideration
Messaging	One way — from brand to customer	Multiple directions — between brand and customer, between multiple customers and prospects
Content	Generated and controlled by the brand	Generated by influencers; can sometimes be guided or suggested by brand, but not controlled
Call to action	Specific and usually related to conversion or sale	Generalized and measured by activity volume as a metric of awareness
Metrics	Return on investment, specific and quantifiable	Return on engagement, largely qualitative, and requiring interpretation
Audience	Target customer	Customer, as well as people who are adjacent to the customer
Research	Who will buy and when, where and how to touch them	Who and what the customer will consider when deciding to make a purchase, and where they find that information
Sample Tactics	Paid search, display ads, telemarketing, coupons, infomercials, catalogs, and direct mail	Blogger programs, Instagram and Pinterest contests, Twitter parties, YouTube video reviews, Facebook amplification

Direct Marketing: Measuring Data and Deliverables

Direct marketing starts with customer data and includes specific, measurable activities. And when we say "measurable," we mean activities that are measured before activation, after activation, and often *during* activation.

For something to be considered direct marketing, you must have a call to action, prompting the target to do something very specific — call this number, click this link, buy this *right now*. Direct marketing is often called direct response, because you're very specifically requesting a response.

When you design a direct marketing program, you must meticulously identify the following:

- ✔ **Who** is most likely to say yes — in other words, your target customer
- ✔ **Where** your target customers are most likely to be receptive to the offer — in other words, the channel where you can reach them
- ✔ **When** your target customers are most willing to take the action — taking into account things like seasonality or purchase patterns

Back in the day (which really is only a few years ago), the most common types of direct marketing were direct mail, coupons, and good old-fashioned telemarketing. Catalogs and infomercials can also be considered direct marketing. As direct marketing evolved, it became more sophisticated and moved online, taking the form of display ads, email campaigns, and couponing (in the form of online discount codes).

Whichever direct marketing tactic you select, the most important part is measuring that call to action. You measure the activity against your goal — for example, increasing visits to a website by 10 percent — before the campaign, during the campaign, and after the campaign to see whether it worked. This type of result is relatively easy to interpret — the target either does or doesn't perform the action.

It may seem like direct marketing is more, well, *direct* and laser focused on the goals of conversion and sales. So, why would you spend time on non-sales-generating conversations and harder-to-measure, open-ended activities that comprise influencer marketing? The answer lies with your customers.

Everybody has become savvy to marketing tactics. We *know* when we're being sold, and to put it simply, we don't much like it. In addition to the issues of awareness and preference, the sheer volume of direct marketing has made it relatively ineffective. Many direct marketing tactics, like display ads, have simply lost their power. People don't even see them! Click-through rate benchmarks are well below 1 percent — you're almost more likely to be struck by lightning than to click a display ad.

Email continues to be effective, in the form of value-added newsletters, but the high volume of spam that everyone receives from virus-infected computers has changed what it takes to make it through customers' email filters, never mind actually get them to open something. As of July 1, 2015, email distribution provider MailChimp reports open rates ranging from the mid-20s to the mid-teens, depending on the industry. Click-through rates from emails range from a high of over 5 percent from senders related to topics like hobbies, to a low of 1.4 percent for emails from restaurants.

Today's customer is smarter and more powerful. With the rise of social media and self-publishing platforms, people are making purchase decisions because they heard their friends talking about it on Facebook, or they read about it on a favorite blog. They're gathering their own information and making their own decisions about what, when, and where to buy.

In other words, customers aren't listening to brands, or responding to their calls to action — but they *are* being *influenced* by friends and family on Facebook, colleagues on LinkedIn, celebrities on Twitter, and even dogs and cats with Instagram accounts. The obvious move was for marketers to say, "How do we get these people talking about *us*?" And that's where influencer marketing comes in.

Influencer Marketing: Getting the Right People to Talk about You

Influencer marketing is a more flowing, iterative style of marketing. Imagine concentric rings, or ripples in a pond. You send out an idea or message, in the hopes that people pass it along. And although customer data plays a role in designing programs, it's usually qualitative data (about things like preferred social media channel) instead of quantitative data (about the annual shopping habits of people in a particular zip code, for example).

This main distinction, going from the unilinear direction of messaging (from brand to customer in direct marketing) to the concentric, two-way conversations between brands and customers, and customers and customers, is what makes influencer marketing so special *and* complicated.

Think of influencer marketing as a multipronged conversation:

- ✔ **The audience talking to you:** In the past, marketing was as simple as brands talking to customers and prospects. Now, that audience can and does respond, telling you when you messed up, suggesting ways to make things better, and celebrating you when you get it right. And they expect you to acknowledge their input, immediately and specifically.

- ✔ **The audience talking to each other about you:** Not only can you talk to customers and prospects, but your customers and prospects can talk to *each other* about your brand, usually with stunning candor and specificity.

- ✔ **You and the audience listening to each other:** The great thing about all these open conversations is that you have free market research, delivered to in real time. The potentially scary thing is that your prospective customers get to see, hear, and take into account all the same positive and negative feedback that you see. They draw conclusions about the brand, based on the content of those conversations, and how responsive, respectful, and transparent you are.

Always be authentic. Your customers know your brand even better than you do. Don't try to fool them with fake positivity or by avoiding issues. They know when you're lying, and they'll tell everyone.

Consumers know that brands control the content of direct marketing, and that it's (understandably) biased. When they make purchase decisions, they want to evaluate content from a variety of trusted sources, not just the brand. By working directly with people who are influential — by trusting influencers to be advocates — brands reach an exponentially larger audience, with content that is seen as more authentic and credible.

It's Not Either/Or: Using Both Influencer and Direct Marketing to Meet Your Goals

Influencer marketing and direct marketing generate entirely different results. So, if you measure influencer marketing using direct marketing goals, you'll be disappointed.

The way to make sure you're measuring the right activity is to start with your goals. Is your target customer ready to get right down to business and convert to sales? Great! Design a direct marketing campaign and get ready to count your money. On the other hand, if your goal is to create awareness and consideration of your product in the market, then an influencer marketing campaign is right for you! Get ready to talk (and listen) to people who are excited about your brand and offering.

What about when your program goes both ways? Life is full of gray areas, and marketing programs reflect that. If you have the time, money, and opportunity, your marketing plan will include activations that overlap and support each other.

Here's an example: Dove #LoveMyCurls is a wide-ranging campaign from Unilever. Part of its larger initiative is to be known as an accessible and body-positive brand for women of all races. It cleverly incorporates a variety of marketing tactics including direct marketing elements like paid search (so people looking for products for curly hair will see a paid link to the Dove Love Your Curls website, as shown in Figure 14-2). This tactic is measured simply by how many people visit the site from the paid link.

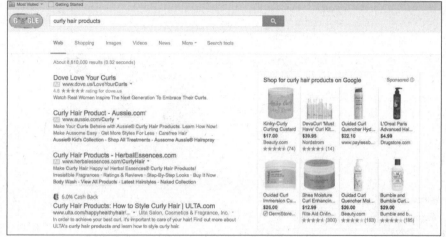

Figure 14-2:
Dove #Love-
MyCurls
paid search.

Source: www.google.com/ - q=curly+hair+products

On the Love Your Curls website (http://promo.dove.us/loveyourcurls),
visitors see an e-book called *Love Your Curls,* written by Taiye Selasi and illustrated by Annick Poirier (see Figure 14-3). Dove hired Ms. Selasi, a well-known
African-American author, to write the text, instead of developing the copy
in-house, because her influence lent cache and authenticity to the project. This
is an influencer marketing tactic, which Dove could measure by the volume
of activity: number of mentions or shares of her name in association with the
hashtag #LoveMyCurls.

Visitors to the website, many of whom likely had been pulled to the site via
paid search, can personalize and download the e-book. This is a straightforward and easily measured direct marketing type of conversion: how many
downloads of the e-book, and how many personalizations of the downloaded e-book.

In addition to the brand-produced e-book, Dove sent samples of their Dove
Quench Absolute range of curly hair products to beauty vloggers — women
who are influential with other women when they're trying to decide which
beauty products to buy. The resulting videos of influencers using and showcasing the pros and cons of the Dove Quench Absolute products, in a way
that is *not* controlled by the brand, was subsequently perceived as very
authentic to the viewers (see Figure 14-4).

This is classic influencer marketing and measured by activity — number of
views, number (and sentiment) of comments, and number of shares of the
videos on social channels like Facebook and Twitter.

Source: http://promo.dove.us/loveyourcurls

Figure 14-3:
Dove's download-able *Love Your Curls* e-book.

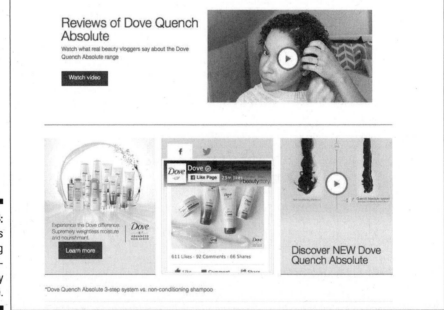

Figure 14-4:
Influencers showcasing Dove's curl-friendly product line.

Source: www.dove.us/Products/Hair/Advanced-Hair-Series/Quench-Absolute.aspx

Coupons: A one-night stand, not a marriage

One way you can measure conversions from influencer marketing is by including a coupon code and call to action to use it to buy the product. Some programs lend themselves to this type of hybrid layering, and give you another way to judge the effectiveness of your program. It's important to remember that, unlike with direct marketing programs, you have no control over who receives the coupon offer — so the conversion rates are lower to start. Plus, you'll probably reach people before they're ready to make a purchase. Reading a blog is a leisure activity that is usually separate from shopping.

If you're looking for a way to enrich an influencer marketing program, coupons are an interesting addition. Just don't fall into the trap of thinking they can change the primary goals and metrics of the program.

Cleverly, Dove helps those activity numbers by amplifying the videos on their own properties, including the official Dove website, and getting them in front of an optimized group of viewers, brought to the site by direct marketing methods.

This multilayered nature of real-life marketing initiatives demonstrates why it's so important to evaluate your tactics by the right metrics. Most people would agree that 26,000+ views of a non-celebrity beauty vlogger is *great* influencer activity. However, if you were to measure it by number of bottles of conditioner sold (conversions), you'd be disappointed. There's no way to track exactly who saw the video and then went out and bought the product. Fortunately, that's not how you measure influencer marketing.

Believing Your Results

As a marketer, you must constantly evaluate how effective your efforts are. After all, you're spending money, with the (ultimate) goal of making more money. Each marketing activity is a step on that journey from awareness to purchase and advocacy.

You have to measure against your goals, because you get what you measure. This is *often* true . . . but what about when it's not? For all the data and metrics, marketing is still more art than science. So marketers make educated guesses about what will work, and sometimes we guess wrong. Or we do something really well, but it works differently from what we expected.

Don't get hung up on the failure — or success — of your program. One of the great things about working with influencers is that everything is out there in real time. That means you know immediately if something didn't work, and you can get in there and address it immediately.

Much of influencer marketing happens as conversations. Which means that your response is as important as your initial activity. If something fails, ask "Why?" and "What could we do differently?" and use the answers to inform your next plan.

Very few marketing plans are "one-and-done" activations. Think of any program as a stage in a marathon. Your results tell you whether your tactics are working. If they aren't, you change them so you can be more successful in the next stage.

Of course, you may be the one in a million that gets it right the first time. Congratulations! The rest of us will be over here, interpreting our results and figuring out how we can do better next time.

Chapter 15

Setting and Measuring the Right Goals for Your Influencer Marketing Campaigns

*M*arketing helps sell stuff. It's the only reason to take the time and spend the money to do it. What makes marketing interesting — and often difficult — is that *how* you do marketing changes with social and technological advances.

Influencer marketing is about getting the right people interested in your products as the first of many nonlinear steps toward purchase activity. This approach is rapidly replacing the more traditional 1-2-3 of "Hey, this exists, you want/need it, now buy it here" of traditional — and particularly direct — marketing (see Chapter 14).

Influencer marketing is still on the bleeding edge. This concept is important to understand for marketers who work with social media in general, and with influencers in particular, because the landscape changes so dramatically, so quickly. What was true a year ago — never mind three years ago — is probably laughably out of date today.

In terms of evaluating the success of your influencer marketing programs, this means

- ✔ Old ways of measuring success don't really apply.
- ✔ New ways of measuring success are still in development.
- ✔ It's hard to know when to use which measurement.
- ✔ You wind up with a lot of trial and error.

Testing and Learning as You Go

The nice thing about using early-stage tactics like influencer marketing is that you aren't alone in your trial and error! Everyone is in the same boat and, generally speaking, willing to share war stories and best practices.

It may *feel* like there's a mysterious "right answer" out there, but believe us: Your competitors are struggling with the same challenges, trying to find benchmarks, struggling to understand how an activity connects to a sale, and whether they're getting it right or horribly wrong.

Don't be afraid to ask questions, and when you can, be generous with information about successes *and* failures. Our industry is young and we have a thrilling opportunity to shape it!

Measuring activity

The easiest, and at times the most relevant, way to measure a program is as simple as listing what you did. In old-school marketing, a campaign produced one piece of content. Influencer marketing produces multiple pieces of content, so the beginning of your success is an inventory of those many pieces. For example:

- ✔ Number of blog posts and comments
- ✔ Number of Facebook posts, comments, shares, and likes
- ✔ Number of Instagram posts, comments, and likes
- ✔ Number of tweets, retweets, favorites, and responses
- ✔ Number of impressions
- ✔ Number of hashtag incidents

This evaluation is purely quantitative, and it's deceptively simplistic. Getting people to engage with a brand is incredibly difficult. *Any* activity is a positive indicator, and from this perspective, the higher your volume of activity, the better your chances of getting a positive result.

If you have user-generated content — which is what all this activity boils down to — you have rich sources of information that

- Other people can use to evaluate your brand.
- You can use for customer research including brand sentiment or areas that need improvement.
- You can repurpose (for example, as Facebook ads or content on your own website).

None of this equals sales. So, if you have an influencer marketing campaign about exciting new flavors of potato chips, don't make the goal to sell a million bags of potato chips, because you're going to get posts, comments, likes, shares, and retweets and not one single sale that you can attribute to your influencer campaign. And that's okay!

Counting comments

You can control the first level of activity — for example, sponsoring influencers to produce a blog post, and then amplifying it on Facebook, Instagram, and Twitter.

The next level of activity — how people respond — is out of your hands, and once you get over the anxiety of this lack of control, it's that much more interesting. Do readers comment on the blog posts? If so, what do they say? How about a Facebook comment with a link that provokes a multiple-comment discussion string?

This second level of activity is where the volume can grow exponentially and tip over into that treasured and coveted virality. You can't control it, but one way to evaluate your program is to see how much of this second level — how many comments — your initial program generated.

The trend for where and how many comments has shifted over the years, and will certainly continue to evolve. In 2009, a popular blog post could garner 100+ comments. By 2015, the same blog post, which could get even more impressions, would be lucky to get ten comments — or even two! But, the Facebook post amplifying the blog post could easily see a mix of 150+ likes and 30 comments.

If only mentions equaled sales . . .

We admit it: Not being able to draw a straight line from a mention to a sale is frustrating. We know people buy things because they read a cool review, because they've told myriad market researchers that it's true. We also know because we all do it ourselves. It's logical. It's anecdotal. It's intuitive.

The problem is, none of these is a methodical, quantifiable reason to attribute activity to a sale.

But don't despair. This industry and discipline are still relatively young. New ways to listen to online activity appear on the horizon literally daily. Someday we'll be able to track activity to sales. We get closer every day!

Your first job as an influencer marketer is to understand the volume of activity and everywhere that it's happening. Then you can dig further and start to interpret what it all means.

A wildly successful campaign would be one in which customers respond to your paid influencer posts with a like, post selfies of themselves with the display in the supermarket, and use your campaign hashtag. But this amazing influencer marketing success *still* wouldn't equal sales . . . yet.

Understanding the Value of Your Influencer Marketing Activity Relative to the Cost

The current inability to say unequivocally that an influencer marketing campaign resulted in sales is a bitter, *bitter* pill for the folks paying for all this activity. This is especially true because brands are used to getting more tangible results for their money with older styles of marketing programs.

This is why it's important to understand your campaign activity, and to take the time to interpret the content of the activity into something meaningful in the context of your marketing and business goals. For example, say you want to sell a juice box, and you know that your best customers are women from 25 to 45, with children between 3 and 5. Your market research (either from paid sources, in-house observations, and analysis of client behavior, or from reading industry articles on trends) shows that this demographic spends a lot of time discussing food on Facebook, and posting pictures of lunches on Instagram. You decide to do a paid influencer campaign that includes blog reviews, which you have the influencers amplify on Facebook and Instagram. Their activity includes 50 blog posts, 50 Facebook posts, 50 Instagram posts, and 5 million impressions. That's 150 pieces of individual content that aligns with your brand that has an opportunity to reach 5 million sets of eyeballs.

Does it mean you sold a single juice box? No.

However, it *does* mean that you sent out a high volume of highly credible content promoting your brand that has an optimal chance of reaching the people most likely to buy your juice box. That's valuable!

Avoid assigning an arbitrary value to activity — for example, saying that a Facebook "like" is worth $124. The truth is that the value depends on a lot of factors, starting with your overall business goals and including the following:

- ✔ Your overall activity in the channel
- ✔ Your other marketing initiatives
- ✔ The goal of this particular program
- ✔ The budget for this program
- ✔ How big/small this program is relative to other programs
- ✔ What your competition is doing in this area

In this section, we cover how you measure and understand the value of your influencer marketing activity relative to your goals. *Return on investment* (ROI) is the traditional analysis of how many sales you get relative to how much money you spent. Because it's hard to quantify sales from influencer marketing programs, the measurement of return on engagement is often used instead. It evaluates the amount of activity generated by your program, as well as the qualitative benefit to your brand.

Return on investment

The traditional way to evaluate a return on investment is to subtract how much the campaign cost from how much you sold or got back. But you simply can't extrapolate that kind of data from influencer marketing campaigns.

But if your marketing activity is connected to your business goals (as it should be!), you can still establish value. Staying with the juice box example, maybe your business goal is $8 million in revenue. To reach this goal, you need to sell 10 million units. Market research shows that you need to reach

50 million of your target market to convert to that many units. This campaign cost $50,000, and got you to 10 percent of that goal, reaching 5 million impressions with your target market. Sounds pretty valuable, right?

The whole trick to return on investment is to have a clear understanding of how influencer marketing fits into the big picture of your business plan.

Return on engagement

Fortunately, the industry has developed a number of sophisticated ways to evaluate influencer marketing campaigns: to measure the *return on engagement* — exactly who saw your content and how much interaction your target market had with your content. Sure, they saw the content, but did they care?

As with so much of influencer marketing, there's no one formula to evaluate engagement. Elements to consider include, but are not limited to the following:

- ✔ **Likes, loves, and favorites:** Easy, built-in functionality that lets people demonstrate their interest or approval with one click.
- ✔ **Retweets and shares:** Easy to facilitate by adding a share button.
- ✔ **Time spent on the page or watching your video**
- ✔ **Repeat visitors, commenters, or engagers**
- ✔ **Positive (or negative) comments:** You should be reading and responding to these anyway.
- ✔ **Clicks on links or downloads**
- ✔ **How you stack up against your competitors:** If you have ten comments, and your competition has two, you're doing great! But if your competition has 100 comments, you have some work to do... .
- ✔ **Increase (or decrease) in any of the above over time and campaigns**

Return on hugs?

Influencer marketing is a new industry, a new discipline, and a developing methodology. That means you can be creative, you can learn as you go, and you can even make up stuff and be right — that's part of the excitement of using leading-edge techniques! By using them, you also get to create them.

At the same time, you'll find there are all kinds of "social media gurus" who are building careers on crazy "innovative" ways to evaluate your influencer marketing. One of the most pervasive of these "creative accounting" approaches is the idea that there is value in having a "relationship" with each one of your customers. We think this is silly.

Yes, you want to be attentive to your customers' needs. Yes, you must deliver service and products that satisfy customers, and bring them back for more. Yes, you want your users to become champions and advocates. Nope, they don't care if you like them back. Sorry.

We hate to be the one to tell you, but your customers and potential customers don't want you to be their "friend," and they don't want to be in a relationship with your brand — at least not in anything but the loosest, most commercial sense of the word. In many ways it's one-way relationship, where the brand does all the work, and the customer enjoys as much or as little interaction as they want.

This does not mean you can ignore your follows or friend requests, and you definitely need to respond to online comments and questions as soon as possible. Consumers will expect to see that brands are "following back" as a sign that you're engaged and listening.

The key word, though, is *listening*. Most people don't want to hear from you, even to acknowledge their birthdays, unless it's to give them a big discount or a cool free gift (that's a *cool* free gift, not some dumb pen or calendar with your logo on it). They care a lot more about what *they* think about your brand because it helps them define their profiles on social channels.

Don't lose sight of this fact. People get to mess around on social media for fun, or to communicate with friends, or to kill time, and play games. But the *only* reason for brands to be active on social media is if it helps you achieve business goals.

Interacting with your customers is a useful tactic because it gives you a direct line into how they feel about your product. It helps to build consideration and can get you in front of the right customers at the right time. Prior interaction can also buy you some leeway, if someone has a problem with your product or service. For example, if an influencer has worked with you and knows she can direct message you and get a response, there is a chance she'll approach you directly rather than complain in public . . . at least at first. But if your product lets them down, if your service stinks, if your competition has a better offer, no amount of "friendship" on social platforms will be able to fix that.

Remember: This is work. Would you expect a hug from your boss as part of your paycheck every two weeks? We didn't think so.

Measuring the Effect of Influencer Marketing Campaigns

Evaluating your influencer marketing efforts can be challenging. It's hard to know when you're doing it right, and it's frustrating when your stakeholders or even the voice inside your own head is asking, "But is this helping me sell anything?"

Keep your evaluation practical, specific, and in the context of your business goals, and you'll have an easier time hanging on to your sanity.

Setting expectations

The most important part of evaluating your influencer marketing programs actually happens long before you start any activity. Get all the stakeholders on the same page with the fact that you'll never be able to track the purchase path. You can't definitively say, "Yup, we sold 10 million units because of these ten blog posts!" Set the expectation that you're doing important, useful, valuable work, which sets the stage for all the wonderful sales to come.

Remind people that if your influencer marketing is done well, it opens the door to exponential growth.

And when you're struggling to explain why it's important to include a consistent hashtag on Twitter *and* Instagram, remember this: You can only close a deal if you start a conversation in the first place.

Top-heavy leads to happy endings: Seeing why you need a full funnel

You can't necessarily track the sales path from an influencer marketing program, but you *can* give yourself some credit for the sales that do happen. The sales cycle starts at the top of the funnel (see Chapter 13).

The better the quality of the leads in the top of your funnel, the better your eventual conversion rate. And influencer marketing is *great* at helping you reach the right people, with the right message, to make them aware of you and to consider your service or product.

Think of it this way: The sales cycle is a beautiful garden filled with white and purple daisies, bright marigolds, and multicolored zinnias. You're the gardener. In the spring, you get out your influencer marketing activities, which include preparing the soil (writing your plan), adding the right kinds of fertilizer (marketing), and planting all kinds of seeds (engaging with influencers and getting them to share their wonderful posts about you). You take care of those seeds by giving them more water if it's too dry (more attention) or less water if it's a rainy week (don't spam them!). When the beautiful flowers bloom (those are sales), you can tell by the flower which type of seed you planted. In this example, let's say daisies were blog posts, marigolds were Instagram, and zinnias are Twitter. So you know which type of program produced which flower, but it's impossible to look into the ground to see which individual seed turned into that gorgeous bloom. You just needed to plant enough seeds, and take good enough care of them, and they bloomed!

Consider your influencer programs the same way. Do enough of them, do them well, notice which flowers bloom best under which conditions, and do more of that!

Part V
Creating Stellar Influencer Marketing Campaigns

Find out how to connect emotionally with your audience in an article at
www.dummies.com/extras/influencermarketing.

In this part . . .

- ✔ Discover the six secrets to influencer marketing success
- ✔ Find out how to elevate any product from boring to engaging through influencer marketing.
- ✔ Learn how to handle an influencer marketing campaign that goes off the rails.
- ✔ Check out the brands that are winning at influencer marketing.

Chapter 16

The Six Secrets to Influencer Marketing Success

*I*n this chapter, we provide six secrets to help you set up your influencer marketing programs for success.

Note: This chapter assumes that you're familiar with previous chapters of this book, which explain in detail how to set up a typical influencer marketing campaign — from goal setting to vetting influencers to gathering metrics. If you're diving into this chapter without having read anything else, feel free to continue, but come back and read it again, after you know how to set up a campaign.

Throughout this chapter, we use our award-winning Batkid influencer marketing campaign (see the nearby sidebar, "Batkid to the rescue!") to help us illustrate our secrets. But we didn't do anything differently for Batkid than we do for all our other clients. What makes a great social media campaign is true across the board. And when you have an amazing story to tell, one that people want to participate in, magic happens!

Batkid to the rescue!

Batkid is the superhero name of Miles Scott, a child and cancer survivor who is in remission. His wish was to be Batkid, a sidekick of the eponymous comic book superhero Batman, the subject of books, radio, TV shows, and films. When Clever Girls created the social media plan and began tweeting requests, thousands of volunteers, city officials, businesses, and supporters rallied to turn San Francisco into "Gotham City," the fictional hometown of Batman, on November 15, 2013, for one of the largest and most elaborate Make-A-Wish Foundation projects ever staged. #Batkid and #SFBatkid were the two hashtags people used on social media (mainly Twitter and Instagram) to tag their posts and show their support. Check out our video at `https://youtu.be/nziKNmmJGgU` to learn more about the campaign.

Secret #1: Set Realistic Campaign Goals

Campaign goal setting is important. Why? Because influencer marketing without goals is a waste of time. And influencer marketing without being tied to business goals is an even *bigger* waste of time. Just as you wouldn't make a capital expenditure without assessing your business need, you wouldn't spend money on an influencer marketing campaign unless your end goal was to move your business forward. In this section, we walk you through a series of questions to ask yourself in order to set realist goals for your campaign.

"Going viral" is not a goal

"We need a viral video!"

"Make it go viral!"

We can't tell you how many times we've heard from our industry peers that their clients, influenced by the constant barrage of viral videos shared via social media, want all their social media programs to "go viral" and think that virality is the key to brand marketing success.

Wanting a campaign to "go viral" is not a viable campaign goal. Going viral isn't realistic — and, besides, it often doesn't map to business goals like engagements or sales. What you want to do is set practical, measurable campaign goals that will (maybe) set you up for virality, but more important, help you achieve your sales and/or marketing goals, whether you go viral or not.

What are you trying to achieve?

When preparing for an influencer marketing campaign, think about what the overall purpose is. For example, is your campaign:

- ✔ Launching your new company, product, or brand
- ✔ Sharing a charitable initiative
- ✔ Amplifying a special offer, like a coupon
- ✔ Promoting a contest or sweepstakes
- ✔ Advertising an event

Your purpose might be one of the above, a combination, or all of the above. Whatever the case may be, start by thinking about what your marketing need is and how influencers will fit into that plan.

When we created the social media plan for Batkid we knew that when a major news event happens in real time, it gains traction and is shared and reshared on Twitter. Twitter, at the time of the Batkid campaign, was the best social channel to get the word out and let people know where and how to support Miles, so our entire social program was based on "advertising" the event on Twitter. We used our network of influencers to get the initial word out on Twitter, and it spread from there.

How will you assess your achievements?

After the purpose of your campaign is set, you need to decide how you'll assess your achievements by selecting a few measurable targets. These targets can be anything you want — from the number of people who download a coupon to how many times a tweet is shared (tracking via your unique hashtag) — as long as they're tied to sales or marketing goals (see Chapter 15).

If you've never done an influencer campaign before, set some metrics so that you can gather baseline data about your campaign, and then use that baseline data to gauge future campaign success.

Here are some suggested targets to get you started:

- ✔ The number of visits to your website
- ✔ The number of increased Twitter, Pinterest, YouTube, and/or Facebook followers
- ✔ The number of likes, comments, and/or shares a Facebook post gets

✔ The percentage of increase in sales due to a coupon or promo code

✔ The number of tickets sold to an event based on a trackable URL

✔ Increase in foot traffic to your retail store

✔ Brand awareness (more people talking about you online)

✔ Better data on your customers

One of the main reasons why it's important to have business goals is so that you can track your return on investment (ROI). Influencer marketing isn't free, and as with any marketing program you run, you want to make sure that the data you gather supports your spend.

How will you achieve your goals?

When you've decided on the purpose of your campaign and how you'll measure your achievements, you need to think about how you're going to git 'er done! Here are the main questions you need to answer:

✔ Do you have the time, expertise, and resources within your organization to not only create your influencer marketing campaign, but also find, vet, and hire the right influencers for the job?

✔ Are you familiar enough with social media analytics to gather and measure the data you'll be collecting?

✔ Would you rather hire expert consultants and/or agencies to do the creative work, manage the influencers, and/or collect the data?

How you answer these questions probably depends on the timing of your influencer marketing campaign, your marketing needs, and your budget. If you're in a hurry, you may want to hire outside help — but keep in mind that most agencies require several weeks of lead time and may charge a quick turn fee if you need a campaign to run sooner.

If you aren't on a timeline, you may want to budget to hire a creative team, which includes a staffer who is knowledgeable about influencer or content marketing or an analytics expert. Think about what's best for your company and your needs, and go from there.

When will the campaign run?

The timing of your influencer campaign is very important. Think about when you'd like your campaign to run. Is it seasonal? Does it correspond to a holiday? Is it tied to an event you're promoting?

Let's take a month-long holiday campaign as an example. You have a product that would make a fabulous holiday gift. Ideally, you want to start promoting that product in November having your influencers marketing your product all month long in advance of the holiday shopping rush. If you're in the United States, you may want to launch your campaign around Thanksgiving and capitalize on the Black Friday or Cyber Monday shopper mindset.

Working backward from there, this means your influencers should be familiar with your product and know what their scope of work is (exactly what's expected of them and what they'll be sharing) and have all assets and materials needed (product photos, videos, and/or descriptions) by the date of your program launch. This means that the creative for your campaign — including goals, assets, and influencer scope of work — needs to be completed at least three to four weeks in advance of influencer selection, vetting, and hiring (including getting all employment contracts signed). Depending on the number of influencers you're hiring, that process alone can take two additional weeks even with experienced professionals doing the selection and vetting.

Six weeks in advance of your November campaign launch puts you in mid-September, which means you should already be thinking about plans to lock down your influencer marketing holiday promotion in the summer.

Even if your influencer marketing campaign isn't tied to a holiday, you should give yourself at least two months to come up with a plan, set goals, figure out how you're going to achieve them, and begin gathering your data. When you've done all that, you're ready to launch your influencer marketing campaign.

Secret #2: Know Your Audience

The second secret to setting your influencer marketing campaign up for success is knowing who is talking about you and where your potential customers are.

Who's talking about you?

If your company has a social media presence, you need to know where your audience — fans and potential customers — is talking about you. Do you have a product or service that people tweet about or share about on blogs? Or are lively conversations happening on your Facebook page? Before starting any influencer program, take the time to investigate and listen in on conversations already happening about your company, product, industry, and/or competitors on social media and focus on who's doing the talking.

How to introduce yourself to an influencer without seeming like a spammer

It's easier than ever to reach out to the influencers you want to work with, but doing it without coming off as a spammer . . . now that's another story. Here are our top suggestions for contacting influencers without turning them off:

✔ **Research the influencer's blog or social media account to see if she does sponsored posts.** If she doesn't, that doesn't necessarily mean she's not interested in starting, but it might be a sign she's not interested.

✔ **Use the influencer's the real name (not her social media handle).** Don't start emails with "Dear Fashion Blogger."

✔ **Show that you're deeply familiar with the influencer's content, interests, and values.** The more specific you can make your message — and the less generic — the better.

✔ **Show that a real person is reaching out.** Infuse your outreach with humor and personality. Don't send a generic tweet or email that makes it seem as if you send 100 notes per day.

Grassroots conversations may already be happening about your brand. Get to know those influencers. Introduce yourself to them, whether via a hello tweet or by leaving a comment on a blog post, as a way to begin a relationship (see the nearby sidebar). People who are already talking about your brand on social media are your *organic influencers*. They have the power to affect your brand in positive or negative ways. Establishing an authentic relationship with them — where you engage their opinions and ideas — is a way to keep their view of your company or brand positive. And when you're ready to start your influencer marketing campaign, you can contact these influencers first to see if they'd like to participate.

Where are they talking about you?

It's not just who is talking about you, but *where*. When you see where the most engaged social media interactions are happening, you can target your influencer marketing campaign to those particular channels.

For example, if you're a fashion or beauty brand, you may want to focus your influencer marketing on Instagram, like Jimmy Choo (www.instagram.com/jimmychoo), Motives Cosmetics (www.instagram.com/motivescosmetics), Flash Tattoos (www.instagram.com/flashtattoos), or Christian Siriano (www.instagram.com/csiriano). All those brands leverage Instagrammers to share their content.

It makes no sense, for example, to focus on Pinterest for an influencer campaign if you sell cloud services. Pinterest is a visual channel, so it lends itself to sharing visual content like recipes, workout ideas, decorating tips, and fashion inspiration.

With our Batkid campaign, we knew Twitter was the best place for people to follow along with a live event. This was the biggest nondisaster local event to happen online, and Twitter helped it to go viral.

Know where your audience lives. If no one is talking about fundraising on Instagram, you're wasting your time doing your campaign there.

Secret #3: Stay on Message

We often joke that our first question when starting any influencer marketing campaign is, "What's the hashtag?" The key message is just as important as the goal, and making sure that everything you do drives activity back to your key message matters. If your marketing plan is a rocket ship, your messaging is the flight plan and social media is the rocket fuel.

Marketing plan = Rocket ship

We love to use the rocket ship analogy when talking about influencer marketing (see Chapter 14). Just as you wouldn't attempt to explore space without a rocket ship, you shouldn't engage in influencer marketing without a plan.

With our Batkid campaign, we made sure that our influencer marketing plan laid out all the social media activity for the entire week leading up to the event — including all the posts we asked our influencers to share — as well as an almost minute-by-minute script for all the social media activity for the entire day itself.

Messaging = Flight plan

With your rocket ship in place, you need a flight plan to get to space, and that's exactly the purpose of your message. What will you be asking your influencers to do? Share a coupon code? Tweet a link for a charitable donation? Post a photo? Whatever it is, your influencer marketing flight plan needs to have one clear, consistent message. Pick one call-to-action so you don't confuse your influencers and/or your potential customers.

For Batkid, our hashtag, #SFBatkid, was essential to our messaging and we put it on everything — every Tweet, every Facebook post, every Instagram photo, and every blog post. We also had one URL that drove everyone back to the Greater Bay Area Make-A-Wish Foundation website, where interested parties could find all the information about Batkid and how to participate in the day (whether in person or online), as well as how to make a donation. The message in all the social media activity was clear: Click here and you'll find everything you need to know.

Social media = Rocket fuel

You've built your rocket ship and your flight plan is solid. Now it's time to take off! The social media channels where your influencer marketing campaign will live are the rocket fuel you need to send your campaign into outer space. By tracking where your influencer conversations are already happening, and by leveraging those channels, you'll be able to give your influencer marketing campaign the fuel it needs to take off. Influencers will be sharing your content in the channels where it makes the most sense, and you'll be able to leverage the influencers' audiences or communities within those channels to spread your message far and wide.

A marketing plan is your rocket ship, and social media is the rocket fuel that sends it to outer space or somewhere amazing. Without a plan, without a ship, you just have a bunch of liquid that can catch fire and burn down your launcher.

Secret #4: Be Agile

It's important to have an influencer marketing plan in place, but be sure to build in contingencies just in case Plan A doesn't work out as planned.

Say you have two dozen influencers contracted to write blog posts, but what happens if three of them get sick, one person's laptop dies, and another has a family emergency and can't complete her work by your deadline? Hopefully, you've also identified five backup influencers who can step in and take their places to get your job done. Even with the best laid plans, anything that can go wrong often will go wrong, but it doesn't have to be a disaster if you're prepared.

For our Batkid project, backup plans were essential. Miles was 5 years old at the time, and on his wish day, he had a packed schedule of rescuing damsels and foiling villains. Just *reading* his schedule was exhausting. Anyone who has a 5-year-old knows that not everything goes according to plan — even on a normal, low-key day. What if Miles didn't want to get out of his Batkidmobile? What if he was afraid of the crowds? What if he wanted a post-lunch nap? The Greater Bay Area Make-A-Wish chapter had contingency plans in place to account for any eventuality, and that meant we needed to be agile as well.

Our main goal in advance of Miles's wish day was to make sure the #SFBatkid hashtag was trending on Twitter before the day started. In case it wasn't trending, we planned a Twitter party for that morning, before the events started, to jumpstart the hashtag and get it trending. #SFBatkid was already trending the night before, so we didn't need to have the Twitter party, but we did it anyway. In this case, Plan B wasn't needed but it's good that we had it in our back pocket.

Don't feed the trolls: How to handle damage control

One of the things we hear from our clients is their fear that, once their messaging is in the hands of influencers, they won't be able to control it anymore. The message is sent out into the social mediasphere where it has the potential to engage people who aren't fans of the brand or message. You can help protect your product, initiative, or service from *trolls* (Internet bad guys — or just really loud critics) in several ways:

- **Make sure your company hasn't had any bad press recently.** Has your product been the subject of a recall? Are you in the middle of a sticky lawsuit? Did your product have a glitch or virus that left lots of people unhappy? Maybe you should postpone your influencer marketing campaign until your brand isn't so exposed.

- **Hire exactly the right influencers for your campaign.** Influencers who are fans or potential fans of your brand are professional and will often be your best cheerleaders, evangelists, and/or explainers if their posts encounter negative attention from trolls. Make sure they're armed with correct information, and let them do their job.

- **Don't feed the trolls with emotional responses.** Engage carefully and respectfully with trolls — even and especially if they aren't being respectful. Your audience is watching, and they're paying attention to how your brand conducts itself on social media. If a troll is spreading untrue information, state the correct information (or a link to the correct information) across social media. You don't have to have the last word, you just have to have the correct word.

As the day went on, we noticed that people had started using the #Batkid hashtag in addition to the #SFBatkid hashtag. By the end of the day, we noticed that #Batkid seemed to have replaced #SFBatkid altogether. We were tracking the success of our campaign by monitoring mentions of the #SFBatkid hashtag so what were to do? When we noticed the dual hashtag use, we immediately reached out to our metrics partner, Simply Measured (www.simplymeasured.com), and let them know to track that hashtag as well. In the end, we were able to gather data and analytics on both hashtags and used that information in our reporting.

Secret #5: Recognize the Power of Emotional Stories

Emotions — from awe and anger to sadness and joy — make content go viral. You want to set up your influencer marketing campaign to go viral, but Psy is busy making another video (plus you can't afford to pay him) and your cat is camera shy. How to create a compelling story that people will want to share? Start with a story people will care about!

Batkid was a ready-made amazing story, so it's no surprise that people felt compelled to share. Who can't relate to the concept of good versus evil or sympathize with a 5-year-old cancer survivor who wants to be a superhero?

If you want your influencer marketing campaign to be set up for virality, you *must* create an emotional angle for your story. What emotion will your brand story elicit? Will it play on humor? Or will you aim to inspire? Brands have spent millions of dollars on creative concepts and marketing plans to ensure virality. If you don't have millions of dollars to spend, you have to come up with a compelling story, formulate a solid plan, and identify the right influencers to help spread your message. Then hope for the best.

Beyond the emotions of virality, two other factors are at play:

- ✔ Good viral content tugs at the heartstrings or makes people feel something, and that's not necessarily tied to any of the emotions we mention earlier.

- ✔ Good viral content is relatable. Content is contagious when people want to feel a part of the story and then share it not only because they relate, but because something about the sharing is a reflection on them as well. President Obama congratulated Batkid for saving Gotham City in a Vine video (see Figure 16-1), generating nearly 50,000 likes and more than 4,000 comments!

Figure 16-1:
President
Obama's
Vine video.

Source: https://vine.co/v/htbdjZAPrAX

Secret #6: You Get What You Measure

Marketing — especially in new spaces and platforms — is *iterative,* which means you make changes and adjust as you go. What worked? How do you do it more? How do you scale? You can answer all these questions by setting goals for your campaigns and tracking those goals. In that sense, you get data from what you measure (see "How will you assess your achievements?" earlier in this chapter).

Let's say the goal for your month-long holiday influencer marketing campaign was to track the number of visits to your website and to sell more of your product by sharing a coupon code across social media. Your influencer marketing plan should focus on having influencers share a link to your website where people can then find a coupon code to use toward a purchase. Before you start your month-long influencer marketing campaign, gather some baseline information about your website traffic and know your typical sales numbers for your product. By the end of the your month-long promotion, you'll check your site traffic and look at your sales numbers.

You get what you measure — and hopefully the results are what you were expecting!

Chapter 17

Putting It All Together

· ·

In This Chapter

▶ Exercising your creativity

▶ Making magic with your personal insights

▶ Avoiding the controversial

▶ Managing "crazy"

· ·

***W**ahoo!* You've read our guide, picking up all sorts of useful ideas, and now you're ready to tackle your influencer marketing programs with gusto! Time to have some fun!

Of course, no one will care if your marketing efforts are "fun" if they don't produce real results. But the best part about social media marketing is that *fun* tends to equal *effective*.

Think you're ready to have some fun? Of course, you are!

Getting Creative and Letting Go

Social media is a loud, crowded space full of millions of people talking over each other. Standing out isn't easy! Engaging influencers to create content that resonates with their audience is a great first step — you know their audiences are receptive. But even the most loyal influencer fan will click or tap to something else if the content they're seeing is something they've seen a million times before. No one wants content that is stale, boring, corporate, or lame.

As with all social media advertising, creating great content is tricky because users are savvy. They don't want to be sold to. They don't want advertising that feels like advertising. At the same time, they don't want to feel "tricked" into reading or engaging with content that is sponsored but tries too hard to pass itself off as non-sponsored.

FTC guidelines require disclosure of sponsored content! Be sure to visit www.ftc.gov for the most recent guidelines on how to properly disclose influencer endorsements on social media.

The happy medium with influencer marketing is in developing a great campaign outline and then letting influencers take over, doing what they do best. In this section, we show you how.

Walking the walk

To be successful at influencer marketing — or social media marketing of any kind — you must stay on top of Internet trends. (Many marketers outsource influencer marketing for this very reason!) You wouldn't hire someone to produce a TV commercial if that person had never seen a TV commercial before, would you? Similarly, you can't run an influencer marketing campaign if you've never seen one, and you can't just guess at what kind of influencers and content will work on social media platforms if you aren't paying attention to them.

Start by expanding your own social networks. How many people *follow you* is far less important than how many people *you follow*. Listen, post, and interact on Twitter and Facebook. Use Instagram every day. Find some Tumblr accounts you enjoy and follow them. Join Reddit. Spend time researching trending topics. If you don't understand a hashtag, click it and find out what the story is. Start using the language yourself.

While you're poking around social media, you'll run into countless "gurus" and experts and people whose only job online is to offer advice. You may benefit from following them, but you'll likely benefit *more* simply by becoming a savvy social media participant yourself. It's about a million times easier to answer the question "What would make this blog post interesting for readers?" if you're a blog reader yourself!

You don't have to be an expert, but you should at least try to understand what's happening in social media by downloading popular apps (for example, Periscope, Snapchat, Whatsapp, and Tinder) and/or talking to people who use them regularly to become versed in what's cool.

Yes, you have to know what's cool. Cool is critical to social media and influencer marketing success. If you're not trendy, you're not relevant.

Are we having fun yet?

For some reason, marketers seem to completely forget how they behave online, and end up creating content they'd never pay attention to themselves.

Social media is, above all, social. It's about connecting, reaching out to people we know in real life and online , and sharing our human experiences through stories and photos. The only way to interject brand stories among all the nonbranded ones is to make them as real and unbrandlike as possible. This doesn't mean you should create programs that are *so* far from your brand or brand message that no one will notice (or remember!) what your brand even is. But there are definitely ways to get out of "corporate box" thinking.

When you're immersed in social media culture, pay attention to your personal trends and preferences:

- ✔ What content do you click on each day?
- ✔ Which headlines spark your interest most often?
- ✔ What content do you actually share?
- ✔ What content do you ignore?
- ✔ What's the last piece of sponsored content you read?

When you can answer those questions, you're on your way to building influencer marketing programs that will pass the cool test!

In the following sections, we walk you through an example of taking an everyday product and transforming an influencer marketing campaign from "boring" (irrelevant) to "fun" (relevant and engaging).

Dental floss is boring

Say you've been tasked with engaging influencers as part of a new product launch for dental floss. Assuming that the program goals and success metrics have already been mapped out, your job is to guide influencers into creating content. About dental floss.

We'd be hard-pressed to think of a more boring blog post than one that outlines the features and benefits of dental floss. A product review of dental floss? Not only would you, as a reader, *never* click that post, but what kind of influencer would be happy to write it?

If you secretly think dental floss is boring, everyone else will think it's boring, too. So, how do you create an influencer marketing program around dental floss that's fun? Start with the questions above and try to make your answers work around a dental floss theme. (Yes, really!)

Making dental floss fun

We started considering what *we* find fun about social media, what type of content *we* share, and we came up with some sample ideas for a dental floss program. Now, we aren't saying all these ideas are good, but they are an illustration of how to get creative and fun with even the most mundane of topics:

- We love to share DIY content! We could ask influencers to showcase other uses for floss, encouraging them to take a creative, DIY spin on a product usually relegated to the bathroom: weaving, making jewelry, dipping floss in paints and decorating jars, dangling cat toys, and so on.

- Recipes are always popular. Why make a special trip to the store for cooking twine when dental floss works just as well for trussing roasted chicken or turkey? There are many ways dental floss can be used in cooking techniques that influencers could illustrate, encouraging new ways for consumers to keep dental floss top-of-mind.

- Getting kids to floss regularly can be really tough. We could ask influencers to share their best tips and tricks to getting their kids to floss regularly, sharing their secret bathroom charts or incentives, plus lots of pictures of really cute kids!

- We could create completely unscientific "flosser profiles" and then develop a "What Kind of Flosser Are You?" type of quiz that people love to fill out.

- Maybe the goal is to make dental floss a more prominent aspect of everyday grooming among consumers. We could ask influencers to showcase new ways in which they're willing to display their floss. Why do soaps and toothbrushes get all the fancy bathroom display tools? Why can't floss be proudly displayed on the bathroom sink as well?

- Best songs to floss to? We could ask influencers to name, or even come up with alternate lyrics to, their favorite songs — songs that they sing to themselves in their heads while flossing so they know they're spending enough time on the job. We could even host a contest for the best song/lyrics for flossing your teeth to!

Go for it!

Not to get too philosophical, but when it comes down to it, the real reason brands don't do a better job of embracing influencer marketing is because they're scared. They're afraid of losing control of their brand's message. What the brands don't realize, however, is that people are using social media to talk about them — whether the brands are participating or not.

Still, this fear of loss of control compromises influencer campaigns that could otherwise be great. To those brands and marketers we say: Let it go!

Don't be afraid to be real

If you're paying attention to us, you're immersing yourself in social media. You're following and interacting with influencers you want to engage professionally. You see what they're posting.

In our earlier example, we encouraged influencers to think of and post creative uses for dental floss. No, ours isn't a traditional approach to promoting dental floss, and probably the brand's manager expects the entire marketing campaign to focus on bathroom-only messaging. But that's so corporate! And everyone knows what dental floss is for. No one will pay attention to a boring bathroom-only program. Not on social media, anyway. But using dental floss for crafts? That's unexpected. That's something people would be interested in. That's a real-life hack and something people on social media are likely to find useful.

So what's "real"? Think of it this way: Would you tell your friend about it? We're not going to tell anyone about a new dental floss just because there's a new dental floss on the market. (In truth, that would be weird! "Hey, buddy! Did you hear about this new dental floss?"). But you might share a fun craft you did with your kid that turned out great and that you photographed and that, oh, hey, happened to use dental floss.

Let the influencers influence

If you're all tapped out of "real" or "cool" ideas but you really want a fantastically successful influencer marketing program, *ask the influencers what kind of posts they'd like to create!*

No one knows an influencer's audience better than the influencer does. Influencers are successful because they create great content. Don't be afraid to let them take the lead! Tell them what your program goals are and ask them how they think they could best achieve your objective.

The influencers care just as much about their posts as you do. They have a reputation to uphold, and they can't come across as inauthentic to their readers. They are (presumably) being paid for the work that they're doing for you. They want to please you because they want to work with you — and other brands — again.

Giving minimal guidance to the influencers and letting them do their thing often results in diverse, interesting, compelling programs that truly engage audiences.

What If It All Goes Wrong?

Brands still worry about handing their precious brand messaging keys over to influencers. *What happens if the bloggers go crazy on us?* We've all heard horror stories of brands failing to use social media correctly, and having the Internet come after them like an angry mob. It does happen from time to time.

The good news is that avoiding Internet disasters isn't difficult! Brands that find themselves in hot water usually do so because they aren't paying attention, or because they forget that social media is a live medium, which means if you put something out there you need to be prepared to respond. Social media and social media marketing isn't a one-way street — you need to be prepared to engage with your consumers as soon as they offer you feedback, even if it's not positive.

Preventing a crisis

No form of social media marketing, including influencer marketing, can be 100 percent brand-safe. Even the most carefully selected influencers following guidelines to a completely innocuous program may have a commenter who says something unkind about the brand. That's okay! This is what makes the medium so real. And truly, a few negative comments here and there aren't a big issue.

Internet backlash from influencer marketing programs occurs for a finite number of reasons. Here's how to prevent this kind of backlash:

- **Don't try to hide the fact that you're working with influencers, or that the influencers are being compensated.** Always be transparent! Besides, the FTC requires that you be honest about this stuff — whether you get backlash or not from consumers, you don't want to be fined by the FTC.

- **Don't underestimate the intelligence of your influencers' audiences.** If your brand or service is controversial, even just among a small group of people, the influencers' audiences may bring this controversy to light. Don't use influencers to try to "spin" something negative into a positive if the positive spin is disingenuous.

  If you do have a product or service that is known to draw Internet ire, do your best to warn the influencers ahead of time.

✔ **Don't hop on social media memes — like using trending hashtags on Twitter — without doing research!** Too many brands use hashtags without researching their origins. Don't ask your influencers to participate in trendy memes or use hashtags if they're appropriating or "hijacking" them from meaningful conversations.

✔ **Be careful, courteous, honest, and professional in all your communications with influencers.** Not all influencers will show you the same respect, but it's always worth it to err on the side of caution. Ask yourself, "What if this blogger decided to post the content of my email to her site?"

✔ **Don't engage influencers in programs that encourage "bad" behavior on the influencers' part or their audiences' part.** For instance, programs where the influencer who get the most votes wins can get downright ugly. In an attempt to get votes, some influencers may start spamming their networks, or find creative ways to get people to vote for them. Meanwhile, influencers who don't get enough votes may feel jealous and/or make accusations of their fellow influencers, and the whole program can end poorly, overshadowed by the angst and anger of the participants.

✔ **If you're asking influencers to review your product and you're afraid of what they'll write if they don't like it, know your options.** If the product isn't great, influencer marketing is probably not the best way to go. If you don't really want influencers to share their honest opinions, don't engage them. You'd basically be asking them to lie for you, and that damages everyone's reputation.

If the product *is* good but you worry about influencer feedback, be upfront about how you would like them to handle it. Don't say, "You may only post your opinion about our product if you like it." ***Remember:*** You aren't compensating people to write good things. Instead, say, "If you were unhappy with this product for any reason, we'd love to hear your feedback directly. We want to know how we can improve it! You're welcome to share your balanced feedback in your post, or you may choose not to post at all." Give them the option of not posting. Consider compensating them regardless.

✔ **Cease all influencer marketing activity across social channels when there is a national or international crisis.** From a brand management standpoint, you don't want influencers touting a product amid sensitive posts about a national tragedy. You don't want your "Fun, flirty looks for spring" mascara tweets next to a tweet from someone who's openly mourning.

Managing a crisis (if it happens anyway)

If you follow our guidelines, you'll deftly avoid any real controversies online. However, on the slim chance that something does go off-kilter with your influencers, we've got you covered:

- ✔ **Respond immediately.** The longer you remain silent, the worse the situation can get. Don't launch an influencer marketing campaign (or *any* social media campaign) if you don't have the resources to monitor it in real time. If someone or something goes off the rails, you need to have someone on hand to respond right away. If the crisis is big and requires more executive-level response than you can give immediately, at least acknowledge that there is a problem and you're looking into it.

- ✔ **Respond with honesty.** Don't lie about how long the issue will take to resolve, or say that the issue was unforeseen if it wasn't. That will only make matters worse.

- ✔ **Apologize.** The internet has a terrible memory! The faster you apologize for whatever started the negativity in the first place, the faster the audience will move on to something else. Negative situations usually get worse when a brand argues with its customers, and the same holds true for influencers and their audiences.

Make sure your apologies are sincere and actual apologies. Don't use words like *if* and *but*. For instance, saying "We're sorry if we offended anyone" is troublesome for two reasons:

- • If you're making an apology because people were offended, there is no need to say "if."

- • Phrases like this suggest that the blame lies with the people who are offended as opposed to the offender.

This may seem like splitting hairs, but bad apologies can add fuel to Internet firestorms.

Try to make your apologies personal. If a program somehow offended many people, do your best to apologize to those people directly, not just in a single blanket statement they may not see. If your influencers are the ones fending off negativity, support them publicly and privately. Publicly, defend your influencers on their posts (by acknowledging the negative comments and apologizing on behalf of the influencer). Privately, email the influencers and offer them support.

None of these steps should be necessary if you've taken the proper care to avoid risky programs in the first place. ***Remember:*** The influencers want their programs to be as successful as you do. You're in this together!

Chapter 18

Five Pros Doing It Right

· ·

In This Chapter

▶ Looking at companies that are nailing influencer marketing

▶ Learning from the very best

· ·

*W*hen it comes to influencer marketing, the five brands in this chapter have mastered it with their recent campaigns. In this chapter, we tell you what they did and what elements made those campaigns such successes.

Case Study: Ford Fiesta

When Ford came out with its 2014 Fiesta, it turned to consumers for all elements of its campaign, including TV, print, and digital. After a successful first pass at user-generated content for its 2009 Fiesta Movement campaign, Ford decided to give its consumers even more say this time around.

Back in 2009, Ford asked its consumers to enter to be one of 100 influencers who would receive a Fiesta for free for six months. Those who were selected participated in monthly challenges and posted about their experiences on blogs, YouTube, and their social media channels. According to *Adweek,* that first Ford Fiesta influencer campaign resulted in 6,000 presales of the car, with 6.2 million YouTube views, 40 million impressions, and 50,000 pieces of content. So, when Fiesta came around again, Ford decided to go even bigger with the user-generated content by making it the first campaign in the auto industry to be *entirely* user generated.

What they did

Ford started out the campaign the same way as it did in 2009: by selecting 100 influencers who would each receive a free Ford Fiesta with covered gas and insurance costs. This time it would be for eight months instead of the original six. In addition to selecting just consumers, this time Ford also featured a few celebrities and some of the influencers who participated in the 2009 Fiesta Movement. Like the first time, the influencers participated in monthly challenges, but only a few involved the Fiesta. Monthly themes revolved around different aspects of the car's appeal and personality. These included adventure, travel, tech, entertainment, healthy living, and social activism. The original content was then used for TV and online commercials, digital ads, social ads, and even print ads for an entire year. Ford curated all the user-generated content on a microsite at `www.fiestamovement.com`.

Why it worked

By not including the Fiesta in each challenge, Ford could subtly promote the vehicle without bashing consumers over the head with it, which ultimately leads to annoyance and inauthenticity. Scott Monty, global head of social media for Ford, told *Forbes* that based on the 2009 experience, the brand wanted to emphasize lifestyle elements "rather than be in your face about product features." He also added that it's a more powerful approach because when people buy cars, especially people in the Fiesta's target demographic, they're interested in what it can do to support their lifestyle and not so much about specific product features. A key tactic to support this strategy was calling for content that would make the users look "cool or funny by discovering a piece of content," because consumers aren't excited to just talk about product features.

Another lesson that Ford learned the first year they asked for user-generated content was that the professionals could only help so much. When something is truly user generated, they couldn't polish it up too well or it would defeat the purpose. That's why, the second time around, Ford took a step back in the production of the content. However, the influencers were all made aware of the messaging that aligns with the Ford Fiesta brand and values. In addition to the advantage of the content being more authentic because it isn't overly produced, Ford also saved money on the production costs — a win-win situation.

Because Ford hadn't sold as many Fiestas in 2009 as it had hoped, the 2013 campaign was supported by paid TV. Although the creative content was drawn from the user-generated material, the paid TV ads also had features messaging intended to drive consumers to the showroom to make a purchase.

In the end, the 2013 campaign was another success. YouTube brand management software Octoly reports that the campaign earned 203 million organic views (versus only 21 million views of the Fiesta videos on its official channels).

Case Study: Lay's Do Us a Flavor

In 2006, Frito-Lay launched its first Do Us a Flavor campaign in which it called for users to help Lay's develop its next new chip flavor. The campaign has now been repeated in 14 different countries.

What they did

The Do Us a Flavor campaign had a highly successful run in the U.K. where many people submitted ideas by mail. In 2012, Do Us a Flavor came to the United States, and instead of mailing in ideas, Americans would use the power of social media to make submissions. The campaign involved an online app that lived on a Lay's microsite (see Figure 18-1 for a screenshot of the microsite). Participants would go to the site to name their flavor, choose the key ingredients, and then write a description or inspiration for the flavor. For those who needed a little push of inspiration, the app also had a Flavorizer component that featured celebrity chef Michael Simon. Chef Simon could recommend a flavor based on people's Facebook profiles by aggregating their posts and photos to give a personalized expert recommendation.

Figure 18-1:
The Lay's
Do Us a
Flavor
campaign.

Source: www.dousaflavor.com

Strategic Facebook sponsored posts also told people if their friends were submitting flavors. Lay's own Facebook page was also full of posts about the contest. The first U.S. campaign was such a success that Lay's brought it back in 2014. This time, the campaign involved all other social channels, such as Twitter and YouTube, and participants could make submissions via mobile as well.

Why it worked

People wanted to share their creations. Not only was it a fun, creative idea without too much production involved, but the winning idea would also take home a $1 million grand prize and, of course, endless bragging rights. And because so much of the promotion was organic word of mouth, from friends' newsfeeds and posts, the campaign caught on and spread rapidly.

The U.S. campaign had 3.8 million submissions total, with 955 million organic story impressions, according to media agency OMD. Following the campaign, Lay's gained 1.2 million new social fans, tripling its original fan base. The number of people talking about Lay's, or PTAT (people talking about this), increased by 4,700 percent. Lay's as a brand earned 1.26 billion PR impressions. All this resulted in a 12 percent increase in sales. As a result of this campaign, Lay's was also able to gather a plethora of consumer insights. For example, 7,200 like the color red in their flavor names as opposed to the 3 who liked beige.

The first U.S. campaign resulted in three finalists: Lay's Cheesy Garlic Bread, Lay's Chicken and Waffles, and Lay's Sriracha. All three of these flavors made it to store shelves, with one (Lay's Cheesy Garlic Bread) being crowned as the ultimate winner. This engaged an even wider audience because, even if you hadn't submitted an idea or voted online, anyone could now go into the stores, pick up one of the limited-time flavors, and have a say in which one was going to stay for good.

This campaign worked so well because it harnessed the influence of everyday consumers, and the marketing grew organically out of that. It was a brilliant idea that everyone could relate to, and there were multiple ways to participate. From submitting an idea, to voting online, to purchasing and trying the flavors, people could engage at all levels. Each of these opportunities was another chance to get buzz about the campaign, and it drove the exact results that Lay's had wanted.

Case Study: Heineken Coachella Snapchat

As of April 2014, Heineken had been sponsoring Coachella music festival for 13 years. Instead of having its usual dome in 2014, Heineken took it a step further and created the Heineken House, a full-on stage complete with its own lineup of Heineken sponsored performers, art, and food.

What they did

Using Snapchat with the name HeinekenSnapWho, Heineken engaged with fans by teasing out live mashups of the performances happening at the Heineken House. Those who added the Heineken user received a prompt to reply back with their birth dates, to confirm that they were at last 21 years old. Once confirmed, users could see Heineken's clues about what surprise guests would be performing in the Heineken tent. If fans sent back a correct guess, they would get a preview of when that performance would be happening, and subsequently, know when to head over to the Heineken House because the surprises were not announced on an official lineup.

In addition to having surprise guests at the Heineken House, there was also a World Fusion bar at which mixologists infused different herbs into Heineken, creating exclusive drinks for fans. L.A.-based chef and former music producer Mark Trombino also served artist-inspired doughnuts. Even more, an artist in the house created live art inspired by fans' Instagram photos tagged #HeinekenHouse.

Why it worked

Heineken is the first beer brand to leverage Snapchat, paving the way for marketers in their category on the platform. Eric Steele, creative director at Wieden+Kennedy (the ad agency that worked on the campaign) told *Time* that "When you're at a music festival like Coachella, a lot of people are kind of fueling the rumor mill of who's going to show up, who's going to be the surprise act." Heineken's marketing strategy was deliberate in placing the brand into that conversation. Moreover, because the campaign required consumers to respond with guesses, there was a high level of natural engagement built into the campaign. In addition, the campaign offered exclusive content, which is always something buzz-worthy and sought after when there is a crowd of close to 100,000 people at the same event.

During a time when brands are still trying to figure out how to use Snapchat as a marketing platform, Heineken was able to successfully leverage the social channel to engage its target audience. As a result, Heineken is setting industry standards and recognized as being at the forefront of innovative social marketing.

Case Study: Blogust

Blogust is Shot@Life's annual digital relay to give life-saving vaccines to children in need around the world. Shot@Life (see Figure 18-2), the UN Foundation campaign behind Blogust, is an organization that educates, connects, and empowers Americans to champion vaccines as one of the most cost-effective ways to save the lives of children in developing countries. Its goal is to decrease vaccine-preventable childhood deaths and give every child a shot at a healthy life.

Figure 18-2: Shot@Life.

Source: www.shotatlife.com

What they did

Shot@Life describes Blogust as "A month-long digital dialogue, bringing more than 25 of the most beloved online writers, photo, and video bloggers and Shot@Life champions together to help change the world through their words and imagery."

Blogust started in 2012 during the Mom 2.0 Summit, when Liz Gumbinner of Mom 101 said, "Comments are our currency." It was from that that Blogust was born, and now it happens every August (BloGUST like AuGUST). Shot@ Life wanted to bring together some of the world's top influencers who cared about the issue of vaccines for children around the world.

For each day during the event, Blogust shares a personal story about Happy and Healthy Firsts. The Blogust contributors participate in a blog relay, with one blogger posting each day and then a Shot@Life champion posting each Saturday of the month. Every time someone comments on a Blogust post, Walgreens provides a life-saving vaccine (up to 60,000) to children in need around the world.

Why it worked

Thirty-one bloggers participated in the first event in August 2012. Comments on the Blogust posts unlocked donations that helped save more than 11,000 lives. The participants and influencers commented and shared enough to donate 36,000 vaccines. Walgreens has also been increasing pledge of donations each year, with the most recent goal of 60,000 donated vaccines.

The event was such a success and for a good cause that it's now an annual event. It's extremely easy to participate in — all someone has to do is comment or share in order to give a child a life-saving vaccination, so why would anyone *not* want to participate? The official hashtag is now #Blogust across all social platforms. The ease of participation coupled with the feel-good factor people get when they're saving a life is unparalleled. And participants can even comment and share each day to keep giving vaccinations.

The campaign is inspiring while simultaneously raising awareness about the need for childhood vaccines. It puts the power in the hands of the people to help those in need, without having to spend a lot of time, money, or even effort to make a big impact. For those reasons, Blogust has been the success it is and has potential to grow year after year.

Case Study: Always Like a Girl

The Always #LikeAGirl campaign was arguably one of the most buzzed about campaigns of 2015. The creative was touching, inspirational, and impactful, earning it a Grand Prix in PR and a Glass Lion at the Cannes Lions International Festival of Creativity, the top honor in marketing and advertising.

What they did

The #LikeAGirl campaign kicked off with a video (see Figure 18-3) that recruited boys and post-adolescent women to run, throw, and fight "like a girl." Then the clip cuts to the reactions of young girls answering the same prompt. The difference was clear. Whereas the young girls embraced the idea of "like a girl" as strong and empowering, the others perceived it as an insult. In its ad, Always reports that a girl's self-confidence plummets during puberty. According to Leo Burnett, the ad agency behind the campaign, only 19 percent of women have a positive association with the expression "like a girl." This campaign was designed "as a stirring rally cry to reverse this connotation and champion girls' confidence."

Figure 18-3: The #LikeAGirl video on YouTube.

My hair, Oh God...

Always #LikeAGirl

Always

Subscribe 74,543

59,579,803

Source: `https://youtu.be/XjJQBjWYDTs`

The #LikeAGirl campaign asked women to share on social media something they proudly do with the hashtag "LikeAGirl" to change the negative perception of the phrase.

Why it worked

This was not just another campaign; this was also a social experiment. The target audience spoke to at least, but likely more than, half the population.

The message was extremely poignant because it pointed out a society-wide issue and asked for a society-wide attitude change. It was a change that many people could feel good standing behind, and it was something girls and women of all ages could relate to. It also had a call to action for everyday consumers to join in the movement on social media. The power of social media and influence today allows for a movement like this to be possible across states and even countries.

The original #LikeAGirl YouTube video earned more than 58 million views. The first video was released in June 2014; another was released in July 2015. As of August 2015, the video has garnered almost 38 million views. Not only is it one of the highest-awarded campaigns in the advertising and marketing space, but it has generated a tremendous amount of conversation about the topic and, naturally, the brand. Always and parent company Procter & Gamble have earned invaluable positive public sentiment and media attention as a result of this well-executed marketing campaign.

Part VI
The Part of Tens

Read about ten pop-culture moments of the '90s that would've been better with Twitter in a free article at www.dummies.com/extras/influencermarketing.

In this part . . .

- ✔ Avoid the most common pitfalls of influencer marketing campaigns.
- ✔ Get the top ten resources for influencer marketing industry news.

Chapter 19

Ten Reasons Influencer Marketing Campaigns Fail

In This Chapter

▶ Avoiding common traps

▶ Measuring for success

▶ Controlling the right things

▶ Focusing your efforts

*L*et's be honest: The Internet likes nothing more than a virtual train wreck. The best influencer marketing campaigns yield tremendous results for brands. The worst, however . . . well, a poor campaign will do nothing for a brand other than waste time and money, but a terrible campaign — one that is so badly executed that it garners negative social media attention — can severely damage a brand's reputation. In extreme cases, that damage can be permanent.

Never fear! In this chapter, we tell you ten reasons influencer marketing campaigns fail — and all ten reasons are easily avoidable. Read on to learn what *not* to do with your campaign.

Valuing Numbers More Than People

Marketing can be a numbers game. If your goal is to build brand awareness, it makes sense that you want to be seen by as many people as possible. After all, the more people who see your brand, the better known you're likely to become, right?

Well, not exactly. Just because you're seen by a million people doesn't mean a million people will remember you.

You can find influencers on Twitter, for example, who have 30,000, 50,000, even 100,000 followers and do nothing but tweet sponsored content, never interacting with their audience. Do you think your message will be remembered amid that kind of noise? Probably not.

One of the key reasons we love influencer marketing is because it allows people to tell your brand story to their followers in a real, authentic, and meaningful way.

Someone with 50,000 unengaged Twitter followers who uses your brand's hashtag 20 times in a day will look great on paper ($50,000 \times 20 = 1,000,000$ potential impressions), but yield no real results. Her followers won't care or take action. On the other hand, someone who has 5,000 engaged followers and creates a unique brand message . . . *he'll* drive engagement and establish brand awareness among his followers.

When it comes to working with influencers, seek out the ones who create good, original content. Find influencers who demonstrate engagement with and from their audience. Find and work with influencers who seem like they *should* be extensions of your brand's marketing efforts.

Don't start off your Influencer Marketing campaign by searching for the biggest influencers. Bigger only sometimes means better.

Pursuing Passively

Sending batches of emails out to email lists as part of your broader PR plan in the vague hopes that influencers will write about you is a) not very effective and b) not influencer marketing. It's old-fashioned "spray and pray," and it doesn't get you anywhere.

True influencer marketing involves establishing an actual relationship between the brand and the influencer. This means keeping outreach personal, customized, and true.

Approach your selected influencers respectfully, as though you're asking them to enter into a professional relationship with you — because you are! State clearly why you've chosen them out of all the other influencers using social media (maybe you like their point of view, their storytelling ability, or their photography skills) and why you think they'll fit with your program. Tell them right off the bat why you're writing them. Don't fall back on marketing jargon.

Spell out what you're asking them to do for you, whether it's writing a single blog post or a series of posts, posting photos to Instagram, or promoting your content on Facebook. Outline clear "asks" of your influencers and state explicitly whether you'll be compensating them (we strongly recommend that you *do*) and how much. You can negotiate compensation with an influencer — just keep in mind that asking influencers to work for free is bad form.

Finally, consider entering into a contractual relationship with the influencer. Why leave results to chance? If you write out exactly what, where, and when the influencer should be posting and have a mutually signed contract saying so, you're pretty much guaranteed to see the results you're expecting. You don't need to approach influencers as though their deliverables have to be a mystery, impossible to predict. You're far more likely to get exactly what you want when you're clear about what that is.

Measuring the Wrong Stuff (Or No Stuff)

Measuring the return on investment (ROI) of influencer marketing is sometimes tricky, but it's not impossible. Most often, the problem is that the people running the campaign don't know what to measure. And if you don't know what to measure, or you measure the wrong stuff, you'll have no way of knowing if your program worked.

As we detail in Part IV, you can't be successful running any kind of marketing campaign without stated goals. Only when you define what success will look like can you shape your program, set measurement expectations, and evaluate whether you met those expectations.

Let's look at an example: Say that a known potato chip brand is introducing a new flavor to the market. Maybe their marketing goal is to encourage widespread product trial. They decide the way to do this is to offer an electronic coupon for a free sample. Their success metrics will center on how many coupons are downloaded and how many of the downloaded coupons are redeemed.

In this scenario, they should identify which influencers will generate the most coupon downloads and product trials. They should reach out to influencers who are known for distributing coupons and have big followings on channels where coupon distribution is quick and easy (like Facebook or Twitter).

Some of the questions we get asked most often when it comes to influencers are: How many monthly impressions do they have? How many impressions will this program generate? Monthly impressions are a fine metric to monitor, but impressions are only meaningful if they track to a goal.

Impressions are a metric, not a goal.

For the potato chip brand in our example, asking "How many impressions will we get?" is very different from and much less focused or useful than asking "Which influencers will generate the most coupon downloads and trials for us?" (that is, the actual goal).

Being a Control Freak

The cornerstone of influencer marketing is handing over the brand messaging keys to your brand's advocates. To be effective, influencers have to be given latitude and control in communicating to their audiences. After all, these are audiences *they* cultivated. They know how to communicate with their followers better than anyone.

Sure, letting go is hard, especially for well-established brands that are used to maintaining complete control of every aspect of their marketplace presence. We're professional marketers. We used to write entire manuals on brand standards. We get it.

But from the second social media became a thing — from the moment consumers had access to the tools and platforms once solely used by big-budget companies — brands lost control of their messaging, whether they wanted to admit it or not. Today, people are posting about brands all day, across all social media platforms, in whatever ways they feel like, whether brands want them to or not. Influencer marketing is a way for brands to take advantage of this new reality and get some (but definitely not all!) control back. Brands work with people who are influential online, encouraging influencers to promote and create sponsored content.

Influencer marketing is successful because consumers trust recommendations from their friends and acquaintances more than they trust messaging from brands. Influencers may not be "friends" in the traditional sense, but readers develop strong affiliations with their favorite influencers and trust them more than advertisers.

Brands that fail to truly hand over the keys are missing the point. And we've seen this happen (over and over) in one of two ways:

- **Making it too professional:** Many brands claim to want influencers to tell their story, but when it comes down to execution, they want to be involved in every aspect of that influencer's content.

   If you, your agency, or your brand is trying to do some or all of the following, you're missing the point of influencer marketing:

   - *Providing art direction for what should be authentic photos:* It's okay to want high-caliber pictures, but detailing exactly how a photo must be arranged is over the top.

   - *Editing influencers' images in Photoshop.*

   - *Requiring that influencers use specific phrases, sentences, or entire paragraphs.*

- *Requiring several URLs and keywords in a single blog post.*

- *Asking bloggers to alter the design of their blogs to better complement the look of their sponsored posts.*

- *Editing blog posts to sound more like the brand's voice.*

- *Requesting or expecting the influencers to edit or alter any of their sites or profiles that are superfluous to the sponsored work they're doing.*

Influencer marketing is supposed to be a surprising, refreshing alternative to canned or glossy ads.

✔ **Faking authenticity:** Sometimes brands can't help it. They get a vision of what a perfect "authentic" post should look like and insist on controlling every aspect of the program to ensure their vision is achieved.

We've worked with several clients who ended up providing pages and pages of instructions to influencers to tell them exactly how their posts should look. Some have gone so far as to say, "Here is how to look authentic"!

Influencer marketing is not owned media (see Chapter 2 for more on the various types of media). The more latitude you give influencers to tell your story, the likelier it will be to resonate with the influencers' audiences.

Setting DUMB Goals

Setting goals is critical to the success of an influencer marketing campaign. Unfortunately, too many marketers set themselves up for failure by setting the wrong goals. You're no dummy, so you don't want to set DUMB goals — goals that are **d**isconnected, **u**nrealistic, **m**uddy, and **b**enchmark-free:

✔ **Disconnected:** Goals need to be tied to actual, meaningful metrics. They can't be self-contained. Too often, social media campaigns are measured in a vacuum and aren't written into (or measured along with) marketing plans. For instance, a disconnected goal would be "We need 2,000 likes on our Facebook page." Why do you need 2,000 likes? So that what? A like without context or connection to anything else is meaningless.

Instead, start collecting data. When you have more engagement on your Facebook page, does that correlate to more traffic to your retail page? Does it correlate to sales? If so, then likes may be meaningful. Just be sure to tie their impact to something worth measuring.

✔ **Unrealistic:** Influencer marketing is a new, exciting marketing tactic, but it's still only a marketing tactic. There is no reason to assume that it will yield wildly different results than other approaches. For some reason, many marketers believe that influencer marketing will be a cheap magic bullet that will drastically impact sales right out of the gate.

Going viral is not a realistic goal. It's not even a good goal. Expect new and improved results from employing new marketing tactics, but keep your expectations reasonable. You should see improvements from any new marketing tactic, but incremental ones. Engaging a handful of bloggers won't double the sales of your product overnight.

✔ **Muddy:** Goals need to be clear and specific, not vague and hard to understand. If your goals don't give you a framework for answering "Was this program successful?," they're too muddy. Here's an example of a muddy goal:

> We want to have bloggers try our new mouthwash and write about it.

Huh? Why? How many bloggers? What kind of bloggers? So that what happens? How will you know if the program is successful?

Here's an example of a clear goal:

> We will engage 15 to 20 bloggers in our target demographic (millennial moms) to receive, test, and write about our new mouthwash using funny pictures that we will repost across our social channels. The bloggers will provide a coupon to their readers as part of their reviews. Our goal is 10,000 coupon downloads with a 20 percent in-store conversion over the first 45 days of the program.

In this example, it's clear what the program's objectives are and how its success will be measured.

✔ **Benchmark-free:** You can't pull goals out of thin air. They need to be based on market research and your own data. Often, this means running test programs to understand how different tactics perform. (This is true for any new marketing program.) When you know what you're going to measure, run a small beta program to gauge the results. Adjust if needed, and then build those expectations into your larger, full-scale plan.

Chasing Shiny Objects

We all know that the social media world moves incredibly fast. As marketers, we're constantly challenged by the desire to be cool, to be first to market, to be pioneers. We want to be the ones to figure out how to leverage the newest, hottest tool in the market to our advantage.

But just because a tool is cool doesn't mean it's effective. And just because it works for one brand doesn't mean it will work for yours. Don't assume that all new platforms, channels, or tools are worth pursuing.

Start building your influencer marketing strategies by identifying who you want to reach and where they are (see the next section). Don't start by identifying which platforms you want to use. When you start with platforms, you run the risk of launching programs that are not only ineffective, but sometimes even obsolete.

Here's an example: Snapchat is a wildly popular tool that amassed over 100 million users in its first four years. According to *Business Insider,* 70 percent of Snapchat users are females under the age of 25. Many brands would love the opportunity to reach that demographic, so they rushed to set up Snapchat accounts . . . only to discover they don't know what to do with them.

Snapchat simply isn't set up to work for brands who want to work with influencers. There is no way to know who the popular Snapchatters are, for instance. And even if there were, it would be very difficult to contact them. Plus, even if it were possible for a brand to find influential Snapchatters and engage them, how would they measure their success? The brevity of Snapchat messaging makes it impossible to measure lasting results.

This isn't to say that Snapchat won't make itself more advertiser-friendly in the future, but too many companies have spent too much time and money trying to be effective on Snapchat with no idea what, if any, impact they had, instead of focusing on improving the way they interact with their existing audiences on Facebook or Twitter.

Bottom line: Unless you have access to tremendous resources, let the big brands work with the new platforms to figure out how it will work for the rest of us.

Picking the Wrong Message or Wrong Medium

Not all social media platforms are created equal. Each has its own unique mode and purpose. This means that the same message won't work the same way across channels. For instance, a recipe will get a lot more traction on Pinterest or Facebook than it will on Twitter. But Twitter can't be beat when you want influencers interacting with an audience in real-time.

The first questions to ask when you're launching an influencer marketing program are:

✔ Where are the people I want to reach?

✔ What are they doing there?

✔ Will my message make sense to them in that medium?

Table 19-1 has some guidelines to help you choose the right medium for your message.

Table 19-1	Which Medium Is Right for Your Message?
Social Media Platform	*Use Social Media Influencers to . . .*
Facebook	Share brand content that has already been created, such as branded videos
	Amplify sponsored images from Instagram or Pinterest
	Share short, easily digestible content, such as coupons or contests
Twitter	Host or participate in scheduled chats
	Encourage people to click through to a brand website
	Promote sponsored posts elsewhere, such as on influencer blogs
Pinterest	Showcase your beautiful products, especially if you're a retailer
	Create and post recipes or DIY projects
	Repin content that your brand has already created or curate boards for your brand
Instagram	Tell stories with photos
	Take photos that look great but aren't perfect
	Share simple visual messages using little to no text
Blogs	Create engaging content with high-quality photos
	Tell stories in long form
	Provide in-depth reviews of a product or service

Letting the Intern Do It

Yes, millennials grew up with the Internet, and social media is second nature to them. But that doesn't mean that young people just entering the workforce intrinsically understand how to use social media from a brand marketing perspective.

Influencer marketing will only be successful if it's tied to a brand's overall marketing plan. "Have the intern send some products to bloggers!" is not an influencer marketing strategy.

You can have your junior-most staff members execute aspects of the influencer marketing campaign, but the strategy must be clear and support your brand's larger goals.

Being Tone Deaf

You can't push brand messages out all day long — you have to engage in two-way communications with your audience. If you do this well, social media can truly humanize your brand, giving you a friendly voice and making you accessible to consumers.

When you've identified your goals, your demo, your preferred influencer platform, and your influencers, don't ruin your program by forcing messaging to be any of the following:

- ✔ **Corporate:** Did someone from your brand actually write the content? If so, it's too corporate. Don't try to pass corporate messaging off as influencer- or user-generated content. Wherever possible, provide guidelines, but then let the influencers create the message themselves. After all, that's why you're working with them!

- ✔ **Spammy:** If your content sounds like an ad, it's spammy. If you're asking your influencers to push a message out more than once or *maybe* twice a day, you're asking them to be spammy. If you're asking them to flood their social channels with the same promotion and language, it's too spammy. Influencers should never direct message (DM) with a promotional message or @reply someone with a promotional message — those methods of communicating are uninvited and definitely spammy.

- ✔ **Unoriginal:** If you're requiring your influencers to use the same language — even if the language is clever — it will come across as unoriginal (especially if you have dozens of people posting the exact same things). Again, let your influencers use their own language and style.

✔ **Fake-cool:** Fake-cool is when a brand swoops into social media and hijacks language or hashtags that are trendy, but does so awkwardly. We can't stress this enough: You can't actually be cool on social media if you don't spend any real time there. Influencers know what will resonate as real and what won't, so don't try to force them to use language or hashtags that don't come naturally to them.

Thinking It Will Be Easy

Influencer marketing is hard to do well. It's time-consuming, it requires genuine human interaction, and there's no guarantee that what you do will work. (But if you follow the recommendations in this book, we think you'll knock it outta the park!)

Remember when social media marketing was new, and brands flocked to Facebook and Twitter because they were "free"? There was so much excitement about reaching consumers in new ways, but so much untried and untested, too. Generally speaking, marketers underestimated how much time, effort, and resources (including budget) it would take to get real brand traction out of these new "free" resources.

Influencer marketing is the next new kid on the social media marketing block, and over and over, we see brands underestimating how much work has to go into launching a stellar influencer marketing campaign.

Don't underestimate what it takes to make influencer magic. Be thoughtful and deliberate in your approach. Take time to work out a plan, goals, and budget. Know what you'll measure and how you'll determine success. Approach your influencers carefully and respectfully, and offer opportunities that are win-wins.

Chapter 20

Ten Online Resources for Influencer Marketing Information

In This Chapter

▶ Keeping current with the latest influencer marketing news

▶ Finding trusted resources amid a sea of junk

*W*e don't have to tell you how hard it can be to find reliable news and information online. You probably know where to turn for your daily diet of general news and information, but what about marketing-specific news? News that's relevant to influencer marketing campaigns? In this chapter, we fill you in on ten trusted resources you can turn to for the news and information you need. Some apply to advertising and marketing in general; others are specific to social media and influencer marketing. But all of these sites are places you can trust.

Advertising Age

If we were to tally up the articles we share with each other in our private, staff Facebook group, the bulk of them would come from *Advertising Age* (or *AdAge* for short). *AdAge* (www.adage.com) is an important source of news and industry information for anyone in the advertising, marketing, and/or social media industry. *AdAge* covers topics relevant to influencer marketing and is particularly useful for people who are interested in where brands are spending their marketing dollars and which agencies are winning what business. *AdAge* coverage includes breaking industry news and information, as well as long-form editorial articles. An *AdAge* subscription is worth every penny.

Digiday

The second-most-shared articles among Clever Girls staffers are *Digiday* articles, and not just because we've received our share of coverage in *Digiday*. *Digiday* (www.digiday.com) is *the* place for daily coverage of advertising (including digital advertising), publishing, and media worlds, and we like that its coverage has a strong (and sometimes sassy) point of view.

The other reason to follow *Digiday* is to learn about its informative events. *Digiday* events are consistently superb, bringing together the best of agency and brand worlds for high-quality networking opportunities. Events are held all over the United States and are often specific to a particular industry (food, fashion, and so on) or audience (millennials, agency executives, and so on), so it's easy to find the event most beneficial to you and your business goals.

iBlog Magazine

We can't say enough how much we love *iBlog* magazine (www.iblogmagazine.com)! *iBlog* is mainly for female bloggers and influencers, but it's also distributed to advertising and PR agencies around the globe. *iBlog* is one way bloggers and influencers can have direct access to agency professionals and vice versa. It's a must-read for anyone wanting to keep up with the latest in blogging industry news. The print magazine is published several times a year and their website is updated with industry news and information daily.

Full disclosure: Clever Girls founder Stefania Pomponi was a founding advisor to the magazine because, as an agency, Clever Girls shares the magazine's mission to inspire "women influencers, bloggers, entrepreneurs, and business owners to actively grow their brands and businesses while balancing work, family, and life."

Clever Girls supports the mission of the magazine to provide access to social media experts who support and guide women throughout all aspects of their social media careers.

Scott Monty

Scott Monty (www.scottmonty.com) is one of the most trusted names in digital marketing. He unofficially helped to launch Clever Girls by giving us our first gig when he was head of social media at Ford Motor Company. Anyone who would give Clever Girls founders Cat Lincoln and Stefania Pomponi keys to a brand new Mustang and Taurus SHO is a friend of ours.

Now, with his consultancy, Scott Monty Strategies, he works with companies needing help with visionary thinking around communications, marketing, and digital strategy.

Plenty of nice things have been said about Scott. He was "ranked by *The Economist* as number one atop the list 25 Social Business Leaders and by *Forbes* as one of the top ten influencers in social media. Not enough? Alan Mulally, the CEO of Ford Motor Company, called him a "visionary."

Scott has been published everywhere, has been quoted everywhere, and is a sought-after speaker. We look to Scott when we want expert analysis on the latest digital, influencer marketing, or content marketing trends.

His weekly column, This Week In Digital (`https://flipboard.com/@scottmonty/the-week-in-digital-m4gqvfv2z`), is a must-read for anyone who wants to stay on top of digital industry news and commentary.

Social Media Club

We always look forward to Social Media Club (SMC; `www.socialmediaclub.org`) events because they're fun (drinks! food!) and informative networking and learning events hosted by our social media industry peers. If you attend an SMC event, chances are, you'll know at least one person there. The organization was founded in 2006 to "host conversations around the globe that explore key issues facing our society as technologies transform the way we connect, communicate, collaborate, and relate to each other." But SMC events are more than just networking events. They provide a real opportunity for personal and professional growth by connecting like-minded social media professionals who want to learn more and do better, together — which is why we're huge supporters.

SMC's mission is to promote social media literary, emerging technologies, and best practices. SMC events are an exciting mix of industry professionals as well as regular business folk who want to learn more about incorporating social media in their work. When social media professionals gather together to share ideas and best practices, we all win. There is a SMC in almost every major city across the United States, so check out an event today!

Social Media Today

We love *Social Media Today* (`www.socialmediatoday.com`) because it's a one-step resource for curated social media news and information from trusted experts, but if you want to take your social media knowledge to the next level, you can also quickly connect to webinars or sign up for one of its global conferences. Founder Robin Carey brings together industry leaders in small group settings and at events to share knowledge and best practices that move the social media industry forward.

Social Media Today conferences and webinars are consistently engaging and an authentic way to connect with the latest social media trends and information.

Social Media Week

Social Media Week (www.socialmediaweek.org) is a site (and conference) that curates social media news, ideas, technology, and insights as they relate to business and culture.

SMW has a broader vision that we find inspiring: to observe and "reimagine" how human connectivity, along with technology, will inform "the ways we live, work, and create." After all, "social" is an important part of social media, and connecting brands with their human fans is an important part of our work. If you don't want to connect with other humans, to communicate and form relationships, then you shouldn't do social media.

To support its vision, SMW hosts conferences in cities all over the globe, connecting physical and online attendees with a community of more than 5,000 speakers.

At Clever Girls, we check in with SMW to keep apprised of global social media trends directly from practitioners in those markets. SMW is also a tremendous resource for our research so we can stay current on trends and analysis for our clients. With just a few clicks, we can access SMW-published original and third-party white papers, case studies, and a host of reports. If you're a research hound, you'll find plenty to keep you busy on the SMW website. But don't forget the human element — connect in person at one of its global events!

SocialTimes

If something is happening right now in social media, chances are, *SocialTimes* (www.adweek.com/socialtimes) has the scoop. Part of the *AdWeek* blog network, *SocialTimes* is one of the longest-running blogs providing coverage of social media news and information, as well as social media industry commentary and analysis. It's truly a "one-stop shop" for all things social.

At Clever Girls, we access *SocialTimes* to stay abreast of the latest social media and digital news. Do the same if you want to impress your colleagues with your knowledge of what's happening in social media today.

Type-A Parent and Type-A Parent Conference

Kelby Carr, founder and CEO of the popular website and influencer network, Type-A-Parent (www.typeaparent.com), which led to the founding of the Type-A-Parent Conference, is a longtime friend of Clever Girls. Bloggers are a tight-knit community and we've known Kelby since she started. Her network attracts bloggers with high ethical standards who create amazing content. Several times a year, they gather together — along with brands — at Type-A-Parent conferences and events. Conferences include a New York City boot camp, and a flagship can't-miss annual conference held in a different city every year.

If you're a blogger and you're interested in upping your game by learning how to improve your writing or photography skills, how to connect with brands, or how to monetize your site, for example, Type-A-Parent should be your first stop. Attend a conference or boot camp, or simply connect with a member of the Type-A-Parent community. You'll get advice and guidance from the blogging trenches from one of the most influential (and supportive) blogging communities on the Internet.

The Word of Mouth Marketing Association

The Word of Mouth Marketing Association (WOMMA; www.womma.org) is the official trade association dedicated to word-of-mouth and social media marketing (which covers influencer and content marketing), and Clever Girls is honored to be a governing member. We're proud to show our support by actively participating in the association that has done so much to shape the word-of-mouth marketing industry for the past decade. Some of the biggest brands and agencies in the world are WOMMA members and look to WOMMA for guidance and leadership on ethical word-of-mouth marketing practices through its education, such as its yearly conference, WOMMA Summit; professional development opportunities like local networking events; and knowledge sharing with top industry marketers via its monthly webinars.

WOMMA is the opposite of a stuffy, walled-off trade association. We've found it to be extremely accessible. Any time we have a question, we can call and talk to a helpful WOMMA representative. WOMMA's membership is made up of the most innovative companies (like ours!) committed to progressing the word-of-mouth marketing industry through advocacy, education, and ethics. Definitely check it out and consider joining if you work in the marketing, PR, or advertising industry.

Appendix

Federal Trade Commission Guidelines

● ●

*B*efore you embark on a full influencer marketing campaign, be sure to review and familiarize yourself with the latest Federal Trade Commission (FTC) guidelines for proper disclosure of paid influencer relationships. Here are the documents you should be familiar with:

✔ **.com Disclosures: How to Make Effective Disclosures in Digital Advertising (2013):** According to this document:

- The general principles of advertising law apply online, but new issues arise almost as fast as technology develops — most recently, new issues have arisen concerning space-constrained screens and social media platforms. This FTC staff guidance document describes the information businesses should consider as they develop ads for online media to ensure that they comply with the law.

You can read the full document at: www.ftc.gov/sites/default/files/attachments/press-releases/ftc-staff-revises-online-advertising-disclosure-guidelines/130312dotcom disclosures.pdf.

✔ **The FTC's Endorsement Guides: What People Are Asking (2015):** In June 2015, the FTC updated the "What People Are Asking" page for its Endorsement Guides for the first time since 2010, because the social media landscape had changed dramatically in the previous five years. You can read the updated page here: www.ftc.gov/tips-advice/business-center/guidance/ftcs-endorsement-guides-what-people-are-asking.

In this appendix, you'll find excerpts from both of these FTC guides. Review them carefully. When in doubt, always err on the side of disclosing to avoid any chance of public shaming by the FTC and potentially hefty fines for failing to follow proper disclosure protocols.

To make sure you're always accessing the most current FTC guidelines, go to `https://www.ftc.gov/tips-advice/business-center/advertising-and-marketing`.

Blogs, Twitter, Instagram, Facebook, or Pinterest

The FTC states that the disclosure must be written in a clear and conspicuous manner that can be understood by the average reader. The disclosure must also be placed directly next to, or as close as possible to, the sponsored content.

In a blog post, this requirement can be satisfied with a simple disclosure statement at the top of each sponsored blog post. On a lengthy blog post, you should repeat the disclosures, as needed (for example, it may be reiterated at the end of the post).

In a social post on Twitter, Instagram, Facebook, or Pinterest, you may use a hashtag such as #sponsored or #ad to indicate the paid relationship. If multiple hashtags are being used, be sure that the disclosure hashtag is within the first three mentions following the endorsement.

Here's what the .com Disclosures document says:

3. Required disclosures must be clear and conspicuous. In evaluating whether a disclosure is likely to be clear and conspicuous, advertisers should consider its placement in the ad and its proximity to the relevant claim. The closer the disclosure is to the claim to which it relates, the better. Additional considerations include: the prominence of the disclosure; whether it is unavoidable; whether other parts of the ad distract attention from the disclosure; whether the disclosure needs to be repeated at different places on a website; whether disclosures in audio messages are presented in an adequate volume and cadence; whether visual disclosures appear for a sufficient duration; and whether the language of the disclosure is understandable to the intended audience.

4. To make a disclosure clear and conspicuous, advertisers should:

   • Place the disclosure as close as possible to the triggering claim.

   • Take account of the various devices and platforms consumers may use to view advertising and any corresponding disclosure. If an ad is viewable on a particular device or platform, any necessary disclosures should be sufficient to prevent the ad from being misleading when viewed on that device or platform.

- When a space-constrained ad requires a disclosure, incorporate the disclosure into the ad whenever possible. However, when it is not possible to make a disclosure in a space-constrained ad, it may, under some circumstances, be acceptable to make the disclosure clearly and conspicuously on the page to which the ad links.

- When using a hyperlink to lead to a disclosure,

- make the link obvious;

- label the hyperlink appropriately to convey the importance, nature, and relevance of the information it leads to;

- use hyperlink styles consistently, so consumers know when a link is available;

- place the hyperlink as close as possible to the relevant information it qualifies and make it noticeable;

- take consumers directly to the disclosure on the click-through page;

- assess the effectiveness of the hyperlink by monitoring click-through rates and other information about consumer use and make changes accordingly.

If you have a lengthy disclosure (for example, one that corresponds to contest or sweepstakes rules) that cannot fit within the status update itself, you may use a hyperlink to drive consumers directly to the disclosure text. Consumers should not have to search for it, and the text should be easy to understand (in layman's terms versus legalese).

Here's what the .com Disclosures document has to say on this subject:

6. Understandable Language

For disclosures to be effective, consumers must be able to understand them. Advertisers should use clear language and syntax and avoid legalese or technical jargon. Disclosures should be as simple and straightforward as possible. Icons and abbreviations are not adequate to prevent a claim from being misleading if a significant minority of consumers do not understand their meaning. Incorporating extraneous material into the disclosure also may diminish communication of the message to consumers.

Contests and Sweepstakes

When sponsoring a contest or sweepstake, you must ensure that even the consumers entering the contest know that they should use a hashtag such as #contest or #sweepstakes when promoting their entry on social media.

Here's what the What People Are Asking document says:

> [Q:] My company runs contests and sweepstakes in social media. To enter, participants have to send a Tweet or make a pin with the hashtag, #XYZ_Rocks. ("XYZ" is the name of my product.) Isn't that enough to notify readers that the posts were incentivized?

> [A:] No. It's likely that many readers would not understand such a hashtag to mean that those posts were made as part of a contest or that the people doing the posting had received something of value (in this case, a chance to win the contest prize). Making the word "contest" or "sweepstakes" part of the hashtag should be enough. However, the word "sweeps" probably isn't, because it is likely that many people would not understand what that means.

Videos

Video reviews and tutorials are an extremely popular avenue for influencer marketing content. If you provide your product free of charge to an influencer for review or you compensated the influencer for the video that she produces, the influencer is required to state the exact nature of the relationship at the beginning of the video. For example, it's acceptable to say, "This video was sponsored by X" or "I received product courtesy of X." An upfront disclosure informs viewers at the start that they're viewing sponsored content. We also recommend that the influencer include a straightforward disclosure in the text of the video description as well, to err on the side of caution.

Here's what the What People Are Asking document says:

> [Q:] My company, XYZ, operates one of the most popular multi-channel networks on YouTube. We just entered into a contract with a videogame marketer to pay some of our network members to produce and upload video reviews of the marketer's games. We're going to have these reviewers announce at the beginning of each video (before the action starts) that it's "sponsored by XYZ" and also have a prominent simultaneous disclosure on the screen saying the same thing. Is that good enough?

> [A:] Many consumers could think that XYZ is a neutral third party and won't realize from your disclosures that the review was really sponsored (and paid for) by the videogame marketer, which has a strong interest in positive reviews. If the disclosure said, "Sponsored by [name of the game company]," that would be good enough.

Online Reviews

Online reviews (even if they're unpaid) must disclose the reviewer's relationship to your business if you offer a service or item of value or discount in exchange for writing the review. The review must reflect the writer's authentic experience of the product or service and disclose any benefits received.

Here's what the What People Are Asking document says:

> [Q:] I'm starting a new Internet business. I don't have any money for advertising, so I need publicity. Can I tell people that if they say good things about my business in online reviews, I'll give them a discount on items they buy through my website?

> [A:] It's not a good idea. Endorsements must reflect the honest opinions or experiences of the endorser, and your plan could cause people to make up positive reviews even if they've never done business with you. However, it's okay to invite people to post reviews of your business after they've actually used your products or services. If you're offering them something of value in return for these reviews, tell them in advance that they should disclose what they received from you. You should also inform potential reviewers that the discount will be conditioned upon their making the disclosure. That way, other consumers can decide how much stock to put in those reviews.

Marketing Agencies and Public Relations Firms

If you're contracting an outside social media/digital marketing agency or PR firm to assist you in your influencer marketing efforts, be sure to do your due diligence to ensure that they have best practices in place to manage their network of influencers, guaranteeing proper disclosure. Any agency worth its salt will have robust monitoring programs to ensure both brand safety and adherence to FTC requirements.

In addition, we recommend looping in your legal team to ensure that they're also up to speed on the FTC guidelines. That way, all departments from PR and marketing to legal are aligned on influencer marketing messaging and publicity.

Here's what the What People Are Asking document says on this subject:

[Q:] Our company uses a network of bloggers and other social media influencers to promote our products. We understand we're responsible for monitoring our network. What kind of monitoring program do we need? Will we be liable if someone in our network says something false about our product or fails to make a disclosure?

[A:] Advertisers need to have reasonable programs in place to train and monitor members of their network. The scope of the program depends on the risk that deceptive practices by network participants could cause consumer harm — either physical injury or financial loss. For example, a network devoted to the sale of health products may require more supervision than a network promoting, say, a new fashion line. Here are some elements every program should include:

1. Given an advertiser's responsibility for substantiating objective product claims, explain to members of your network what they can (and can't) say about the products — for example, a list of the health claims they can make for your products;

2. Instruct members of the network on their responsibilities for disclosing their connections to you;

3. Periodically search for what your people are saying; and

4. Follow up if you find questionable practices.

It's unrealistic to expect you to be aware of every single statement made by a member of your network. But it's up to you to make a reasonable effort to know what participants in your network are saying. That said, it's unlikely that the activity of a rogue blogger would be the basis of a law enforcement action if your company has a reasonable training and monitoring program in place.

At the end of the day, remember that the FTC guidelines are in place simply to protect consumers from false and misleading claims or unintentional bias that may be introduced in a paid influencer relationship.

Index

• T •

Notes

Notes

Notes

Notes

Notes

Notes

Notes

Notes

Notes

Notes

Notes

Notes

Notes

Notes

Notes

Notes

Notes

About the Authors

Clever Girls is an esteemed content marketing and multi-million-dollar social media advertising agency that specializes in connecting top brands with influential women online. Clever Girls connects large brands such as Disney, Proctor & Gamble, Unilever, Ford, GAP, and Office Depot with its network of more than 7,000 women to create award-winning and data-driven influencer campaigns.

Kristy Sammis: Kristy Sammis is Founder and Chief Innovation Officer of Clever Girls. Kristy co-founded the company in 2009 because she is passionate about the ways in which friends, strangers, and organizations intersect online. She is a staunch advocate for keeping social media social.

In her Chief Innovator role, Kristy has been responsible for developing Clever Girls' network, platform, product and service offerings, marketing and sales strategies, and brand voice.

Kristy has spent the better part of the last decade translating the amazing aspects of social media — those embodied by the #Batkid phenomenon that Clever Girls spearheaded — into business principles: notably, that authenticity rules, "users" are actually human beings, and great stories always win the day.

An industry pioneer, Kristy has been instrumental in shaping how brands connect with women online. Prior to launching Clever Girls, she was an integral member of the original team at BlogHer.com, responsible for ensuring the success of the world's first and largest women's blogging conferences (which means she developed and delivered some of the earliest monetized influencer programs basically ever).

Before joining BlogHer.com, Kristy spearheaded and managed the Internal/ Employee Communications team at Walmart.com, the online division of the retail giant and "Fortune 1" company.

Kristy honed her online marketing skills at a boutique media agency in San Francisco, after successive marketing roles at a strategic consulting firm in New York City.

Kristy lives in Napa, California, with her husband and two young children, whose births she live-Tweeted.

Cat Lincoln: Cat Lincoln is Founder and CEO of Clever Girls, an esteemed content marketing and native advertising agency specializing in connecting top brands with influential women online. Cat's specialty is crafting social media programs with data-driven goals that achieve business results.

Leveraging 20+ years of Fortune 500 marketing experience with cutting-edge social media immersion, Cat and the Clever team have built an award-winning practice. In November 2013, Clever Girls was proud to partner with Make-A-Wish and lead the online strategy and execution of the global phenomenon #BatKid.

A respected marketing professional, Cat's pre–Clever Girls experience includes roles at Wells Fargo and ADP, as well as in the nonprofit sector. In addition to prolific personal Twitter, Instagram, and Facebook accounts, Cat has blogged professionally on AOL lifestyle sites StyleList and GreenDaily, travel site Uptake, and parenting site Babble.

Cat is an in-demand speaker, presenting on social media strategy and leadership at conferences including CES, The Economist Big Rethink, Mom 2.0 Summit, PBS Brandmasters Seminar, Springboard Summit, Wells Fargo Social Media Summit, the Radian 6 Users Conference, and the Syracuse University/Whitman School of Management V-WISE Conference as the opening keynote speaker. Recently, Cat gave the TEDxTalk #Batkid, Social Media & Global Participation.

When she's not working, Cat enjoys photography and traveling with her husband. She also has a not-at-all-secret addiction to reality TV. You can get the full scoop on her strong opinions about rose ceremonies by following @DearBadKitty.

Stefania Pomponi: Stefania Pomponi is Founder, President, and Chief Evangelist of Clever Girls. She co-founded the agency in 2009 because she is passionate about the ways in which content creation via compelling storytelling can achieve business goals.

Taking Clever Girls from a bootstrapped Silicon Valley startup to an award-winning social media agency, Stefania has been responsible for leading sales/business development, inking key partnerships, and leading corporate communications and PR efforts. As Chief Evangelist, she is also the public face of the company.

For the last decade, Stefania has been shaping the influencer marketing industry as a blog editor and producer for Fortune 100 media companies hiring, quite literally, thousands of bloggers and championing their rights to be paid for their influential work. She is also a pioneer in the world of social media marketing and scalable content marketing, best exemplified by the viral #Batkid phenomenon spearheaded by Clever Girls. Stefania is an ally to content creators everywhere and believes that authenticity rules, "users" are actually human beings, and great stories deserve great storytelling.

Jenny Ng: Jenny Ng is a senior project manager at Clever Girls, where she manages influencer marketing campaigns on behalf of Fortune 500 consumer brands such as Disney, LEGO, and Ford. Jenny holds more than nine years of B-to-B and B-to-C social media marketing and public relations experience across technology, healthcare, and consumer industries.

Additionally, Jenny has also served as an independent PR manager and consultant, led communications and brand marketing strategy for early stage startups, and worked for a number of PR agencies including SutherlandGold Group, Schwartz Communications (now a part of MSL Group), and Fleishman Hillard.

Edita Gassmann Rodriguez: Edita is a client services specialist with more than ten years of experience across TV, public relations, marketing, and tech. She is currently the Vice President of Client Services & Membership at Clever Girls, where she is responsible for client retention and growth, organizational strategy and development, and program execution. Edita sits on the Clever Girls Leadership Team with executive-level staff across departments.

Edita lives in Northern California with her husband and two miniature dachshunds. When she's not working, she enjoys spending time with her family, working out, traveling, and drinking micheladas.

Judy Zhou: Judy Zhou is PR and Corporate Communications Manager at Clever Girls, where she tells the Clever Girls story and oversees external and internal communications.

Specializing in agency public relations and corporate communications, Judy is experienced in branding on a B2B level for agencies both big and small. Prior to Clever Girls, she worked at the advertising agency Deutsch Inc., where she supported the PR department and managed the agency's corporate social strategy.

A graduate of the University of Southern California, Judy currently resides in Los Angeles and enjoys going to the beach and reviewing boutique fitness studios on her blog WerkoutLA.

Dedication

Kristy Sammis: For my darling, patient, good-humored Family Support Team: Peter, Eve, Townsend, Ammy + B, Carol, Healy, Juanita, and Virginia. Thank you for loving me (through so many crazy-making, unshowered days) and giving me the space to make this book — and our whole business — a reality. It's probably my turn to do the dishes.

Cat Lincoln: For my partner in "real" life and all of my adventures, my husband, Jeff. Years ago you encouraged me to start a business with my best friends, and continue to support me through every twist and turn. You never complain about the long days and nights, and always tell me how proud you are of every accomplishment. I am incredibly lucky to have you at my side. Thank you!

Stefania Pomponi: For Anouk, Wallis, and Dashiell who put joy into my life and magic into my world every single day. Over the years, you put up with so many conference calls where you had to be quiet in the background, endured the times when I had to travel for work, and learned to be responsible and independent maybe a little earlier than you had to. I do this for you — and because I love what I do. But most of all, I love you three so incredibly much. This book answers all your questions about "what Mamma does for work."

Jenny Ng: For my wise and loving grandmother Yu Y Ma and my parents Tin Kee and Yun Mui, who supported my decision to study liberal arts and take the nonlinear career path.

Edita Gassmann Rodriguez: For my dad, Nick, thank you for volunteering to be my fifth-grade student council campaign manager, and for always encouraging me to go for it. Also, for my husband, Eric, thank you for your unwavering patience and support — even when (and especially when) I go into zombie work mode. You're amazing.

Judy Zhou: To my wonderful parents, Shanqin and Guoliang, for always being supportive and letting me escape the cold by running away to L.A. for journalism school. Also, to my grandparents, who I don't get to see as often, and my furry ball of love, Winston, for always bringing joy to everyone.

Authors' Acknowledgments

Clever Girls founders — Cat Lincoln, Stefania Pomponi, and Kristy Sammis — would like to acknowledge the following people without whom this book would not be possible: First and foremost, we would like to thank the most supremely talented, hardest working, most dedicated, "clever-est" staff in the industry. This book is a direct result of six years of kicking ass together every single day. We are unstoppable as #onecleverteam because of you:

Jennifer Bateh, Mel Bergman, Suzanne Browne Mead, Geri Camp, Elyse Collett, Kristen Conley, Kayla Doty, Vin Gonzales, Jody Hart, Jocelyn Hudak, Ashley James, Robin Johnson, Adam Juratovac, Asta Karalis, Scott Lyon, Sarah Matthews, Melissa McGreevy, Monica Murphy, Jenny Ng, Ngan Nguyen, Leah Nielsen, Monica Padilla, Justin Robinson, Edita Rodriguez, Frank Schneider, Sarah Schwoerer, Carmen Shiu, Sheila Tabuena, Judy Zhou

We'd also like to thank everyone who's been a member of Clever Girls over the years. Thousands of influencers strong, millions of impressions represented, your creativity, professionalism, and social media magic has allowed us to build a successful, award-winning influencer marketing agency that continues to lead the industry and define what it means to do what we do. One of our favorite things *ever* is to show our clients just how dazzling our network is. We have the privilege of doing it every day and you always make us look good. We thank you for that.

We could not have built a successful, thriving business without the support and advice from these special people who have been our biggest champions over the years, and not all of them are our family members:

Larry Durso, Jim and Sue Bartlett, Tom and JoAnn Pottberg, John and Linda Sammis, Peter Pomponi, Jill Paldi, Camille Paldi, Heather Thomson, Susan Kimberlin, Deborah Ludewig, Ronald Lesniak, Scott Monty, David Hornik, Laney Whitcanack, Peter Wooster

This book absolutely would not have been possible without the opportunity and guidance provided by Stacy Kennedy and Elizabeth Kuball, our editors at Wiley, who graciously allowed us to redefine what the word deadline means over and over (and over) again.

Thank you to Kelby Carr for your incomparable technical editing skills and for ensuring that every word we wrote is true because if anyone would know, you would.

It's because of all of you that we can say, "We wrote the book on influencer marketing . . . literally!"

With gratitude,

Cat, Stefania, and Kristy

Publisher's Acknowledgments

Acquisitions Editor: Stacy Kennedy

Project Editor: Elizabeth Kuball

Copy Editor: Elizabeth Kuball

Technical Editor: Kelby Carr

Project Coordinator: Kinson Raja

Cover Image: 3dts/iStockphoto

Apple & Mac

iPad For Dummies,
6th Edition
978-1-118-72306-7

iPhone For Dummies,
7th Edition
978-1-118-69083-3

Macs All-in-One
For Dummies, 4th Edition
978-1-118-82210-4

OS X Mavericks
For Dummies
978-1-118-69188-5

Blogging & Social Media

Facebook For Dummies,
5th Edition
978-1-118-63312-0

Social Media Engagement
For Dummies
978-1-118-53019-1

WordPress For Dummies,
6th Edition
978-1-118-79161-5

Business

Stock Investing
For Dummies, 4th Edition
978-1-118-37678-2

Investing For Dummies,
6th Edition
978-0-470-90545-6

Personal Finance
For Dummies, 7th Edition
978-1-118-11785-9

QuickBooks 2014
For Dummies
978-1-118-72005-9

Small Business Marketing
Kit For Dummies,
3rd Edition
978-1-118-31183-7

Careers

Job Interviews
For Dummies, 4th Edition
978-1-118-11290-8

Job Searching with Social
Media For Dummies,
2nd Edition
978-1-118-67856-5

Personal Branding
For Dummies
978-1-118-11792-7

Resumes For Dummies,
6th Edition
978-0-470-87361-8

Starting an Etsy Business
For Dummies, 2nd Edition
978-1-118-59024-9

Diet & Nutrition

Belly Fat Diet For Dummies
978-1-118-34585-6

Mediterranean Diet
For Dummies
978-1-118-71525-3

Nutrition For Dummies,
5th Edition
978-0-470-93231-5

Digital Photography

Digital SLR Photography
All-in-One For Dummies,
2nd Edition
978-1-118-59082-9

Digital SLR Video &
Filmmaking For Dummies
978-1-118-36598-4

Photoshop Elements 12
For Dummies
978-1-118-72714-0

Gardening

Herb Gardening
For Dummies, 2nd Edition
978-0-470-61778-6

Gardening with Free-Range
Chickens For Dummies
978-1-118-54754-0

Health

Boosting Your Immunity
For Dummies
978-1-118-40200-9

Diabetes For Dummies,
4th Edition
978-1-118-29447-5

Living Paleo For Dummies
978-1-118-29405-5

Big Data

Big Data For Dummies
978-1-118-50422-2

Data Visualization
For Dummies
978-1-118-50289-1

Hadoop For Dummies
978-1-118-60755-8

Language &
Foreign Language

500 Spanish Verbs
For Dummies
978-1-118-02382-2

English Grammar
For Dummies, 2nd Edition
978-0-470-54664-2

French All-in-One
For Dummies
978-1-118-22815-9

German Essentials
For Dummies
978-1-118-18422-6

Italian For Dummies,
2nd Edition
978-1-118-00465-4

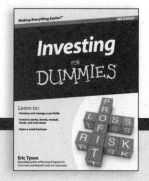   

Available in print and e-book formats.

Available wherever books are sold. **For more information or to order direct visit www.dummies.com**

Math & Science

Algebra I For Dummies,
2nd Edition
978-0-470-55964-2

Anatomy and Physiology
For Dummies, 2nd Edition
978-0-470-92326-9

Astronomy For Dummies,
3rd Edition
978-1-118-37697-3

Biology For Dummies,
2nd Edition
978-0-470-59875-7

Chemistry For Dummies,
2nd Edition
978-1-118-00730-3

1001 Algebra II Practice
Problems For Dummies
978-1-118-44662-1

Microsoft Office

Excel 2013 For Dummies
978-1-118-51012-4

Office 2013 All-in-One
For Dummies
978-1-118-51636-2

PowerPoint 2013
For Dummies
978-1-118-50253-2

Word 2013 For Dummies
978-1-118-49123-2

Music

Blues Harmonica
For Dummies
978-1-118-25269-7

Guitar For Dummies,
3rd Edition
978-1-118-11554-1

iPod & iTunes
For Dummies, 10th Edition
978-1-118-50864-0

Programming

Beginning Programming
with C For Dummies
978-1-118-73763-7

Excel VBA Programming
For Dummies, 3rd Edition
978-1-118-49037-2

Java For Dummies,
6th Edition
978-1-118-40780-6

Religion & Inspiration

The Bible For Dummies
978-0-7645-5296-0

Buddhism For Dummies,
2nd Edition
978-1-118-02379-2

Catholicism For Dummies,
2nd Edition
978-1-118-07778-8

Self-Help & Relationships

Beating Sugar Addiction
For Dummies
978-1-118-54645-1

Meditation For Dummies,
3rd Edition
978-1-118-29144-3

Seniors

Laptops For Seniors
For Dummies, 3rd Edition
978-1-118-71105-7

Computers For Seniors
For Dummies, 3rd Edition
978-1-118-11553-4

iPad For Seniors
For Dummies, 6th Edition
978-1-118-72826-0

Social Security
For Dummies
978-1-118-20573-0

Smartphones & Tablets

Android Phones
For Dummies, 2nd Edition
978-1-118-72030-1

Nexus Tablets
For Dummies
978-1-118-77243-0

Samsung Galaxy S 4
For Dummies
978-1-118-64222-1

Samsung Galaxy Tabs
For Dummies
978-1-118-77294-2

Test Prep

ACT For Dummies,
5th Edition
978-1-118-01259-8

ASVAB For Dummies,
3rd Edition
978-0-470-63760-9

GRE For Dummies,
7th Edition
978-0-470-88921-3

Officer Candidate Tests
For Dummies
978-0-470-59876-4

Physician's Assistant Exam
For Dummies
978-1-118-11556-5

Series 7 Exam For Dummies
978-0-470-09932-2

Windows 8

Windows 8.1 All-in-One
For Dummies
978-1-118-82087-2

Windows 8.1 For Dummies
978-1-118-82121-3

Windows 8.1 For Dummies,
Book + DVD Bundle
978-1-118-82107-7

Available in print and e-book formats.

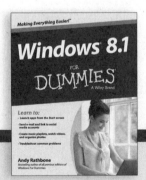

Available wherever books are sold. **For more information or to order direct visit www.dummies.com**

Take Dummies with you everywhere you go!

Whether you are excited about e-books, want more from the web, must have your mobile apps, or are swept up in social media, Dummies makes everything easier.

For Dummies is the global leader in the reference category and one of the most trusted and highly regarded brands in the world. No longer just focused on books, customers now have access to the For Dummies content they need in the format they want. Let us help you develop a solution that will fit your brand and help you connect with your customers.

Advertising & Sponsorships

Connect with an engaged audience on a powerful multimedia site, and position your message alongside expert how-to content.

Targeted ads • Video • Email marketing • Microsites • Sweepstakes sponsorship

Custom Publishing

Reach a global audience in any language by creating a solution that will differentiate you from competitors, amplify your message, and encourage customers to make a buying decision.

Apps • Books • eBooks • Video • Audio • Webinars

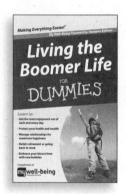

Brand Licensing & Content

Leverage the strength of the world's most popular reference brand to reach new audiences and channels of distribution.

For more information, visit www.Dummies.com/biz

Dummies products make life easier!

- DIY
- Consumer Electronics
- Crafts

- Software
- Cookware
- Hobbies

- Videos
- Music
- Games
- and More!

For more information, go to **Dummies.com** and search the store by category.

FOR
DUMMIES
A Wiley Brand